New
First
Certificate
Masterclass

Student's Book

Simon Haines

Barbara Stewart

OXFORD UNIVERSITY PRESS

UNIT	TOPICS	GRAMMAR	VOCABULARY
1 Description pages 9–20	Unusual activities Places	Habitual actions in the present and past Present continuous with *always* *Would* and *Used to* + infinitive *Be / get used to* + *-ing*	Places Introduction to phrasal verbs
2 Future pages 21–34	Weather Old age	The future: *will, going to*, present simple/continuous, future continuous/perfect Articles	Weather Age Phrasal verbs *break up / put up*
3 Opinion pages 35–48	Famous people Art	Gerunds and infinitives	The arts Crafts *See / watch* Noun suffixes Phrasal verbs *put on/put off*
4 Comparison pages 49–62	Television Men and women	Comparative and superlative adjectives and adverbs *The . . . the . . .* *So* and *such*	Family relationships Jobs Compound nouns Phrasal verbs with *take*
5 Narrative pages 63–76	Mishaps Sport	Past tenses and time expressions Participle clauses	Sports Compound adjectives Phrasal verbs
6 Conditions pages 77–90	Twentieth century problems Telling lies	Conditional sentences types 0, 1, 2 and 3 Mixed conditionals	The body Compound adjectives *Say, speak, talk, tell* Colours Phrasal verbs as nouns
7 Description pages 91–104	Jobs people do Appearance and character	Defining and non-defining relative clauses	Describing people *Fairly, rather, quite*, etc Negative prefixes Phrasal verbs with *turn*
8 Points of View pages 105–118	Smoking Crime and punishment	Reported speech	Crime Noun suffixes Phrasal verbs with *go* *Rob / steal*
9 Interaction pages 119–130	Computer games Holidays	Suggestions, advice, warnings *Should, ought to, could* Regrets and criticisms Contrasting conjunctions	Travel and holidays Colloquial language Word roots Phrasal verbs with *bring*
10 Restrictions pages 131–144	Rules and restrictions Space	Obligation and necessity *must, have to, need* Lack of necessity *didn't need / needn't have* Prohibition and permission *can, can't* Adverbs *Too, enough, very*	Clothes Prohibition Phrasal verbs
11 Speculation pages 145–156	Science and technology The environment	Expressing certainty and possibility *must, can't, could,* *might* Wishes	Gadgets and appliances Adjectival suffixes Phrasal verbs with *come*
12 Information pages 157–170	Sleep Festivals	The passive	Celebrations and festivals Food and drink Sleep *Raise, rise; lay, lie* Phrasal verbs with *up* and *get*
13 Skills and Abilities pages 171–182	Memory The cinema	Expressing ability *can, be able to, manage / succeed* Question tags	The mind and the senses Money *Remind / remember* Phrasal verbs related to money
14 Cause and Effect pages 183–196	Education Music and health	*Make* Expressions of purpose Causative verbs *have/get something done*	Education Health Three-part phrasal verbs

EXAM TECHNIQUES	READING	LISTENING	WRITING	SPEAKING
Reading: Multiple choice questions Paper 1 Part 2	A hard act to swallow	Descriptions of places	Paragraphing and punctuation	Picture discussion Problem solving Opinion Description
Reading: Gapped text (missing sentences) Paper 1 Part 3 Listening: Short extracts Paper 4 Part 1	Long life	Story about British weather Extracts about the weather	Formal and informal styles Informal letter	Opinion Prediction Discussion
Use of English: Cloze Paper 3 Part 2	Talking to Elton John	Artists and opinions on art	Giving an opinion Exam training: Articles 1	Opinion Narrative Role play interview Description
Speaking: Personal information; talking about photos Paper 5 Parts 1 and 2	Whose finger is on the button in your house?	Interview about men's and women's abilities	Describing an object Exam training: Transactional letters 1	Discussion Opinion Problem solving
Reading: Matching headings Paper 1 Part 1 Use of English: Word formation Paper 3 Part 5	I flew to Brazil by accident	News report on caving	Exam training: Stories 1	Picture discussion Discussion Narrative Opinion
Listening: Note-taking and blank-filling Paper 4 Part 2 Reading: Gapped text (missing paragraphs) Paper 1 Part 3	The shape of things to come	People talking about lying	Exam training: Reports 1	Picture discussion Opinion Discussion Problem solving Narrative
Use of English: Error correction Paper 3 Part 4 Listening: Multiple matching Paper 4 Part 3	Living dangerously	Descriptions of someone in different contexts	Exam training: Applications 1 Describing people	Picture discussion Opinion Description
Reading: Multiple matching Paper 1 Part 4	The hangman's rope	Views on tobacco advertising	Presenting an argument Exam training: Compositions 1	Opinion Discussion Debate Role play
Use of English: Vocabulary cloze Paper 3 Part 1	Eurorailing	Advice phone-in	Exam training: Transactional letters 2	Discussion of texts Discussion Role play Opinion Narrative
Use of English: Key word transformations Paper 3 Part 3	What it takes to be an astronaut	Extracts about clothing and fashion	Exam training: Articles 2 Bringing descriptions to life	Picture discussion Discussion Role play Opinion
Listening: Selecting from two or three answers Paper 4 Part 4	Living on the edge	Radio game show 'Follow that'	Connecting ideas Exam training: Compositions 2	Discussion Description Picture discussion Narrative
Speaking: Shared task; topic-related discussion Paper 5 Parts 3 and 4	ZZzzz	Radio broadcast on Bonfire Night Extracts about Bonfire Night	Reporting an opinion Exam training: Reports 2	Picture discussion Narrative Description
	Memories are made of this	Extracts about the cinema	Exam training: Set book (Paper 2 Part 2 Question 5) Exam training: Applications 2	Discussion Opinion
Taking the First Certificate Exam	The stars who did their own thing	Extracts about music	Checking your work Exam training: Stories 2	Picture discussion Opinion Problem solving Discussion

Exam Factfile

Introduction

The First Certificate in English (Cambridge Level 3) has five papers. Each of these papers is worth 20% of the total. A, B and C are pass grades, D is a narrow fail, E is a fail and U is an unclassified result.

General practical advice about taking the exam is covered in the Exam techniques section of Unit 14 on pages 195-196.

Paper 1 Reading (1 hour 15 minutes)

Paper 1 consists of four parts, which are always in the same order. Each part contains a text and a comprehension task of some kind. In total there are 35 questions. The type of texts used include newspaper and magazine articles, advertisements, brochures, guides, letters, fiction, messages and reports.

Summary

Part	Task type	Questions	Task format	Masterclass example
1	Multiple matching	6 or 7	A text preceded by multiple matching questions.	Unit 5 page 72
2	Multiple choice	7 or 8	A text followed by multiple choice questions with four options - A, B, C or D.	Unit 1 page 14
3	Gapped text	6 or 7	A text from which six or seven sentences or paragraphs have been removed and put in jumbled order after the text. The task is to fit the missing text into the gaps.	**Sentences** Unit 2 page 26 **Paragraphs** Unit 6 page 88
4	Multiple matching	13-15	As in Part 1.	Unit 8 page 110

Paper 2 Writing (1 hour 30 minutes)

Paper 2 consists of two parts. Part 1 is compulsory - it must be answered by all candidates. In Part 2, candidates can choose one of four questions (2-5). Part 1 is a 'transactional' letter. In Part 2, writing tasks may include letters, articles, reports, applications, stories and compositions. These will have a 'real' purpose and a particular reader in mind.
Across the two tasks, candidates are expected to write between 240 and 360 words in all.

Summary

Part	Task type	Number of tasks and word length	Task format	Masterclass example
1	Question 1 Transactional letter	One compulsory task of 120-180 words	Candidates write a letter related to a situation outlined in one or more short texts, rubric* and sometimes visuals.	Unit 4 page 54 Unit 9 page 127
2	**Questions 2, 3 and 4** From the following: • an article • a report • an informal/ non-transactional letter • an application • a composition • a story	Choice of three tasks, each 120-180 words	A 'real-life' situational task presented through rubric.	**Article** Unit 3 page 46 Unit 10 page 136 **Report** Unit 6 page 82 Unit 12 page 169 **Letter** Unit 2 page 32 **Application** Unit 7 page 96 Unit 13 page 182 **Composition** Unit 8 page 116 Unit 11 page 156 **Story** Unit 5 page 68 Unit 14 page 193
	Question 5 Write one of the above types on a set book.	Choice of two tasks, each 120-180 words	A task presented through rubric.	**Set Book** Unit 13 page 176

* rubric: language describing or explaining what students should do

Paper 3 Use of English (1 hour 15 minutes)

This paper consists of five parts, which test the candidate's knowledge of grammar and vocabulary.

Summary

Part	Task type	Questions	Task format	Masterclass example
1	Multiple choice gap-fill, testing mainly vocabulary	15	A text with 15 gaps followed by a choice of four answers for each gap.	Unit 9 page 128
2	Open gap-fill, testing grammar and vocabulary	15	A text with 15 gaps; no answers are given.	Unit 3 page 40
3	'Key' word transformations, testing grammar and vocabulary	10	A complete sentence followed by a gapped sentence, which must be completed using a given word.	Unit 10 page 142
4	Error correction, testing mainly grammar	15	A text with some correct lines and some lines containing an extra and unnecessary word. Candidates must identify the extra words.	Unit 7 page 100
5	Word formation, testing vocabulary	10	A text containing 10 gaps, each of which must be filled with a word formed from a given root word.	Unit 5 page 76

Paper 4 Listening (about 40 minutes)

This paper contains four parts. Each part contains one or more recorded texts and accompanying comprehension questions.

The recorded texts used may include the following:

Single speakers: answerphone messages, commentaries, documentaries, instructions, lectures, news, public announcements, advertisements, reports, speeches, stories, talks.

Two or more speakers: chats, conversations, discussions, interviews, quizzes, radio plays, transactions (for example, in a shop).

The speakers will have a variety of accents. Background sounds may be included before the speaking begins, to give information about context.

Summary

Part	Task type	Questions	Task format	Masterclass example
1	Multiple choice	8	Short unconnected extracts each about 30 seconds long. Multiple choice questions have three options, A, B or C.	Unit 2 page 34
2	Note-taking or blank-filling	10	A monologue or a text involving more than 1 speaker, lasting about 3 minutes.	Unit 6 page 81
3	Multiple matching	5	Short connected extracts, each about 30 seconds long. Candidates match extracts with prompts.	Unit 7 page 104
4	Selecting from two or three possible answers	7	A monologue or a text involving more than one speaker, lasting about three minutes. Task types may include yes/no; true/false; three-option multiple choice; which speaker said what.	Unit 11 page 155

Paper 5 Speaking (about 15 minutes for 2 candidates)

This paper - the speaking test - contains four parts. Normally, there are two examiners and two candidates*. One examiner only assesses, the other gives instructions and talks to the candidates. Candidates should talk mainly to each other.

* In certain circumstances it may be possible for the speaking test to be between one examiner and one candidate. This type lasts about 10 minutes.

Paper 5 tests the following language abilities:
- accurate use of grammar
- range and use of vocabulary
- pronunciation
- communication
- successful completion of tasks

Summary

Part	Task type	Time	Task format	Masterclass example
1	The interviewer asks each candidate some questions.	about four minutes	The interviewer encourages candidates to give information about themselves.	Unit 4 page 60
2	Each candidate in turn talks to the interviewer and the other candidate for one minute. Candidates then exchange information with each other.	about four minutes	Each candidate is given two pictures to talk about, both factually and in relation to themselves. Each candidate comments briefly on the other candidate's pictures.	Unit 4 page 60
3	Candidates talk to each other by doing a task such as: • making plans • solving a problem • making a decision • discussing an order of importance • speculating	about three minutes	Candidates are given pictures or diagrams to help them start the communication task.	Unit 12 page 162
4	Candidates exchange opinions with each other.	about four minutes	The interviewer encourages discussion related to the topic of Part 3.	Unit 12 page 163

Description

Old habits die hard

Introduction

A The people in these photographs have unusual skills. The man on the left is Stevie Starr, a professional entertainer. What do you think he does?

B Make a list of all the objects you can see in the photograph of Stevie. What are these objects normally used for?

C The people on the right are practising a traditional skill for doing something. Do you know what they are doing? What are the modern scientific techniques for doing this?

D Do you know of any other traditional skills which are still practised today?

E Do you, or does anyone you know, have unusual skills or abilities?

Reading

1 Think ahead You are going to read about Stevie Starr. Look at the title of the article. Does this help you to guess what his stage act consists of? If you have already made a guess, are you still confident that you are correct?

2 Reading Read the article to find out if your guess is correct. How many of the objects in the photograph on page 9 are mentioned in the article?

A hard act to swallow

STEVIE grew up in a children's home in Scotland. Every week, the staff took a proportion of the children's pocket money to pay for holidays. Little Stevie developed a daring strategy to hang
5 on to what little money he had. He laughs about it now. 'I used to swallow all my coins. That got them really furious, so they'd put me in a room on my own as a punishment. After a few minutes in there, I'd hit myself on the chest and
10 cough the money back up.'

Since then, Stevie has turned into Stevie Starr, a professional regurgitator who does up to four shows a day, and can demand fees of £500 – £2000 a show.

Everything Stevie swallows comes back dry, except
15 for the goldfish. They swim about in his stomach in the water that he swallows for them first. After ten minutes they resume their normal lives in a goldfish bowl. 'People are always accusing me of cruelty,' says Stevie, 'but the fish never die.'

20 Medical experts might have a few worries about Stevie. The sight and sound of him swallowing and bringing back a snooker ball sometimes causes even normally calm people to panic. He also smokes a cigarette, retains the smoke in his stomach, then
25 swallows some butane gas and mixes the two. Next he swallows some washing-up liquid, blows a huge bubble, brings up the smoke and gas inside the bubble, cuts the bubble off, gets someone to set light to it, and BANG!

He enjoys watching audience reactions. 'I tend to start
30 by swallowing a light bulb. There might be a thousand people watching, but once I've done that, you can hear a pin drop.' He loves performing off-stage as well. 'I often go into a pub, order a couple of drinks and then cough up the money to pay for them.'

35 Watching his routine is an uncomfortable experience.

'I can feel my stomach moving around while I talk to you,' says Stevie. He swallows some sugar, followed by a glass of water, and brings the sugar back dry.

He swallows a locked padlock, followed by the key, opens it in his stomach and returns the padlock.

He changes the pattern of a Rubik cube inside his 40 stomach, and regurgitates piles of money selectively. When members of the audience, who have checked the dates of coins beforehand, ask for a 1978 10p or a 1988 20p, he extracts it from the pile of coins in his stomach and brings it up. 45

Physically, Stevie doesn't believe he is any different from the rest of the human race, who use their stomachs simply to digest food. 'It's all done by muscle control,' he says. 'I imagine a little pair of hands in there doing everything, controlled by my brain. I'm sure I could 50 teach anyone to do what I do.' ●

3 Points of view

1 Would you go and see Stevie's act? Why? Why not?
2 Do you think he really does what he says, or do you think he cheats in some way?

4 Comprehension

A Here are two general questions about Stevie. Each question has a choice of four answers. For each question, choose the best answer according to the text.

1 Which is the best summary of Stevie's life to date?
  A He has done what everyone expected him to do.
  B He is making a living out of something he was taught at school.
  C He has disappointed the people he grew up with.
  D He has succeeded despite early disadvantages.
2 Which is the most suitable description of Stevie's character?
  A He is basically a shy person.
  B He is extremely hardworking.
  C He is generous with his money
  D He thinks he is specially talented.

B Now read the text again and answer these questions.
1 Why was Stevie punished in the children's home?
2 What is the connection between Stevie's life in the home and his job now?
3 What effect does Stevie's swallowing the light bulb have on his audiences? *Quietness*
4 Why are the members of the audience important to Stevie's trick with the coins?

C Vocabulary
Find words, phrases or expressions in the article which mean:

staff

1 group of people who work somewhere together (1 word)

daring strategy 2 brave plan (2 words)
hang on to 3 keep (3 words)
furious 4 very angry (1 word)

5 payment for a service or job (1 word) *fee*
6 continue, carry on with (1 word) *resume*
7 react in a frightened or alarmed way *panic* (1 word)
8 take out, select (1 word) *extract*

D Reading between the lines
When you read, you will often need to understand more than is actually written down. These questions will help you to read between the lines.
1 'Stevie grew up in a children's home.' What does this sentence tell you about Stevie's early childhood?
2 'They'd put me in a room on my own as a punishment.' What does this sentence tell you about the children's home?
3 Why do you think Stevie can ask for such a lot of money for a performance?
4 How do you think Stevie would try to teach other people his skill?

5 The show's over

Imagine you have just been to Stevie's show, or have seen it on television. Write 40–60 words to a friend, describing the show and your reactions to it.

> 7th May 1996
>
> Dear Tom
> I'm glad you enjoyed the weekend. It's a pity you couldn't stay longer – I've just seen an incredible performance by a professional regurgitator called Stevie Starr

Grammar and practice

1 Habitual actions and events

A Do these sentences from the article refer to Stevie's life now or to his life in the past? *N*

now 1 'I <u>tend</u> to start by swallowing a light bulb.'

now 2 'I often <u>go</u> into a pub, <u>order</u> a couple of drinks and then <u>cough up</u> the money to pay for them.'

past 3 'They'd <u>put</u> me in a room on my own as a punishment.'

now 4 'People <u>are</u> always <u>accusing</u> me of cruelty.'

past 5 'I'd <u>hit</u> myself on the chest and cough the money back up.'

now 6 'The fish never <u>die</u>.'

past 7 Every week, the staff <u>took</u> a proportion of the children's pocket money.

past 8 'I <u>used</u> to swallow all my coins.'

B Now or past?

1 How did you decide that a particular sentence referred to the past or the present? Was it the form of the verb, or another word in the sentence, or something else?

2 How can you tell that all the sentences refer to actions or events that are habitual or repeated?

C Now read sections 1 and 2 in the Grammar reference on page 200.

2 Practice

A Use of English

Complete the second sentence so that it has a similar meaning to the first sentence. Use up to five words including the word you are given. Do not change this word.

Example: When I was six, I spent all my spare time with my friends.   **used**
I *used to spend* all my spare time with my friends when I was six.

1 In the winter we played football.   **used**
We *used to play football* ~~football~~ in the winter.

2 I hardly ever play football these days.
often
These days *I don't often play* football.

3 Every Saturday afternoon I'd go to a football match with my father.   **always**

My father and I *always went to* a football match on Saturday afternoons.

4 At the age of eight, I always sat next my best friend at school.   **used**
When I was eight, *I used to sit next* to my best friend at school.

5 My brother and I caught the bus opposite the library.   **would**
My brother and I *would catch* the bus opposite the library.

6 If the weather was bad, the bus was always late.   **used**
The bus *used to be late* whenever the weather was bad.

7 On Saturday mornings my brother and I used to go into town to spend our pocket money.   **would**
My brother and I *would go into town* on Saturday mornings to spend our pocket money.

8 These days I usually travel everywhere by car.   **tend**
These days *I tend to travel* everywhere by car.

B Now and then

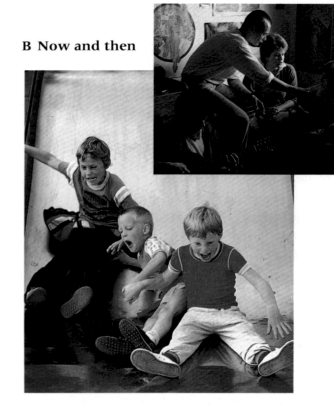

Compare aspects of your life as a child of six or seven with the same aspects of your life now.

Think about these situations and make brief notes.

1 your favourite way of spending free time, like a public holiday or a day off school or work

Example then – *got up early, played with friends*
now – *stay in bed, get up late, listen to music*

2 your attitude to money and buying things
3 favourite food and drinks
4 tastes in music and fashion
Compare your ideas in pairs or small groups.

C Think of at least three different ways of answering these questions about the way people behave in certain circumstances. How do people behave in these situations?

1 when they are tired

Example *They tend to forget things, fall asleep, and get bad-tempered. Sometimes they drop things or lose things.*

2 when they are in a hurry
3 when they are nervous or embarrassed
4 when they want to impress someone
How do you react in these circumstances?

D Repeated actions
In the text, Stevie Starr says: 'People are always accusing me of cruelty.'
The present continuous tense with *always* is used to refer to a repeated action. Here, Stevie is complaining about the frequent accusations, which he probably finds rather annoying.

1 Make similar complaints about people you know – they can be family or friends. Tell your partner.

Example *My brother is always leaving his clothes around the house.*

2 What do you do that other people, and perhaps you yourself, find irritating?

Example *I'm always losing my keys.*

3 Fluency

You and your partner are going on a three-week trekking holiday in the Himalayas. One person has had to drop out of the party at the last minute and you need to find a suitable replacement. The trek is for people of average fitness, and involves no climbing. The group will walk for six hours each day, which will mean an early start every morning. You'll share a tent at night. There will be a local guide, who speaks English, and Sherpas to carry your equipment.

A Before you read about the people who applied to join your expedition, decide what kind of person you are looking for. Write a list of important personal qualities.

B Student A, read the notes on page 198. Student B, read these notes about the good and bad points of three applicants. Choose who you would most like to join the expedition. You decide whether these people are male or female.

WM Peters
+ Physically fit, experienced climber. Works hard and is completely reliable. Speaks the local language.
− Talks a lot and is not a good listener.

L Palmer
+ fit and physically strong. A trainee nurse who gets on very well with other people, and is not easily offended.
− Has a tendency to be rather forgetful. Quite lazy and likes to lie in in the morning.

F Trueman
+ Is very enthusiastic about joining the group despite lack of experience. Never complains about anything and keeps a cool head in emergencies. Can keep secrets.
− Has no sense of humour and is not good at relaxing.

C Explain and justify your choice of new team member to your partner. Discuss each other's preferences and try to come to an agreement.

D Finally, compare choices with other pairs.

Exam techniques

1 Guidelines

Do	Don't
● Read the text quickly from beginning to end.	➡ Don't stop to think about individual words you do not understand.
● Read the questions very carefully. Work out whether they are asking for specific or general information.	➡ Don't rush this process or guess the answers yet.
● Read the text again, this time more carefully. Look for the parts that contain the information you need.	➡ Don't hurry this second reading. Understanding individual words is more important now.
● Choose the answer you think is correct: A, B, C or D.	➡ Don't guess. Look for real evidence.
● Try to eliminate the other three answers by finding reasons why they are wrong.	➡ Don't be too confident about the answer you have chosen until you have evidence that the others are not correct.

2 Practice

A Try out the guidelines on the passage opposite. As you read for the first time, decide what sort of passage it is and where it might be from.

B Read the questions and decide whether they are asking for specific or general information. Then, for each question, choose the answer which fits best according to the text. Note why the other three answers are wrong.

1 The writer of the passage wished
   A she had Sam's job.   C she looked like Sam.
   B she was called Sam.   D she was an art student.

2 In the mornings Sam used to
   A take a long time to put on her   C choose her clothes carefully.
     make-up.   D lie around before going to work.
   B get ready for work very quickly.

3 The writer went back to sleep in the mornings because
   A she couldn't face the day ahead.   C she always went to bed late.
   B she was always tired.   D she had no reason to get up.

4 The writer got to work late because
   A she always had a big breakfast.   C she wasn't keen on her job.
   B she spent a long time getting ready. D she didn't get up in time.

5 Eventually the writer left her job because
   A she wasn't very good at teaching.   C she got married.
   B her employer dismissed her.   D she knew she couldn't get to work
                                            on time.

6 The writer felt that Sam was
   A too tidy for her.   C a good person to share a flat with.
   B a very fortunate person.   D unsympathetic towards her.

7 What do we find out about the writer of the passage?
A She didn't get on with her flatmate.
B She lacked self-confidence.
C She paid great attention to her appearance.
D She was a well-organized person.

The Perfect Flatmate

When I was 21, I came to live in London. I shared a damp basement flat with a beautiful ex-art student from Brighton. Her name was Sam.
5 She had long brown hair and a slim figure that I was madly jealous of. She ate three chocolate bars for breakfast every morning.

I used to lie in bed looking at
10 her eating and getting dressed, wondering how she could possibly consume so much sugar without losing her teeth, her figure or her complexion. She'd put on her make-
15 up in under a minute, throw on whatever clothes happened to be lying around the room, and rush off to work looking like a model on the cover of a fashion magazine. Like
20 me, she was just an art teacher in a secondary school.

I, on the other hand, used to put on weight if I even smiled at a bar of chocolate. I'd already lost several
25 upper teeth, my face was spotty and I looked like a heavyweight boxer whatever I wore.

My morning reaction to Sam was always the same. I'd shut my eyes,
30 pull the blankets over my head and force myself back to sleep. I knew that I really ought to get up too, and make use of the early start to have a shower, iron my blouse, polish my
35 shoes, paint my nails and eat something for breakfast.

But I have never been what you'd call a morning person. The teaching job I was doing at the time
40 was the only period of my life, thank goodness, that I've had to be anywhere by 8.30 a.m. Anyway, I needed a few extra comforting dreams after the shock of seeing Sam
45 looking so beautiful. Going back to sleep to shut everything out, and using my bed as a favourite means of retreat, became an addiction – my worst habit.

50 Of course, I overslept and was late for work every single day of the week. Eventually I was told if things didn't improve I might be given the sack. So I gave up my job and got married
55 instead. I blame it all on Sam and her beauty.

3 Key words

Some words are more important than others in understanding a text. What are the key words in the story you have just read? Choose three words from each of these lists and be prepared to justify your choices in the light of the whole story.

Paragraph 1   London / flat / beautiful / slim / jealous / chocolate
Paragraph 2   bed / teeth / complexion / make-up / rush / model / teacher
Paragraph 3   weight / smiled / teeth / spotty / heavyweight boxer
Paragraph 4   morning / blankets / sleep / shower / blouse / breakfast

Choose your own key words from paragraphs 5 and 6 and compare your choices with other students.

rickshaw   FAR EAST

Description

Where on earth?

Introduction

A Which countries or parts of the world do you think these places are in? Look at the photographs and describe each place.

Example
This looks like the centre of a largish town or city. It's probably in a modern western country. Places like this are very busy because almost everyone has their own car. Too much traffic makes cities like this noisy and polluted.

B Which of these places is most like the place where you live? Have you ever lived in or visited places like the others?

C If you had to move, which of the places would you most like to live in, and which would you least like to live in? Give your reasons.

Listening

1 Think ahead

People go to new places for many different reasons. How many can you think of?

2 Listening

摘錄引用.

You are going to hear four extracts.
For the first and second extracts, say why the speakers are in the places they are describing.
For the third and fourth extracts, say where the speakers are.

3 Comprehension

A Read the questions below. Then listen to the four extracts again and choose the best answer, A, B or C.

1 Someone is talking on the radio about a place she is visiting. What sort of place is it?   the country 郷村
   A a village   B a city   C a country

2 You hear one half of a telephone conversation. What is the speaker describing?
   A an airport lounge   B an office block   C a hotel room

3 This speaker is living and working abroad. What was her main reason for wanting to do this?
   A She wanted to learn a foreign language.
   B She wanted to make a lot of money.
   C She wanted a change.

4 Listen to part of a TV interview. What is the interviewer asking the woman about?
   A a country the woman is visiting for a holiday
   B the country the woman is living in
   C the woman's own country   → what different from your country

4 Listening

A You are going to hear a man talking about living in Thailand. Read the statements below. As you listen to the recording, decide whether they are true or false.

1 The speaker started working in Thailand in 1969.
2 The restaurant was especially popular with people who worked for the government. *and everyone*
3 The speaker thinks that Number One was a good name for the restaurant.
4 The cooking was done in a small room behind the restaurant.
5 The cooks wore very few clothes.
6 None of the cooks was a woman.
7 The food was cooked in advance and then reheated before being served.
8 The owner of Number One and his family lived in a house next to the restaurant. *back*

B You are going to hear someone talking about living and working in Zimbabwe. Before you listen, read these unfinished sentences. As you listen, complete the sentences in your own words. What you write must make sense and be grammatically correct.

cobweb 蜘蛛網
pandemonium 鷹舍

1 The speaker works at . . . *Bombenay University*
2 He lives about a minute's walk away from . . *his work*
3 Before they moved to their chalet, the speaker and his family lived in *flat*,
4 According to the speaker, people get coughs and colds because of the difference between the *temperature changing daytime and nighttime (baⁿgh be careful)*
5 Some people compare the climate of Zimbabwe with . *South of California*
6 The fact that it isn't too hot at night helps *people sleep very well*

5 Over to you

From your point of view, what would be the advantages and disadvantages of living or working abroad? What would you miss about your own country? Are there aspects of your country that you would definitely not miss?

Grammar and practice

Used to

get used to + Ving
be used to + Ving
used to + V

A What are the different meanings of *used to* in these three sentences from the listening section?
1 You get *used to* seeing the sun every day.
2 We're already *used to* living here. *present*
3 This is about a restaurant which I *used to* go to when I was working in north-east Thailand.

B Which sentence:
a refers to a past situation? 3
b refers to a present situation? 2
c refers to a change of situation? 1

C Now read the Grammar reference on page 200.

D *Be* and *get used to* are followed by *-ing* (or a noun) when *used to* means accustomed.
Do you know any other verbs like this? There is a list in the Grammar reference on page 200 (*Used to*: C).

look forward to ving
object to ving

E Practice
Complete these sentences in two different ways.
1 No matter how hard I try, I'll never get used *to speaking English.*
2 When I was ten, I used *to go to school everyday.*
3 People who have just retired are not used *to staying at home.*
4 When my parents were young, they didn't use *to smoke.*
5 When foreigners visit my country, they aren't used *to being wraped*
6 When people get married, they have to get used . . . *to cooking for each other.*

F Fluency
How do these major changes affect people? For each one, think about the effect on the individual making the change and the effect on his or her family.
- changing school *get used to making the new friend.*
- leaving home *get used to cooking for yourself*
- getting married
- starting work

Discuss how these changes would affect you. What things would you find strange or different? How easy would you find it to get used to them?

Vocabulary

1 Describing places

Vocabulary reference p 215

A The place of my dreams

As you read the three descriptions of places, fill the gaps with one of these prepositions.

close to   from   in   on

1

My dream home would be a large flat 1 _____ the top floor of a luxury apartment block 2 _____ a quiet residential part of a large city. There would be parks and other open spaces around, and it would be quite 3 _____ the mountains. I wouldn't want it to be a seaside resort, but it shouldn't be too far 4 _____ the coast .

2

If I could live anywhere I liked, I'd choose an old house 1 _____ the centre of a medium-sized town. The town would have all the normal modern facilities, like banks, cinemas and supermarkets. Ideally it would also be of historical interest with a castle or an old church, but it shouldn't be too popular with tourists. It would be 2 _____ water of some kind – perhaps a river or a lake.

3

If I could choose, I'd live 1 _____ a small cottage 2 _____ a country lane 3 _____ the outskirts of a village. The village would have a few small shops and a friendly pub. It would be surrounded by countryside and be about ten miles 4 _____ the nearest town. Ideally, it would be 5 _____ a hilly area 6 _____ a forest.

B This illustration is a view from a building showing the immediate neighbourhood, the community and the wider geographical region. Which of the three descriptions in A does it best illustrate?

C Scan the three descriptions and underline all the place words you can find. List the words under the following headings.

housing, e.g. *flat*

facilities, e.g. *shop*, bank, cinema

communities, e.g. *town*, church, resort

parts of a community, e.g. *outskirts*

natural features, e.g. *mountain* lake .

Add any other words you know, then compare your lists with those in the Vocabulary reference on page 215.

D Think about your dream or nightmare home, and describe it to your partner.

E Write 60–70 words about the place you have been describing.

F Use of English

Read the text and decide which word A, B, C or D best fits each space.

At the seaside

Clacton and Frinton are holiday (1)_____ situated ten kilometres from each other on the east (2)_____ of England. Despite their proximity, they couldn't be more different in character from each other.

Clacton is a typical (3)_____ town with cheap fish and chip cafes, ice-cream stalls (4)_____ the seafront, bright amusement arcades and, of course, a traditional pier jutting out (5)_____ the sea. For a few weeks in the summer its (6)_____ are packed with young families; parents relax with a newspaper and a cup of tea, while their children play in the water or build sand castles.

Frinton, by contrast, is much more refined. Tasteful apartment (7)_____ overlook the undeveloped beach. It's ideal for elderly holiday-makers who enjoy a gentle stroll (8)_____ the seafront. It is quiet, some would say dead, compared to Clacton with its noise and bustle.

1 A	ports	B	resorts	C	places	D	districts
2 A	sea	B	beach	C	shore	D	coast
3 A	sea	B	coast	C	seaside	D	resort
4 A	to	B	on	C	over	D	in
5 A	into	B	on	C	to	D	at
6 A	seas	B	coasts	C	beaches	D	shores
7 A	houses	B	blocks	C	flats	D	castles
8 A	among	B	from	C	in	D	along

2 Phrasal verbs

A Phrasal verbs are two- or three-part verbs which are frequently used in informal English, for example, Stevie **grew up** in a children's home. Read these sentences and fill each gap with the correct form of one of the phrasal verbs from the list below.

get through   go on   grow up   pick up   settle down   turn into

1 While we were watching the film we _____ two bars of chocolate and two cans of Coke each.

2 Look at all those people. They're looking at something in the street. I wonder what's _____ .

3 My parents can't understand why I keep changing jobs. They'd really like me to _____ .

4 I've got a terrible cold. I think I might have _____ it _____ from someone at the party.

5 It took me years to get used to living in London – probably because I _____ in a quiet country area.

6 What started as a friendly conversation quickly _____ a full-scale argument.

B There is a list of the most useful phrasal verbs on page 222.

Writing

Paragraphing and punctuation

My least favourite place

Croydon is a largish town on the outskirts of London. It's a popular shopping centre and several large businesses have their headquarters there. Many of the people who live there work in London, which is about half an hour away by train.

I went to school in Croydon for six years and I never liked it. In the first place, there are hardly any historical buildings, so it is a rather dull town. Secondly, it is full of unfriendly people who are too busy to stop and chat. Lastly, because it is on a main road into London, the streets are always full of traffic and sometimes the air is so polluted that it's almost impossible to breathe.

As far as I'm concerned, I wouldn't mind if I never went to Croydon again.

1 Writing in paragraphs

A Read this description which appeared in a regular magazine feature called 'Favourite and least favourite places'. Do you know any towns like this?

B When you work on a piece of connected writing, it is important to divide what you write into paragraphs. Each time you change the subject, or your focus of attention, you should start a new paragraph. What is the subject or focus of each of the three paragraphs in the text above? Choose one of these titles.

1 The reasons I don't like Croydon
2 The reasons for Croydon's popularity
3 Final thoughts
4 The future of Croydon
5 A description of Croydon

2 Basic punctuation

A This unpunctuated description is intended for the same magazine feature. As you read it for the first time, divide it into three paragraphs.

My favourite place

chateauneuf is in the centre of brittany in north-west france and is on a hill overlooking a river most of the inhabitants are farmers or shopkeepers but there are a few businessmen who work in quimper which is 22 kilometres away everybody lives in stone houses or cottages with whitewashed walls ive visited chateauneuf every easter for six years now because i love the atmosphere and the friendly people chateauneuf is not on the coast so it hasnt been spoilt by tourists there are two small hotels where you can eat traditional french food quite cheaply at easter chateauneuf has a festival of traditional breton music if youre in brittany book into the gai logis hotel try the local food and then go for a walk along the river bank you wont regret it

B Read the text again and add the necessary punctuation. The missing punctuation marks are capital letters, full stops, commas and apostrophes. Check how these punctuation marks are used by looking at the Grammar reference on page 199.

3 Think, plan, write

Now write your own contribution to 'Favourite and least favourite places' for the magazine. You should write a description of 120–180 words with the title *My favourite place* or *My least favourite place*. Follow this paragraph plan.
Paragraph 1: a physical description of the place. Paragraph 2: reasons for liking or disliking the place. Paragraph 3: final comments.
When you have finished, check your punctuation carefully.

2 Future

The outlook for tomorrow

Introduction

A Which of the scenes above show weather conditions most similar to those in your country?

B What do you like and dislike about the climate of your country?

C How does the climate of a country affect the people who live there? Think about these aspects of people's lives:
- their daily routines
- their eating and drinking habits
- their clothes
- their homes and other buildings
- their character and attitude to life

Listening

1 Think ahead

You are going to hear an American talking about British weather and about the attitude of British people to the weather. What do you think he might say? Make notes and discuss your ideas.

2 Comprehension

A Now listen and say whether these statements are true or false.
F 1 The speaker lived in Britain for less than two months.
A 2 One July day, he took a pullover as he thought the evening might be cool. *chilly*
F 3 It was warm and sunny all morning.
F 4 In the afternoon, it rained very heavily.
F 5 People had to walk home because they couldn't start their cars.
A 6 Later in the day the fine weather returned.
F 7 According to the speaker, the British believe weather forecasts are reliable.

B You are now going to hear five short extracts, which are all related in some way to the weather. As you listen, match each of the extracts with one of these sentences A–F. There is one extra sentence which you do not need to use.
4 A Someone is asking for a lift.
3 B Someone is making predictions about the next few days.
C Someone is describing life on a farm.
1 D Someone is giving health advice.
5 E Someone is talking about travel plans.
2 F Someone is describing non-scientific ways of predicting the weather.

C Listen again and answer these questions.
1 In which two extracts is the colour red significant? *red hair is very white skin* so they must take care of sun *very much*
2 Which two extracts mention regions of countries? *coast*
3 Which two extracts mention methods of transport? *bus is late, ferry*

D Vocabulary
Read these phrases from the extracts and match the words in italics to meanings a-f. There are two more meanings than you need.
d 1 You don't need me to tell you to *take great care*.
a 2 After that, *all being well*, you can double the time . . .
e 3 That's the phone, I'll *get it*. *answer*
b 4 Just *hang on*, I'll ask Mum. *wait a moment*
a if there are no problems   b wait a moment   c put the phone down
d be very cautious   e answer it   f if you're not feeling ill

3 Over to you

1 Has the weather ever affected your life in a dramatic way?
2 Do you know any old sayings about the weather, like 'Red sky at night, shepherds' delight'?

Grammar and practice

1 The future

A As you know, there are several different ways of talking about the future in English. Look at these examples from the listening section.

1 We're going to try canoeing this year.
2 The ferry leaves at noon.
3 Temperatures will be around normal for the time of year.
4 We're setting off really early and driving down to Southampton.
5 That's the phone, I'll get it.
6 Cows lying down in the fields means there's going to be a thunderstorm.

Match the sentences with the kind of future they refer to.

4 a an action or event that has been arranged
3 b a prediction or expectation
5 c an instant decision about the immediate future – frequently an offer of help
2 d a scheduled or timetabled event
6 e a prediction based on evidence or knowledge
1 f an intention or plan to do something

B Before continuing, check your understanding of the different ways of referring to the future in the Grammar reference on pages 200–201.

2 Practice

A Read this letter and fill gaps 1–15 with the appropriate future form of the verbs in italics. Fill gaps a–j with one of these prepositions.

at before for in on

Dear Jo,

Sorry it's taken me so long to reply to the letter you wrote (a) _for_ May. The trouble was it arrived (b) _in_ the middle of the summer exams and I was just too busy to write back. That's my excuse anyway.

(c) _On_ Friday that's (d) _in_ three days' time, we (1)_____(break up) (e)_____ the holidays. I can't wait. My friends and I have got a great weekend planned. (f)_____ Friday evening we (2)_____(have) a party to celebrate the end of the school year. Then we (3)_____(start) our mini adventure - (g)_____ Saturday morning we (4)_____(get up) early to drive to Dover to catch the ferry to France. The boat (5)_____(leave) (h)_____ 9.30 and

(6)_____(get) to Calais a few minutes (i)_____ eleven o'clock.

I expect we (7)_____(stop) for something to eat in a little café, and then we (8)_____(drive) to Amiens. We're not quite sure how long it (9)_____(take). You're probably wondering why we (10)_____(go) to France at all. Well, the thing is there's a Slur concert in Amiens (j)_____ the evening - at a place called Megacité - and it seemed like a really exciting idea. It (11)_____(begin) at nine o'clock, so, as long as we keep driving, we (12)_____(get) there in good time.

We (13)_____(probably spend) Sunday and Monday looking round that part of France, and then catch the Tuesday morning ferry back to Dover. I (14)_____(send) you a postcard if I have time.

Hope you have a good summer. (15)_____(you do) anything exciting? Write soon.

Love, Sue

B What would you say in the following situations? Use appropriate future forms in your answers.

1 Your friend is having difficulty with her homework. Offer to explain it to her. _I'll help you_
2 You are always tired. Tell a friend what you plan to do about it. _I am going drinking more tea._
3 Someone asks your age on your next birthday. _I'll be 43._
4 Someone asks you to go on holiday with them. Apologize and tell them that you have already arranged to visit relatives. _I visit_
5 A friend wants to know about the next train to London. Tell them the departure time (8.00) and the time of arrival in London (10.00).
6 It has been raining all day. Suddenly the temperature drops to below freezing point. Make a prediction. _Temperature is going to snow_

C Arrangements
Work in pairs. The instructions for Student A are on page 198.
Student B
You have missed all your English lessons for the last two weeks, because you have been on holiday. You decide to phone a classmate (your partner), to ask him or her to meet you one evening next week to go through all the work you have missed. When you phone, tell your friend a little about your holiday and then arrange an evening meeting.

Example
Are you doing anything on Monday evening?

D Look at this picture and make predictions, using *will* or *going to*.

The D.J. is going to change the CD *He is going to switch off the light.*

The cake are going to falling down *The lady's hair is getting wet.*

E Fluency

1 Weather forecasters are warning that your town is about to be hit by storms, with unusually high winds and heavy rain. In groups, predict the effects of the storm on the town and its people. What *will* and *won't* happen?

If you are not sure about your predictions, you can use some of these expressions.

It will probably . . .
It probably won't . . .
It will almost certainly *an argument to happen*
It's quite likely that . . .
I should think it will . . .

F What'll happen to me?

Write 40–60 words about your own future. Choose one of the following subjects.

- things that are already arranged for the next year or two
- intentions and predictions for the next five years
- personal and career ambitions

3 Articles

A Look at these extracts from the listening section and fill the gaps with the definite article *the* or the indefinite article *a* or *an*.

1 It was __a__ day in July last year.
2 I remember __the__ day really well.
3 It was __a__ bright sunny morning.
4 I took __a__ thin pullover, just in case it turned chilly.
5 By two o'clock in __the__ afternoon, it felt like mid-December.
6 Don't stay out in __the__ hot sun for too long.
7 After that you can double __the__ time of __the__ previous day.
8 That's __the__ phone, I'll get it.
9 He wants to know if you can pick him up at __the__ station.

B Look at the gaps you have filled with *the*. Why did you decide to use *the* in each case? Choose one of these reasons.

1 It is not the first time this thing or person has been mentioned.
2 The speaker and the listener know what or who is being referred to.
3 There is only one of these things or people – in the world or in this context.

C Now decide whether the gaps in these sentences need *the* or no article.

Example   The QE2 takes passengers on __∅__ voyages across __the__ Atlantic.

1 Liam Neeson was born in __∅__ Ireland, but now lives in __the__ United States.
2 __∅__ film reviewers spend much of their time mixing with __the__ rich and famous.
3 When they're very young, __∅__ babies only drink __∅__ milk.
4 In __the__ evening, I met my girlfriend, we went for a walk, looked at __the__ moon and talked about __∅__ love.
5 Just before __the__ plane landed __the__ pilot told us that one of __the__ engines was on __∅__ fire.

D Compare answers with a partner. Work out some rules which explain when no article is used.

E Check your understanding of articles in the Grammar reference on page 201.

Vocabulary

Weather
Vocabulary reference p 215

A Arrange these weather words in order from the coldest to the hottest.

cold   cool   freezing   hot   mild   scorching   warm

B Fill the gaps in sentences 1–5 with the correct form of one of these verbs.

blow   fall   pour   shine   strike

1 When I looked out of the window this morning, snow _____ .
2 It _____ with rain all day, so the match was cancelled.
3 Can you hear the wind _____ outside?
4 During the storm last night our school was _____ by lightning.
5 The sun didn't _____ once during our two-week holiday.

C Fill the gaps in the sentences below with an adjective meaning the opposite of the adjective in italics. The first letter is given, together with the number of letters for each word.

1 Yesterday was *fine*, but today it's been w _ _ all day.
2 It was *bright* in the morning, but it became quite d _ _ _ later on.
3 The day started c _ _ _ _ , but became *cloudy* by midday.
4 The atmosphere in the west is quite *damp*, unlike the east, which has a reputation for staying d _ _ .

D Collocations
Match these adjectives with suitable weather nouns.

gentle   heavy   high   light   loud   strong   thick

Example   a **light** wind

1 a wind   4 snow   7 thunder   10 a breeze
2 rain   5 drizzle   8 clouds
3 fog   6 a shower   9 a downpour

E How many weather nouns can you think of that can be made into adjectives by adding the letter *-y* ? Write a list. Remember that sometimes the final consonant has to be doubled, e.g. su*n – sunny*.

F   Weather idioms
Guess the meanings of the idioms in italics in these sentences.

1   Ever since Laura's party, I've felt *under the weather*.
2   Did you see that dog chase those two cats? It *went like the wind.*
3   I'm going to get up early tomorrow morning *come rain or shine.*
4   I'm certainly not going to spend all my money in one go. I'm going to *save some for a rainy day.*
5   I don't know what all the fuss is about. As far as I'm concerned *it's a storm in a teacup.*
6   Our teacher has tried to explain it to me several times, but *I'm still in a complete fog.*
7   I've enjoyed living here, but now *there's a cloud on the horizon.* They're planning to build a new office block right opposite our apartment.

Exam techniques

Reading: Gapped text (missing sentences) Paper 1 Part 3

1 Guidelines

Do	Don't
• Read through the gapped text quickly. Think about what information might be missing.	➡ Don't try to fill any gaps until you have a general understanding of the text.
• Read the list of missing sentences. Remember, there is one extra sentence that you do not need.	
• Try to fit the sentences into the gaps. Match the topic of a missing sentence with the topic of the sentences before and after each gap.	➡ Don't look for language connections, for example grammatical links, until you have matched the subjects.
• Check your guesses by looking for language connections, e.g. matching verb tenses; pronouns which refer to nouns already mentioned.	➡ Don't rely only on subject connections. There may be more than one missing sentence on the same subject.
• Read the whole text with the missing sentences you have chosen, to check it makes sense.	➡ Don't forget to check that the extra sentence will not fit in any of the gaps.

2 Practice

fickle

A Follow the guidelines as you do this exercise. First read the article quickly and make a note of the main dangers and difficulties facing Arctic explorers.

The struggle to beat the cold

Last week, Stephen Martin, David Mitchell and Clive Johnson, all members of Transpolar Expedition, were forced to abandon their 1400-mile walk across the North Pole from Siberia to Canada.

The Arctic circle in winter is a hostile zone, as everybody knows. The polar bears spend much of their time sleeping, the birds fly south and many of the whales move to California. **[0 H]** The Arctic climate has been so severe this year, that several expeditions have been abandoned for safety reasons.

Martin, Mitchell and Johnson were overcome by exhaustion, cold and almost impossible travel conditions. Ironically, in one of the coldest spells in the north, with temperatures falling to –50 degrees C, the trio have had to deal with the polar traveller's nightmare – open water. In very strong wind, the Arctic ice will move and break up. Even though it is very cold, large

cracks can develop in the ice and expose the sea. **[1 G]**

The wind is another problem: no matter how low the temperature is, the wind will make it even colder. Sea water freezes at –1.8 degrees C, so falling in is extremely hazardous. Even if you are fully clothed, the water begins to soak through fairly quickly, so you have a limited amount of time to get out. **[2 A]** In this way a lot of body heat is lost.

And then there is the risk that one of the party could get cut off.

Even on one ice floe, this danger exists. If the weather is bad, the ice floes split. There have even been instances of a split appearing through the middle of a camp, which means that explorers must be prepared for the worst. **[3 C]** In these circumstances, it is difficult to relax.

After the struggle with heavy equipment across broken ice, in high winds and impossible temperatures, there is another problem: how do you rest? **[4]** Instead, there is ice in the

sleeping bag caused by frozen breath and perspiration. This can make sleeping extremely uncomfortable.

Martin, Mitchell and Johnson were prepared for all these problems. **[5]** They also took care to protect the parts of their body most at risk from frostbite: the hands and especially the feet. Their feet were protected by four layers of socks and three kinds of boots.

Their hands were also protected by several layers, with a huge pair of overgloves to finish. The problems came when they had to put up a tent or open a flask. **[6 E]** Hands are more vulnerable to frostbite than other parts of the body.

Unfortunately, all this careful preparation was not enough, and Martin, Mitchell and Johnson had to give up their expedition. They are not, however, the only explorers to have met with such bad luck: defeat and disaster have been part of polar history ever since Sir John Franklin sailed north in 1846 with the loss of 129 lives.

floe = a sheet of floating ice

B Gap-filling

1 Read through the missing sentences A–H. Then, using the content clues for these missing sentences to help you, choose the sentence which fits each gap.

2 A Once back on the ice, at –50C, anyone who has fallen in has to change their clothes rapidly, before the water begins to freeze.

B They wore the most up-to-date thermal clothing and carried a spare set each.

3 C So their belongings are always packed and they are ready to move quickly to one side or the other.

D One of the problems is, that even though it is constantly moving, Arctic ice has nowhere to go.

E Of course the more they could do with their gloves on the better.

F The body desperately needs heat of some kind.

G Although the water begins to freeze quite quickly, it is unsafe to cross for some time.

H In fact the only warm-blooded creatures in the region are scientists and explorers.

Content clues

A What effect would changing your clothes at a temperature of –50°C have on your body?

B What do their *thermal clothing* and their *spare sets* tell you about these people?

C Why might people have to be ready to move quickly?
How do you think this state of constant readiness makes people feel?

D If this ice has nowhere to go, what do you expect the next sentence to tell you?

E What would happen if gloves were taken off in conditions of extreme cold?

F In what situation might someone desperately want a hot water bottle?
Is it likely that a hot water bottle would be available in the Arctic?

G Which water would begin to freeze quite quickly?

H Does the text mention any other warm blooded animals?

2 Now check that the language of the missing sentences matches the language of the text. Use the language clues for the missing sentences to help you decide. What is the answer to the clue for H, the example sentence?

Language clues

A Why does the author write **the** water and not *water*?

B Who are *they*?

C *One side* of what?

D What could follow a sentence which starts *One of the problems. . .*?

E This sentence starts with *Of course. . .* What might the next sentence add?

F Whose *body*?

G What is the most common use of this verb tense (Simple present)?

H Which *region*?

C In pairs, compare answers. If you disagree with your partner, try checking to see if you answered the clue questions in same way as each other.
You can practise this technique again when you do the next reading text.

2

Congratulations! You're 130 today.

Introduction

A What is your personal definition of the age expressions *middle-aged, elderly, old* and *very old*? When do each of these ages start and finish?
At what age are people regarded as old in your country?

B How are old people treated in your country?

C Think of an old person you know well, perhaps a member of your own family. Describe the appearance and character of this person to another student.

Reading

1 Think ahead

What would be the best things and the worst things about living to be 130 years old? Make two lists of ideas.

2 Reading

A Before you read this article, look back at the guidelines for dealing with a gapped text on page 26.

B As you read the article for the first time, think about what kind of information may be missing.

Long Life

Scientists are finally beginning to unlock the secret everyone has been dying to know: just how long can we live? They confidently predict that in the 21st century people will be living to the incredible age of 130. And this is just the start.

Experts studying the process of ageing believe it is possible that people will live long enough to have great-great-great-great-great-grandchildren. **1** □ There are around 4000 people over the age of 100 in Britain – ten times more than 30 years ago.

Dr Vijg, a Dutch biologist, is the head of a project studying the growing number of old people in the population. **2** G

A century ago average life expectancy in Europe was 45. Today, providing we look after ourselves, drive our cars carefully, and cut down on things like butter, alcohol and cigarettes, we can add nearly 30 years to that figure. **3** X

But that is nothing, compared to what will happen once scientists have discovered our genetic secrets. **4** □ Dr Vijg says: 'Nobody dies from old age – just diseases that affect people as they get older.' And he forecasts that within 30 years, science will be preparing people for a longer life. 'Already the killer diseases are being eradicated,' he says. 'About 50% of cancers are curable, and I really believe that this will increase to 80%.'

Doctors also believe that the death rate from the biggest killers – diseases of the circulatory system – will decline as man comes to his senses by giving up smoking and eating more healthily. Dr Vijg points to experiments with animals in laboratories. **5** E

Dr Vijg believes that as life span increases, so will other expectations. Women will be having babies at an older age. **6** I 'In another ten years people might think it normal for a woman of 50 to be having her first child.'

What about living forever? Will eternal life ever become a reality? 'So far, that is science fiction,' says Dr Vijg. 'Theoretically it is possible, but it will be another hundred, perhaps two hundred years before we know all the secrets of our genes.'

3 Comprehension

Choose from sentences A–G the one which fits each gap in the article. Remember, one of the sentences does not fit anywhere.

A Within the next ten years, we may all have added a couple more years on top of that.

B Some of the problem genes, like those that cause haemophilia, have already been tracked down. 查出

C Their work is being carried out by biologists in laboratories all over Europe.

D This belief is based on research and on the fact that more and more people are living to be 100 as our general health improves.

E 'Those given less food, but of a higher quality, lived to the human equivalent of 150 years.'

F 'Already, more and more are having their first child when they are over 30,' he says.

G He and his team are focusing their attention on human genes, which they think may hold the key to what kills us, early or late in life.

4 Vocabulary

The words in this table are from the article. Fill as many of the gaps as you can with related words.

	Noun	Verb	Adjective	Adverb
1	confidence	X	confident	confidently
2	prediction	predict	predictable	predictably
3	health	X	healthy	healthily
4	improvement	improve	X	X
5	cure	cure	(in)curable	X
6	caution	X	cautious	cautiously
7	expectation	expect	expected	X
8	reality	X	real / realistic	really / realistically

5 Over to you

Find out how many students in your class or group would like to live to be 130. What are their reasons?

Grammar and practice

1 The future continuous

In the first part of the unit the future continuous was used to talk about actions or events which will be in progress at a specific time in the future.

Example   . . . *this time next week, **we'll** probably **be having** our first lesson.*

This tense can also be used to predict future trends, developments or tendencies.

Example   *In the 21st century people **will be living** to the incredible age of 130.
Women **will be having** babies at an older age.*

2 The future perfect

Another way of expressing predictions about the future is to talk about actions or events which will be completed by a particular time in the future. The future perfect tense is used for this purpose.

Example   *Dr Vijg reckons that **by** the year 2000 **we will all have added** a couple more years to our lives.
By early in the next century the disease **will have been brought** under control.*

3 Practice

A Predict some possible 21st century trends. Here are some subjects to think about.
- education   number of years at school, university

Example   *In the 21st century, more students will be going to university.*

- employment   working hours, holidays, retirement age
- leisure   facilities, hobbies, TV, sports
- diet   meat, cost, health, convenience foods

B Look into your own future. Think about this time tomorrow, this time next week and this time next year. Think about all the things you will or won't do in the period between now and these times. Now talk to a partner about what you will or won't have done by these times.

Example   *What will you have done by this time next year?
By this time next year, I'll have left school, but I won't have started work.*

If you are not sure about the future, use the word *probably.*

Example   *I'll **probably** have left school, but I **probably** won't have started work.*

4 Fluency

New Year's Eve 1999 will be a momentous occasion. It will be a thousand years since the start of the last new millennium.

A Make some predictions about your life in the year 2000. Think about things you will have done by this time, and things you'll still be doing. Compare ideas with other students.

B What do you think your country or town will do, or should do, to celebrate this occasion? How do you intend to celebrate?

Vocabulary

1 Age

A Prepositions

Fill the gaps in these sentences with appropriate prepositions. There are similar sentences in the article 'Long Life' on page 28.

1 My father retired from work just before the age _____ 65.
2 In the future, many women will have their first child _____ an older age than they do now.
3 My grandfather lived _____ the age of 82.
4 Currently, many people die _____ diseases of the circulatory system.
5 Only people _____ the age of 18 can see this film, because it's very violent.

B Expressions

Guess the meanings of the age idioms in *italics* in these sentences.

1 My father always says *You're only as old as you feel.* *the age but still young*
2 I've heard that joke before – it's *as old as the hills.* *very old.*
3 Anna always has such sensible ideas. She's certainly got *an old head on young shoulders.* *old experience.*
4 Paul keeps on making the same mistake – but you can't *teach an old dog new tricks*, can you? *change the habit. not easy.*
5 My friend talks just like his father. In fact he's *a real chip off the old block.* *the same character as the father or family*
6 You wouldn't think my mother was nearly 60, would you? She's very *young for her age.* *looks very young.*

2 Phrasal verbs

The article about the Arctic on page 26 contains the sentence 'In very strong wind, the Arctic ice will move and *break up.*'

Like many phrasal verbs, *break up* has an obvious, literal meaning and several idiomatic meanings. It can mean break into pieces, come to an end, separate, finish school for the holidays.

Put up can mean lift, raise, increase, provide accommodation for, display, build and tolerate (*put up* **with**).

Fill the gaps in these sentences with the correct form of either *break up* or *put up*.

1 Over the last six months garages *have put up* the price of petrol three times.
2 A group of American students are coming to stay next year. We've offered *to put up* three of them.
3 Although the meeting lasted nearly six hours, it *broke up* _____ without agreement.
4 To get the teacher's attention, you've got to *put up* your hand.
5 Last night I went round to complain about my neighbour's TV. I just couldn't *put up* the noise any longer.
6 When do you *break up* for the summer holidays?
7 It was lucky that the pilot jumped out when he did – the plane *broke up* _____ and burst into flames as soon as it hit the ground.
8 Mark's really fed up. He and his girlfriend *broke up* last night.

Writing

Formal and informal styles

1 Formal or informal? Think of some everyday situations in which people write *formally* and *informally*. Make two lists.

2 Models **A** Read these short texts quickly. Decide where they are from and who they might have been written to or for.

1 Having a snack before going on the mountain railway. Weather perfect – bright sun, clear. Hotel excellent. See you when we get back. I'll ring.

2 There is one difference between what I cook and the food I was brought up on – I don't use meat, but it tastes as good, if not better, than using (to put it bluntly) dead animals.
Which brings me to the reason I've written this book.

3 Thanks for the pics. They're brilliant – specially that one of Mum and Dad just before they set off for the airport! I might get that one blown up and then put it up on the wall somewhere!

4 A **video camera** is used for recording electronically encoded visual images. Video cameras can be separate portable units or video-tape cassette recorders, incorporated with the camera in devices which are known as camcorders.

5 We are delighted to hear that you've made a complete recovery and that you'll be able to make it on Friday. It doesn't matter when you get here, and if you feel like leaving early, that's quite alright, too.

6 I have worked at Datascreen for eight years. For most of that time I have been in charge of the main office, which has meant resolving staff problems, managing the accounts and ordering stationery. I understand that this is the kind of experience you are looking for.

7 Considering his last album was made in his kitchen, Blueboy Jones has got used to studio technology pretty quickly. This is an impressive collection of songs. My favourite track is Barefoot Blues.

8 I'm writing to thank you for having me to stay. I really appreciate all the trouble everyone went to to make me feel at home. When I told my friends what a fantastic time I'd had, they were really envious.

B Now decide whether each text is written in formal or informal language. Which are the most formal and the most informal texts?

3 Analysis Which features of the texts helped you to decide how formal or informal they were? Here are some questions to help you to distinguish between formal and informal language. For each question, compare the two texts in brackets. Which kind of writing is more likely to

1 have shorter sentences? (1 and 6)
2 have a more impersonal style or tone? (3 and 4)
3 use fewer shortened verb forms? (7 and 8)
4 include polite phrases? (3 and 5)
5 use passive verbs? (4 and 8)
6 use phrasal verbs rather than single-word verbs? (3 and 6)
7 leave out words, such as pronouns? (1 and 2)
8 use slang or colloquial words? (3 and 5)

pics

4 Practice

A Read this informal reply to a party invitation and fill the gaps by choosing one of the phrases below.

(1)_____ for the invitation to your party on Thursday. (2)_____, but (3)_____. My boss has just (4)_____ that I've got to (5)_____ a training course in Birmingham from Monday to Friday. As you can imagine, (6)_____ about it – I was really looking forward to seeing all my (7)_____ again.
I'll (8)_____ you for (9)_____ when I'm back. (10)_____ to everyone.

1 I am very grateful / thanks
2 Sorry / I apologize
3 I can't make it/ I will not be able to be there
4 let me know / informed me
5 attend / go on
6 I am most depressed / I'm really fed up
7 old mates / ex–colleagues
8 ring / telephone
9 a conversation / a chat
10 Say 'Hi' / Give my regards

B This is a more formal letter cancelling an arrangement. Choose the appropriate word or phrase to fill the gaps.
(1)_____ I shall not be able to (2)_____ the interview (3)_____ for next Wednesday. (4)_____ a staff shortage at work. All full-time employees have been (5)_____ to be at work every day next week. (6)_____ that I am still (7)_____ the job I have applied for (8)_____ and I would be most grateful if (9)_____. (10)_____ this causes you.

1 Sorry to say / I am sorry to inform you that
2 attend / be at
3 we fixed / that was arranged
4 This is due to / It's all because of
5 asked / requested
6 I'd like to point out / I should make it clear
7 very interested in / really keen on
8 in your company / at your place
9 we could fix another time / a new interview date could be arranged
10 I apologize for any inconvenience that / Sorry for any fuss

5 Think, plan, write

You are going to write an informal letter to an English-speaking pen friend. Thank your friend for an invitation to visit his or her family in the summer. Explain that you are unable to go, as you have already made other plans.

A Before you write, decide what to say. What plans have you made for the summer?
List the informal expressions you could use to thank your pen friend for the invitation and to apologize for having to turn it down.

B Write the letter in 120–180 words. Here is a brief paragraph plan to follow:
Paragraph 1   Greetings and thanks for the invitation.
Paragraph 2   Apologies for being unable to accept, with reasons.
Paragraph 3   Conclusion. Say when you hope to see your pen friend again.

Exam techniques

Listening: Short extracts Paper 4 Part 1

1 Guidelines

Do	Don't
• Read all the questions and the three possible answers for each one. This may help you to predict the content of each extract.	➡ Don't waste time before the recording starts. You can get a lot of useful information from the questions and possible answers.
• As you hear an extract for the first time, listen for words associated with one of the three answers. Be careful – the wrong answers may also include some of these words. Choose what you think is the right answer.	➡ Don't worry if you don't understand everything the first time, as each extract is repeated.
• Listen to the extract again and check your choice of answer.	➡ Don't decide on your final answer until you have heard the extract twice.
• Keep calm. You can answer a question correctly even if you don't understand every word.	➡ Don't leave any questions unanswered.

2 Practice

Follow the guidelines above as you do this listening exercise. Note that in the exam there will be eight extracts in all.

You will hear people talking in six different situations. For questions 1–6, choose the best answer, A, B or C. There are clues in *italics* about the questions or extracts to help you as you listen.

1 A man is talking about a work routine. What is his job?
   A postman
   B dustman
   C delivery driver
   What do each of these people do in their jobs?

2 What is the relationship between the speakers in this conversation?
   A mother and son
   B employer and employee
   C teacher and student
   *One of the speakers uses the word **terms**. What places have time periods called terms?*

3 If you overheard this conversation, where would you be?
   A in a vet's surgery
   B in a doctor's surgery
   C at a hospital
   *What is the difference between a **vet** and a **doctor**?*

4 A man is talking about aspects of his work. What is his occupation?
   A actor
   B dentist
   C surgeon
   *What different kinds of **theatre** are there? Who might wear a **mask** in a theatre?*

5 A man is talking about a frightening experience he once had. What was the situation?
   A a bomb scare
   B a driving accident
   C a mining accident
   *What is **coal dust**? Where might you find it **in the air**?*

6 Where might you overhear a conversation like this?
   A at a hairdresser's
   B in a clothes shop
   C in a school
   *What can have **highlights** and a **natural wave**?*

3 Opinion

The rich and famous

Yacht

paparuzzA

paperazzu

Introduction

A In your opinion, what are the advantages and disadvantages of being famous? Make two lists.

B Do you think the lives of all famous people are affected by the points on your lists? Name some people who are, or have been, most affected.

Reading

1 Think ahead   What do you know about Elton John? Do you think he is happy with his life? Why? Why not?

2 Reading   Read the article as quickly as you can to find out if you were right. Don't worry about the missing headings.

wig — perruka (注記)

Talking to... Elton JoHn

1 C

aimlessly =
When I'm not working, I like <u>plodding round</u> the kitchen doing the things everybody else does. I love going to the
5 supermarket to do the shopping. I come back with far more stuff than I need. When I am on holiday in St. Tropez, I love to get up at six in the morning to
10 get the fresh bread. People often see me wheeling my trolley round the supermarkets in the town.

2 D

I've tried going out (in disguise –
15 <u>dark glasses,</u> hat, that sort of thing – but nine times out of ten it doesn't work. Most people are very pleasant and polite. But it's frustrating if you get out of bed
20 on the wrong side – and you do some days – and someone asks you for an autograph and they haven't got a pen or a piece of paper. But I enjoy my popularity;
25 I don't see the point in being a recluse. 隱居者
rustic

3 A

That's a tricky one to answer.
I've always been a bit of <u>a loner.</u>
By that I don't mean that I'm
30 lonely. It's just that I like to be my own boss all the time. Don't confuse that with being lonely because I'm not. I've lots of great friends around me. But I'm
35 terribly <u>set in my ways</u> and, at my age, it's very hard to change. I don't particularly want to, either. Being successful has given me the confidence to do things I
40 wouldn't have had the courage to do otherwise. But I still retain that shyness when I first meet people. I'm never going to get rid of that.

4 F

45 I'm one of those people who only has to look at a doughnut and I immediately put on a kilo without even eating it. I've always had a problem with my
50 weight. It doesn't bother me too much, although I get depressed when I'm very overweight. I dieted once and I became so obsessed that I nearly made
55 myself ill. But I'm happy with the way I am at the moment. If you exercise at least three or four

surgundi 65

times a week and play tennis, then it's no problem, but you
60 have to keep at it.

5 E

When I get up in the morning, I go on this exercise machine I've got and walk four or five miles in an hour. That burns off the
65 calories for the rest of the day. When I'm on tour, I eat three meals a day and don't snack. I can't eat before or after a show so that helps. It's when I'm at
70 home – the worst thing is the fridge and snacking. I'm a terrible snacker. I'm a big bread fan and I love curry.

6 B

I can't keep touring and making
75 records for the rest of my life – I've got to try something different now and then. One thing I am interested in doing is writing a musical.

7 H

80 That's highly unlikely. I'm not interested in going into a theatre and performing every night. You may find that strange but if you're on tour, at least
85 you're changing cities. I played at the Hammersmith Odeon once for fourteen nights and by the end of it I was going crazy. It was like going to the office. So
90 people who actually appear in plays and musicals for two to three years have my greatest sympathy and admiration. I never consider what I do as
95 work.

3 Comprehension

A The journalist's questions are missing from the article. Choose the most appropriate question from the list A–H for headings 1–7. There is one extra question which you do not need to use.

A Has fame changed you as a person?

B Will you be doing what you're doing now in ten years' time?

C What sort of things do you enjoy?

D How do you avoid being recognized?

E How do you keep yourself fit?

F You like your food, don't you?

G Have you ever wished you weren't famous?

H So, will we see you in your own production one day?

B Vocabulary

Choose the correct definitions for these words and expressions from the article.

1 a recluse (line 26)
   A an ordinary person
   B a celebrity
   ✓C a person who avoids other people

2 a loner (line 28)
   ✓A a person who likes being alone
   B a bossy person
   C a person who is unhappy without other people around

3 set in one's ways (line 35)
   A used to living with other people
   B bad-tempered and difficult
   ✓C having fixed habits

4 to get out of bed on the wrong side (line 19)
   ✓A to wake up in a bad mood
   B to wake up in a good mood
   C to be away from home

C Reading between the lines

1 'You like your food, don't you?'. What question is the interviewer really asking?

2 Why do you think Elton John 'can't eat before or after a show' (line 68)? *nervous*

3 Elton compares playing at the Hammersmith Odeon to working in an office (line 89). What does this tell us about his attitude to work? *routine*

4 Find evidence in the article which suggests that Elton John is basically happy with himself and his lifestyle.

4 Over to you

1 Have you ever met a famous person or received a letter from someone famous? Tell the class about it.

2 If you saw someone famous in a public place like a restaurant, what would you do?

3 What would you most like and most dislike about being famous?

5 A night out

You have won first prize in a competition – an evening out in a place of your choice with the celebrity of your choice. Write a paragraph explaining who you have chosen and where you have chosen to go.

Grammar and practice

1 Gerunds 动名词

A Form and use

Gerunds are verbs which behave like nouns. They can be used in different ways. Look at these sentences from the interview with Elton John. Underline the gerunds.

1 The worst thing is the fridge and snacking.
2 I can't keep touring and making records for the rest of my life.
3 Being successful has given me the confidence to do things I wouldn't have had the courage to do otherwise.
4 One thing I am interested in doing is writing a musical.

Match the gerunds with their uses, a–d, below.

a after prepositions (verbs and adjectives can be followed by a preposition + gerund)
b as the object or complement of a clause or sentence
c after certain verbs
d as the subject of a clause or sentence

B Find more examples of these uses of the gerund in the interview and underline them. Are there any other -ing words which are not gerunds? What are they?

C Subject and object

Complete the sentences by adding a verb in the gerund form and some more words. Finish each sentence in two different ways. Look back at the reading text and the Introduction for ideas. The first one has been done for you.

1 *Being a well-known pop star* means you are recognized wherever you go.
   Being a celebrity means you are recognized wherever you go.
2 _Wearing dark glasses_ is a trick used by many stars to try to avoid recognition.
3 When you are rich and famous, _giving photo / being busy_ becomes an ordinary everyday thing.
4 Most famous people find _being recognized by people_ an extremely boring, but unavoidable part of being famous.
5 _Having no peace / Being followed / Keeping good figure_ is another disadvantage.
6 But for the majority, _being a rich / earning money_ more than compensates for any disadvantages fame brings.

2 Gerunds after prepositions

Complete each sentence in an appropriate way. Choose the correct preposition from those below and add a suitable verb in the gerund form, with any other words you need. The first one has been done for you.

1 Andrea's parents congratulated her _on winning_ .
2 Jamie hates sport. Because he's overweight, he's particularly bad _at running_
3 Sally's a brilliant athlete and is capable _of winning_
4 The athlete was banned for life. She'd been warned _about taking a drug_ 禁止
5 Having made two false starts already, Colin was terrified _of being disqualified_
6 It was Pete's first final and he was excited _about racing_
7 She retired from competitive sport because she got bored _with going on a diet / keeping fit_
8 Carl doesn't care about the prize money. He's only interested _in winning / competing_

about   at   with   in   on   of

3 Verbs followed by gerunds

A The verbs in the following exercise can be followed by a noun or a gerund verb form. Example:
*She couldn't resist **the chocolate cake**.*
*She couldn't resist **having** another slice.*
Use verbs from the list below to fill the gaps in these sentences. You will need to put the verb in the correct tense. There are two extra verbs.

1 I've decided that I really must _____ smoking. I just can't get rid of this cough.
2 I'll never get this finished if you _____ interrupting me!
3 I know Paul didn't take it. Sara has _____ stealing it.
4 I'm getting so fed up with my job that I'm seriously _____ handing in my notice.
5 Would you _____ repeating that? I didn't catch what you said.
6 You can't _____ going to the dentist forever. You'll have to go sometime.
7 You _____ losing your job if your boss finds out you weren't really ill.
8 You can go home as soon as you've _finished_ typing those letters.

| admit | finish | keep | miss | put off _=postpone_ |
| consider | give up | mind | prevent | risk |

enjoy = love = be crazy about
= like = be into = keen on
= be dying for ...

今吨功⇒早

B Now read section 1 in the Grammar reference on page 201.

不喜 = dislike = don't mind
hate = loathe = detest = can't stand = can't bear

4 Gerunds after verbs of liking and disliking

A There are several verbs and expressions in English which express how much or how little we like something, e.g. *enjoy*, *can't stand*. How many others do you know? Make a list, then put them in order from extreme liking to extreme disliking.

B Tell the person sitting next to you about your likes and dislikes, using as many of these verbs and expressions as you can. Think about films and TV, music, sports and games, travel, food, other people, duties and obligations.

Example   *I enjoy watching horror films.*
         I can't stand people smoking while I'm eating.

Do you share any likes and dislikes with your partner?

5 Use of English

A Read the following text through quickly. What does Roger Black enjoy doing?

B Think about the kinds of word that are missing in gaps 1–10, e.g. prepositions, articles. Then choose the correct word for each gap from the words below. There are two extra words which you do not need to use.

C Underline the gerunds in the text and classify them according to the uses described in 1A.

A day in the life of an athlete

Most of my day revolves around my training schedule. I never have a day off unless I'm unfit, (1)_____ at some point I'll head off to see my coach and spend two hours either on the track (2)_____ in the gym. If I'm not training in the morning, I'll spend about two hours sitting (3)_____ my desk sorting out my finances and answering letters – I get (4)_____ of fan mail.

I try to keep the evenings for myself and, although I really enjoy spending time alone at home, I like to see my friends (5)_____ well. We might go out to (6)_____ movie, or entertain in one another's houses but it's always fairly low key.

One important thing (7)_____ being an athlete is that you can't really afford to live it up very much. I know someone who did and (8)_____ really affected his running. As (9)_____ as he stopped partying, he performed much better. One thing I have to do is look after (10)_____, which is not compatible with going out to lots of parties. Rest and recovery are important parts of my day and my favourite form of relaxation is sitting down and playing my guitar.

a	about	as	at	it	lots
myself	on	or	so	soon	the

6 Fluency

Changing places

Work with a partner. Decide which of you is Student A and which is Student B and read your instructions.

Student A

Imagine you can change places with someone you like for a week. This person can be famous or ordinary, a man or a woman. Don't tell your partner who you have chosen. Now imagine yourself in this person's shoes. Think about what you do, where you live, what you do in your spare time, what you like/ dislike about your new lifestyle, and make notes. Your partner will interview you and try to guess who you have changed places with.

Student B

You are a reporter and you are going to interview Student A. Student A has changed places with another person for a week. This person may be famous or not. Prepare the list of questions you will ask Student A to find out what they like and dislike about their lifestyle. For example, ask about where they live, what they do in their spare time, what they can do now that they couldn't do before, what they do in their job.

You cannot ask who they have changed places with. You must guess this at the end of the interview.

Exam techniques

Use of English: Cloze Paper 3 Part 2

1 Guidelines

Do	Don't
• Read the whole text through quickly first.	➡ Don't read the text too slowly.
• Read the text again. Decide what it's about.	➡ Don't worry if you haven't understood everything.
• Think what kinds of words are missing, e.g. verbs, articles, prepositions, etc.	➡ Don't worry yet about what the missing words are.
• Read the text one sentence at a time, filling the gaps you are confident about first. Remember to add one word only.	➡ Don't panic if you can't fill all the gaps immediately.
• Read the text again and fill the remaining gaps. If you aren't sure, make sensible guesses.	➡ Don't leave any gaps empty.
• Check for accuracy of grammar and spelling.	

2 Practice

A Read the text through quickly and decide which of these three titles best describes what the text is about.
1 Men still at top of earnings league
2 The price of fame
3 Million dollar kids

B Now use the guidelines above and the questions and clues opposite to help you complete this text. There is an example (0) at the beginning.

In the 1960s women tennis players received little or no prize money at all. Nowadays, (0) _however_, although prize money for women is still less (1) _than_ for men, top women players can earn twice as much in a fortnight (2) _as_ a successful company director does in (3) _an_ entire year.

But official prize money only accounts for a fraction of the total earnings of both men (4) _and_ women players these days. Most (5) _of_ a top tennis player's income comes (6) _from_ sponsorship contracts with fashion and sportswear companies rather than major championships. Players (7) _are_ paid huge sums of money to wear anything from tennis shoes (8) _to_ a wristwatch.

These massive sponsorship deals have turned tennis stars, some still only (9) _in_ their teens, into millionaires. With (10) _so_ much money in the bank and the world at their feet at (11) _such_ an early age, it is not really surprising (12) _that_ some young stars have not been able (13) _to_ cope with the pressure that fame (14) _has_ brought and have become victims of (15) _their_ own success. What promised to be brilliant early careers have ended in personal failure and psychological trauma for more than a few.

Questions and clues

0 The writer is contrasting the situation of women tennis players in the 60s with nowadays. The conjunction which introduces a contrast and can come between commas is *however*.

1 The amount of prize money which women tennis players receive is compared with the amount that men get. What word is used with *less* (and its opposite *more*) in comparative structures?

2 This is another comparative structure. Top women players' earnings are compared with those of a company director.

3 What clues are there that tell you the missing word is an article?

4 This word joins words or phrases together and frequently occurs with *both*.

5 This word comes after quantifiers like *most, several, some* and before an article + noun.

6 This preposition frequently follows *come*.

7 Which part of the verb is missing? An alternative way of expressing the same idea is: 'fashion and sportswear companies pay players huge sums of money to wear . . .'

8 Which other preposition often occurs with *from* ? Here, the two prepositions introduce the range of things players promote.

9 This is a preposition and part of a phrase used to refer to people's approximate age.

10 Look at the word after the gap. Together, they mean an unspecified quantity.

11 This word intensifies the meaning of the adjective *early*. The whole phrase could be expressed as: 'when they are so young'.

12 This conjunction occurs after some adjectives, e.g. *surprising, interesting, important,* and introduces a clause in which more information is given.

13 What structure follows the verb *to be able* ? What kind of word is *cope* ? What is missing?

14 Part of the verb is missing. Look at the word which follows. The tense of the previous verb will also help.

15 This is a possessive adjective. Whose success is being talked about?

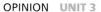

3 Art for art's sake

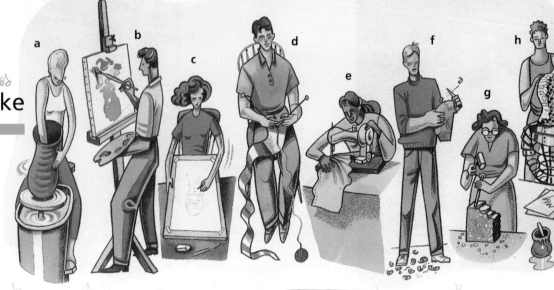

(handwritten notes, left margin:)
pottery – clay
painting – canvas
drawing : charcoal
knitting = wool
sewing = cloth
carving = wood
sculpture = stone
Sculpture : < steel

canvas   carving   charcoal   clay   cloth   drawing   knitting   painting
papier-mâché   pottery   sculpture   sewing   steel   stone   wood   wool

Introduction

A Match the materials and the names of the arts and crafts with the drawings.

B Have you ever made anything? What did you make it from? Was it useful or decorative or both? Were you pleased with the result?

Listening

1 Think ahead

Look at these photos of sculptures made by two British sculptors. Which sculptures do you think were made by the same sculptor? Why? What materials do you think the sculptors used?

2 Listening

You are going to hear a sculptor talking about one of the sculptures above. As you listen, decide which sculpture she is talking about.

3 Comprehension

A You are going to hear another sculptor talking about one of her sculptures. As you listen, complete these notes with a word or a short phrase.
1 The sculpture represents the elements of _____ .
2 The sculpture is made of _____ .
3 She wanted it to represent what happens in _____ .
4 She left the sculpture unfinished so that people could _____ .

B You are going to hear a conversation between a man and a woman, which takes place in an art gallery. Decide whether the following sentences are true or false.

Sculpture 1   1 The man thinks the name of the sculpture is appropriate. *T*
              2 The sculpture is taller than a real person. *T*
              3 Both of them like the colours. *T*   *junk*
Sculpture 2   4 The man compares the sculpture to rubbish. *The like the colour*
              5 The man doesn't like anything about the sculpture. *F*
Sculpture 3   6 The man thinks 'The Giant' is more realistic than this piece. *T*
              7 The man thinks art is about beauty. *T*

4 Points of view

1 Do you agree more with the man's idea of art or the woman's ?
2 Do you think art treasures should be kept in their places of origin?

regret, remember, stop, go on

Grammar and practice

Gerunds and infinitives

A Change of meaning

1 Several verbs can be followed by either the gerund or the infinitive but there is a change of meaning. An example of this is the verb *remember*.
   I don't remember *inviting* him = I have no recollection of inviting him.
   I didn't remember *to invite* him = I didn't do what I intended to do.
2 Try to match these sentence beginnings (a and b) with their endings (c and d). Then choose the best explanation (e or f) for each sentence.

Example   1 – a, d, e and b, c, f

1 a *I've tried taking the pills the doctor prescribed . . .*
  b *I've tried to take the pills the doctor prescribed . . .*
  c *. . . but I just can't swallow them.*
  d *. . . but I still can't sleep.*
  e I've done the action as an experiment.
  f I've made an effort to do the action.
2 a *I stopped to speak to Richard . . .*
  b *I stopped speaking to Richard . . .*
  c *. . . after he lied to me.*
  d *. . . to ask him about the weekend.*
  e I interrupted one activity in order to do another.
  f I finished an activity.
3 a *I regret to tell you . . .*
  b *I regret telling her . . .*
  c *. . . that I am unable to offer you the job.*
  d *. . . I was sacked from my last job.*
  e I am sorry about something I did in the past.
  f I am sorry about something I am doing now or am about to do.

4 a *He went on talking . . .*
  b *He went on to talk . .*
  c *. . . even after he'd been told to keep quiet.*
  d *. . . about his solutions after he'd outlined the problems.*
  e He finished one activity and started another.
  f He continued to do the action.

B Now read section 3 in the Grammar reference on page 202 before you do the practice exercise.

C Practice

Fill the spaces with an appropriate verb in the gerund or infinitive.

1 I hope he's remembered _____ the tickets.
2 UK Air regrets _____ the late arrival of flight UA127.
3 He's tried _____ the window but it's stuck.
4 Will you stop _____ while I'm talking!
5 Shall we go on _____ the next item on the agenda?
6 She doesn't remember _____ to babysit.
7 He's tried _____ less but he still hasn't lost weight.
8 Do you regret _____ school at 16?

D Fluency

1 Have you ever forgotten to do something important? What was it? What was the result?
2 Is there anything in your life you regret doing or not doing ?

Vocabulary

1 The arts
Vocabulary reference p. 215

h aisle
g audience
i circle
d conductor
b curtain
m drummer
f footlight
j gallery
n guitarist
p loudspeaker
q microphone
c orchestra pit
l screen
e set
a stage
k stalls

A Venues
Match the words in the box with the correct features in the illustrations.

B Use of English

Read this text and decide which of the four alternatives best fits each gap.

King Lear
Adrian Noble's modern production of William Shakespeare's 'King Lear' opened last week at the Barbican Theatre in London to enthusiastic (1)_____ .

   Robert Stephens, heading an impressive supporting cast, gives a moving and powerful (2)_____ as Lear, and David Bradley, who (3)_____ the Earl of Gloucester, is so convincing in the (4)_____ that several members of the (5)_____ who were sitting in the front (6)_____ are reported to have fainted during one particularly realistic (7)_____ .

   (8)_____ its length – the play runs for three and three quarter hours with two half-hour (9)_____ – Noble's production is anything but tedious. 'King Lear' will run at the Barbican until March and (10)_____ booking is recommended.

1	A	reports	B	statements	C	reviews	D commentaries
2	A	act	B	demonstration	C	show	D performance
3	A	represents	B	plays	C	interprets	D acts
4	A	character	B	representation	C	part	D impersonation
5	A	audience	B	observers	C	spectators	D crowd
6	A	files	B	lines	C	chairs	D rows
7	A	scene	B	episode	C	section	D place
8	A	However	B	Although	C	Despite	D While
9	A	gaps	B	intervals	C	pauses	D rests
10	A	ahead	B	previous	C	forward	D advance

Writing

Giving an opinion

1 Target reader

Read the four extracts below and fill in the information which is missing from this table.

	Writer	Target Reader	Purpose
1	teenager		
2		Town Council	
3		newspaper readers	
4	market researcher		

1 *I went to see 'T-Bone Stake' on Saturday with Chrissie. It wasn't bad. Chris thought it was brilliant, but then it was only the second live concert she's ever been to. Have you heard their new single? I'm not very keen on it, but maybe it'll grow on me.*

2 **I am writing to complain about the open-air concert which took place at Eastman Road football stadium last Saturday. I think it is a scandal that such events should be allowed to take place. The noise was absolutely deafening!**

3 *In our view, the council should not have agreed to the concert taking place without first consulting local residents. There is a huge difference between the noise made by a football crowd and the racket made by a heavy metal band.*

4 In short, of the local residents interviewed, 98% felt that the noise level was unacceptably high, while over 75% were of the opinion that concerts of this type should not be held at Eastman Road in the future.

2 Language of opinion

A Underline the words and phrases which express the writers' opinions in extracts 2, 3 and 4. This has been done for you in extract 1.

B Now underline any words and phrases which show that the writer is going to give an opinion, e.g. *I think* . Make a list of other words and phrases which could replace the ones you have underlined.

C Rank the four extracts in order of formality, from the most formal to the least formal. Give reasons for your order.

D Suggest other words and phrases for the opinions underlined in extract 1. They should be similar in meaning and in style. How could the same opinions be expressed more formally?

3 Practice

Write a paragraph to a friend (40–50 words), telling him or her about a concert you have been to recently or have seen on TV. Give your opinion of the concert, saying what you liked and didn't like.

Writing

Exam training: Articles 1 Paper 2 Part 2

1 Introduction

An article is a piece of writing on a particular subject, which has been written for publication in a magazine or newspaper. Articles can be written in a lighthearted or more serious style. They can express the writer's point of view or be written in a more impersonal way. An article has a title or heading.

2 Titles

A Decide which of the following you think are essential features of an article title. Give reasons for your choice.
1 It should attract your attention.
2 It should make you want to read the article.
3 It should tell you exactly what the text is about.
4 It should give you an idea of what the text is about.
5 It should be short.

B Read the article titles below and answer these questions.
1 Which titles would make you want to read the accompanying article? Which wouldn't? Give your reasons.
2 What do you think each article will be about?
3 Which title or titles suggest that the article will be light-hearted? Which one suggests that the article will be serious?

a Art should be where it belongs: in the gallery
b Can some art be 'rubbish' and some rubbish be 'art'?
c Recycling with a difference
d What people think
e Our town's new sculpture

3 Opening sentences **A** Read this exam question.

You have seen this notice in an international college magazine.

> **CHANGES IN YOUR TOWN**
> Has a new work of art or a modern building caused mixed reactions in your town? Write us an article about one of these subjects, telling us about the positive and negative opinions of local people.

B Now decide whether sentences 1–3 are good or bad examples of opening sentences for this question. Say why.
1 People have very different views of what art is.
2 What do you do with your rubbish?
3 I don't think that most people in my town are really interested in art.

C Match the following features with sentences 1–3.
a an interesting statement
b an opinion
c a rhetorical question (a question which does not expect or need an answer)

4 Model

Read the model answer to the exam question. As you read, decide which of the opening sentences in 3B belongs to this answer. Give reasons for your choice.

homework to write

5 Analysis

A What is the purpose of each of the paragraphs in the article?

B The article is written in a light-hearted and fairly informal style. Look back at the text and find some examples of this style. Why is it appropriate? Would a serious and fairly formal style be equally appropriate, in your opinion?

semi-formal

Can some art be 'rubbish' and some rubbish be 'art'?

⬚⬚⬚⬚⬚⬚⬚⬚⬚⬚ Most of us throw it away, but if you're an artist maybe you don't.

get A few weeks ago I woke up to find that our town had acquired a new sculpture. Surprisingly, it wasn't in the town's art gallery. It was in the main street - on the pavement, to be precise.

No one knows what it is exactly. This is partly because no one can see it very well. The sculpture stands on yellow scaffolding above everyone's heads and looks as if it might be four horses, made out of old tin cans and plastic bottles!

Everyone in the town's talking about it but opinion is divided. Some people think it's 'interesting', while others say it's 'an eyesore'. Most young people think it's 'fun', although one or two think it must be a joke. Several people have even written to the local paper to complain that it's an obstruction. But the question no one can answer is: is it art?

C The exam question asks for people's opinions. How does the writer indicate that she is going to give an opinion? Why does she use inverted commas?

6 Think, plan, write

Now answer the exam question in 3A, writing about a newly constructed modern building. Use the model to help you and follow these steps.

A Think of some ideas and jot them down. Use the photos and these questions to help you.

1 Are there any buildings in your town which fit this description? If there aren't, choose one of the buildings in the photos to write about.

2 What do people like or dislike about the building? Think about its design; what it is made of; whether it fits in with the other buildings around it.

3 What might people might say about it? Think about both positive and negative opinions.

B Spend a few minutes thinking of possible titles.

C Decide how you are going to start. For example, with a selection of people's comments; with a description of the building; with a rhetorical question. Then make notes on what you are going to write in the rest of the article. Remember to divide your ideas into suitable paragraphs.

D Expand your notes into a full article of between 120 and 180 words. Write in an appropriate style. Finally, check spelling, grammar and punctuation.

Articles 1

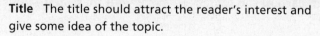

Title The title should attract the reader's interest and give some idea of the topic.

Opening sentence There should be a link between this and the title. The opening sentence should introduce the topic and make the reader want to continue.

Paragraphing Each new point should start a new paragraph.

Style This can be light-hearted or more serious, depending on who is going to read the article. Remember to keep to the same style throughout the article.

Articles 2 covers beginning and ending an article. **p 136**

Vocabulary

1 See and watch

A Complete these sentences with the correct form of *see* or *watch*. Sometimes both are possible.

1 The average teenager in Europe now spends more time playing computer games than _watching_ TV.
2 One of the funniest films I have ever _seen_ is 'Mr Hulot's Holiday' by Jacques Tati.
3 I first _saw_ 'Swan Lake' performed by the Bolshoi Ballet.

see Ballet

4 John decided he was too tired to _watch_ the late night film. (T.V.)
5 We're taking the children to _see_ the latest Spielberg film on Saturday.
6 The class _saw_ two Shakespeare plays when they visited Stratford.
7 You must _see_ the exhibition that's on at the Tate Gallery.
8 I only _saw_ half the match. I didn't _see_ the goal.

B Check your answers. Then try to work out some rules of use for *see* and *watch*.

2 Word building

Noun suffixes

Four of the most common noun endings in English are *-tion*, *-ence*, *-ness* and *-ity*.

1 Find an example of nouns with each of these endings in the interview with Elton John on page 36. What are the corresponding adjectives?
2 Make the following adjectives into nouns.

   *intelligent lonely educated secure sincere dark*ness

Remember that getting a feel for what is right is important, so try saying your ideas to yourself and see how the words sound. Then check your answers in a dictionary.

3 Phrasal verbs

A Elton John says, 'I only have to look at a doughnut and I immediately *put on* a kilo.' Phrasal verbs with *put* have many different meanings. Fill in the gaps in the following sentences with *put on* or *put off* in the correct tense and make any other necessary changes.

1 He quickly _put on_ his clothes and rushed out.
2 She _put on_ all the lights if she is in the house on her own.
3 When you get toothache, you can't _put off_ going to the dentist any longer.
4 He can't concentrate if people talk to him while he's driving. It really _put him off_
5 He _put on_ at least seven kilos since he got married.
6 She thought of becoming a nurse but she changed her mind. She _was put off_ by the long hours and poor pay.

B Match the phrasal verbs in each of the sentences above with these definitions.

a delay
b increase weight → lost
c switch on → off

d get dressed in
e discourage
f distract

C Which uses of *put on* can you find opposites for?
took

Comparison

Power games

Introduction

A Television

1 How many hours of television do you watch in an average day or week? Do you think you watch more television than when you were younger?

2 What is your main reason for watching television?

3 What are the best and worst features of television programmes in your country?

B Reading

The British TV schedule below is for a typical weekday evening.

1 Which channel seems to

a be the most serious? *BBC 2*

b be the most light-hearted? *BBC 1*

c have the most news and current affairs programmes? *CH 4.*

2 Which programme or programmes would you recommend for these people?

a a money-conscious consumer *C 4 : 8:30.*

b someone interested in the performing arts *BBC 2 = 11/25*

c someone who is a compulsive TV watcher *BBC 1 = 7:30*

d someone who likes a good laugh *CF = 10:00   ITV = 11:10*

e someone interested in old buildings *BBC 1 = 9:30.*

*can laughter.
哄的笑声*

BBC 1	BBC2	ITV	CHANNEL 4
7.30 Telly Addicts Weekly quiz show for families who watch too much TV.	**7.30 Young Musician of the Year** Five young performers compete for this year's top prize of £10,000.	**7.30 Coronation Street** Will Don leave Ivy? Don't miss this moving episode of the ever-popular soap opera set in Manchester.	**7.00 Channel 4 News** Political comment and current affairs.
8.30 2 point 4 children A repeat of Sunday's situation comedy.	**8.10 Rembrandt** A programme to mark the opening of the London exhibition of the master's best-known portraits.	**8.00 Inspector Morse** Tonight's story follows the detective to the island of Crete.	**8.00 Brookside** Who is the father of Sammy's baby? All is revealed tonight.
9.00 News **9.30 QED: Pisa** Tonight's documentary asks 'How much longer will the tower last?'	**9.00 Film: Casablanca** (1942) Bogart and Bergman making magic in classic wartime adventure romance.	**10.00 News at Ten** **10.40 Spitting Image** Political satire with your favourite puppet friends.	**8.30 The Food File** An investigation into supermarket prices. Ex-employee alleges price-fixing on a massive scale.
10.20 Sportsnight Cycling – highlights from the Tour of Wales. Golf – the US Masters from Atlanta.	**10.40 Newsnight** **11.25 The Late Show** Arts round-up. The latest and best in theatre, music and literature.	**11.10 Film: Four Weddings and a Funeral** (1994) Englishman Hugh Grant meets American Andie MacDowell in romantic comedy.	**9.00 Anderson's people** The chat show with a difference! **10.00 The Golden Girls** Comedy American style.
11.30 Weather			**10.30 Psycho** (1960) Despite its age this Hitchcock movie never fails to thrill. (B/W) **12.20 Midnight Special** The day's big news stories again.

C Plan and discuss

1 Imagine that you have decided to spend the evening at home watching TV. Look through the schedule again and note down the programmes you would watch.

   Example   *7.30 BBC 2 Young Musician of the Year*

2 Work with two or three other students. You are spending the evening at home together. Say which programmes you each want to watch. Try to agree about the evening's viewing. There is only one television and no video recorder. Make a note of the programmes you agree to watch.

zap = remote control
channel hopping = surfacing

Reading

1 Think ahead Look at the title and the picture below and then guess what the article is about.

2 Reading Read the article through once, quickly, to see if you guessed correctly.

Whose finger is on the button in your house?

Imagine the scene: you and your family are relaxing after a hard day's work. You've just watched the news on TV. What are you going to watch next? Or, perhaps more importantly, who decides what you are going to watch next? Whose finger is on the button?

Deciding what to watch on TV is a battle of wills that is fought in homes all over the world. According to psychologists, it is much more serious than simply deciding between a soap opera and a sports programme, or between pop music and politics. This television conflict is part of a bigger power game which goes on in homes, even though most of the players are unaware that they are playing a game at all. The game is called *Who's Boss?*

'It's such a subtle game,' says psychologist Dr David Lewis, 'that many people don't even know they're playing it. It's all about the balance of power in the home, and who's in control.'

Unconsciously, people begin to play the game as soon as they meet their future husband or wife. By the time the couple get married, the rules of the game are already well-established. The big decisions, like where to live and which school to send the children to, are usually joint decisions. When it comes to less important things, like deciding where to go on holiday, or what sort of car to buy, it's a different matter. Here's just one example of this process at work. He looks through a pile of holiday brochures and announces his preference: 'The South of France'. She quickly agrees before he realizes that the only brochures she gave him were those for the South of France. Similarly, she may decide what time the children should go to bed, and on how the home should be decorated, but he chooses the new car and decides what the family does at weekends.

'Family power struggles are fascinating,' says Dr Lewis. 'Of course, some people are naturally more dominant than others, and the most dominant personality in a family tries to lead. These days, even though so many couples make a conscious effort to have a true and equal partnership, men generally have a greater need to appear to be in physical control. Women, on the other hand, are not as interested in physical control as in emotional control. On the whole, they're more manipulative and can make the man think something was his idea in the first place.'

The tussle over what to watch on TV is a good example of this fight for control. Recently, research psychologists persuaded 400 families to have a 'C-Box' installed in their living rooms. This is a video machine which watches you as you watch TV. They found that 80% of the time it was the man in the house who had his finger on the button, followed by the eldest child, then the youngest child, and only then the woman of the house.

'A child with a strong personality can totally dominate a family,' says Dr Lewis. 'Most kids are far less innocent, far more knowing than their parents realize. Many of them are so sensitive to non-verbal communication that they can pick up atmospheres and sense the strengths and weaknesses of the adults around them. They can be very stubborn and they soon realize that the more stubborn they are, the more quickly they get their own way. When the 'C-Box' was used to study groups of children on their own watching television, the researchers found that the children who had the remote control liked to show off their power by irritating everyone and changing channels every two or three minutes.'

So, next time you've got your finger on the button ready to ZAP the rest of the family with your assertiveness, think about the power game you're playing.

3 Points of view   Who decides which TV programmes you and your family watch?

4 Comprehension   **A Multiple choice**
Read the questions to find out what kind of information is needed. Then read the article again to find the parts which contain this information and choose the correct answers.
1 The arguments people have about what to watch on TV are
   A part of a larger conflict.   C related to people's ages.
   B insignificant disagreements.   D a sign of very bad family relationships.
2 According to Dr David Lewis, the most important family decisions are taken by
   A the husband.   C the husband and wife together.
   B the wife.   D the whole family.
3 The article claims that in personal relationships, most women are interested in
   A controlling other people's feelings.
   B controlling other people's actions.
   C complete control over other people.
   D complete equality with men.
4 What does research mentioned in the article show about family viewing?
   A Women usually decide what the family watches.
   B Men usually decide what the family watches.
   C Children usually decide what the family watches.
   D The whole family usually decides what to watch.
5 What does Dr Lewis say about children in family relationships?
   A They are insensitive to their parents' needs.
   B They find it difficult to communicate their feelings.
   C They are capable of getting exactly what they want.
   D They are unaware of power relationships in families.
6 What did the experiment with the C-Box prove?
   A People find it difficult to decide what to watch on TV.
   B People change TV programmes very frequently.
   C Children find most TV programmes very boring.
   D Children change programmes to assert their authority.

B Vocabulary
Guess the meanings of these words and phrases from the article.
1 a battle of wills (paragraph 2)   5 non-verbal communication
2 the balance of power (paragraph 3)   (paragraph 7). Give examples of
3 a joint decision (paragraph 4)   this kind of communication.
4 a power struggle (paragraph 5)   6 to get your own way (paragraph 7)

C Reading between the lines
1 What does the article imply about the lifestyle of these families?
2 Do you think that the women in the families in the C-Box experiment were really the least influential people in their families?

5 Over to you   Do you think that television has an influence on the way you behave or think?

Grammar and practice

1 Comparisons

The reading text includes a number of comparison phrases. Without looking back at the text, try to fill the gaps in these extracts. The first one has been done for you.

1 When it comes to *less* important things, like deciding where to go on holiday, it's a different matter.
2 The battle of wills is *much* more serious *than* simply deciding between a soap opera and a sports programme.
3 Some people are naturally *more* dominant *than* others.
4 The *most* dominant person in the family tries to lead.
5 Men generally have a g*reater* need to appear to be in physical control.
6 Women are not *as* interested in physical control *as* in emotional control.
7 Most kids are far *less* innocent, far *more* knowing than their parents realize.

Now look back at the text and check your answers.

2 Comparative and superlative adjectives

A What are the comparative and superlative forms of these adjectives?

bad common* far friendly* good
high* important* old strange* thin*

* Think of two or three more adjectives which have comparative and superlative forms like these.

B Here are some phrases which are used with comparative adjectives.

a bit far *a little* a lot much *slightly*

Which phrases are used to compare two things which are very different from each other, and which are used to compare things which are almost the same?

C Before continuing, check your understanding of comparative and superlative adjectives in the Grammar reference on pages 202–203.

3 Practice

A Compare these pairs of famous partners using as many different expressions of comparison as possible.

Examples *Tom is heavier than Jerry. Tom is (just) as clever as Jerry. Tom is less loveable than Jerry.*

B Write sentences comparing these three photographs of people at work.

1 First, compare pairs of jobs, e.g. the disc jockey and the priest.
2 Now compare all three people's lives, using superlative expressions.

Examples *I think the fisherman has **the hardest life**. The disc jockey is probably **the richest of the three**.*

4 Family likenesses

A Look at the photograph and work out who's who.
Paul, 2   David, 11   Jeremy and Clive, 8
Judy, 38   Rachel, 5   Mike, 42   Becky, 16

B Now look for similarities and differences between the eight people. Compare their age, build, hair and height.

C Ask other students to compare themselves with members of their family.

5 *The . . . the . . .*

A Look at this sentence from the article.

The more stubborn they are, the more quickly they get their own way.

The comparative phrase in the first part of the sentence is balanced by a comparative phrase in the second part. How are the two parts of this sentence related to each other in meaning? Here are some more examples of double comparatives.

The harder he worked, the more money he earned.
The richer he became, the more food he ate.
The more he ate, the fatter he got.
The fatter he got, the more slowly he worked.
The more slowly he worked, the less he earned.
The less he earned, the less food he could afford.
The less food he bought, the thinner he got.

B Notice how many different kinds of words can follow *the*. There are notes on these comparative expressions in the Grammar reference on page 203.

C Make up your own sequences starting with these sentences.
1 The later she became, the faster she ran.

2 The less work he did, the more free time he had.
3 The more worried he was, the more cigarettes he smoked.

6 *So* and *such*

A What do these extracts from this unit show about the use of *so* and *such*?
1 It's *such* a subtle game that many people don't even know they're playing it.
2 Many children are *so* sensitive to non-verbal communication that they can pick up atmospheres . . .

How else can *so* and *such* be used? Think of what types of words can follow *so* and *such*. Compare ideas with a partner.

B Before continuing, check your understanding of *so* and *such* in the Grammar reference on page 204.

such + adj + noun

7 Use of English

so + adj.

Complete the second sentence so that it has a similar meaning to the first sentence. Use up to five words including the word you are given. Do not change this word.

1 Maria works so hard that she always gets the highest exam marks.   **such**
   Maria is _such a hard worker_ that she always gets the highest exam marks.
2 As the heat increased, we drank more water. **hotter**
   The _hotter it became the_ more water we drank.
3 Some people have such boring jobs that they can't wait to retire.   **so**
   Some people have jobs which _so boring that_ they can't wait to retire.
4 I am more interested in politics than I am in history.   **as**
   I am not _as interesting as_ _in history_ I am in politics.
5 Nobody in our class can read as fast as Claudia.
   fastest
   Claudia is _the fastest read in_ our class.
6 If you don't take much money with you, you won't be able to spend too much.   **less**
   The _less money you take_ with you, the less you'll be able to spend.

Writing

Exam training: Transactional letters 1 Paper 2 Part 1

1 Introduction

A 'transactional letter' has a specific purpose and a result. For example, a letter of invitation is a transactional letter because it requires a reply. How many more common types of transactional letters can you think of? Make a list.

2 Sample question and model answer

A Read the Situation and the List of dates below, noting the main points you would include if you were writing a letter of complaint to the shop where you bought the stereo.

Situation

You bought a new stereo system, but it went wrong almost immediately. You returned it to the shop and you were told that the repair would take a week. In the end, it was eleven weeks before the stereo was ready. Even then, one of the faults had not been put right. You were unhappy with this situation and decided to write a letter to the shop manager asking for your money back. Before you wrote the letter, you made a list of important dates and problems.

List of dates

 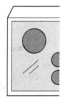

2 Jan	Bought new stereo (£250)
4 Jan	Fault 1 - CD drawer went wrong
5 Jan	Fault 2 - Recorded cassette - sounded terrible
6 Jan	Fault 3 - Pause button stopped working
7 Jan	Took to shop for repair - was told one week
14 Jan	Not ready
2 Feb	Still not ready - 'waiting for spare parts'
9 Apr	Collected stereo - CD and pause OK, recording still terrible

B Now read this model letter and see how many of your points are included.

Dear Sir or Madam,
Re: VGC Stereo Unit Z500

I am writing to complain about this stereo, which I bought in January. After only two days things started to go wrong.

The first problem was the CD drawer, which opened and closed far too quickly. I nearly trapped my fingers in it. The next day I recorded a CD on to a cassette. Everything worked, but the sound quality was very poor. On the following day, the CD Pause button stopped working.

Naturally, I returned the stereo to you for repair. Your assistant said I would have to wait only a week. After two weeks, the necessary spare parts had still not arrived. Eventually, nine weeks later, I collected the stereo. The CD player worked properly, but there was no improvement in the recording quality.

I am not satisfied with the equipment nor with the service I have received. I am therefore writing to ask for a full refund. I will return the stereo to your shop on Monday and I expect to receive a cheque for £250.

Yours faithfully,

3 Analysis   Read through the letter again and do the following tasks.

A Make a note of the main purpose of each paragraph. What is the purpose of the first and last sentences of the letter?

B Circle the key facts in the letter. Then check to find out where they are from, the Situation or the List of dates.

C Write a list of the examples of formal language used in the letter.

4 Practice   **A** Read this exam task and write your own letter of complaint. Refer to the model and 3 above. Write 120–180 words, but do not include addresses.

B Read through your letter carefully, thinking about these questions:
1 Have you included all the information that is necessary?
2 How many paragraphs have you written? Is the purpose of each one clear?
3 Have you used appropriate language for the person you are writing to?

C Finally, check your letter for grammar, spelling and punctuation.

You recently won a competition organized by a satellite TV company. Unfortunately, there are a number of problems with the prize you have received. Read the original advertisement for the competition, on which you have made some notes. Then write to the television company explaining the situation and asking for the things you need.

Transactional letters 1

Key facts   Include all the important factual information provided in the question. Use your own words.

Paragraphing   Each paragraph should have a clear topic and purpose. The first sentence should say why you are writing, the final sentence should make clear to the reader what you expect to happen next.

Style   This is a formal letter, so start with *Dear Sir or Madam* and end with *Yours faithfully*.

Transactional letters 2 covers less formal letters.   p 127

Just for fun

Introduction

Working with a partner, time yourselves to see how long you take to solve these problems.

1 'The day before yesterday I was 18, but next year I'll be 21.' Can you work out the date of the speaker's birthday and the date on which this statement was made?

2 Two friends on the beach are sharing a personal stereo. They work out that they will be able to listen for exactly 48 minutes each in the time they have. Suddenly, four more of their friends arrive. They all want an equal go at listening to the stereo in the same amount of time as the first two had already agreed. How long will each one be able to listen for?

Listening

1 Think ahead

You are going to hear about a TV programme called 'Just for Fun' in which contestants try to solve mathematical problems. The speakers compare men's and women's ability to solve these kinds of problems. Do you think men or women are better?

Compare and discuss ideas in pairs or groups. Use any evidence you have to back up your opinions.

2 Listening

A Listen to the recording for the first time to find out whether your ideas are supported by the speakers.

B Do you find the ideas convincing or not? Give your reasons.

3 Comprehension

A Listen again to the first part of the recording in which John Tams talks about his experience. Finish these sentences with information you hear. You'll need to use three or four words in each case.

1 For 15 years John Tams has been _____
2 He says that, as they get older, girls don't seem to _____
3 When they leave school, very few girls _____
4 Maths is still regarded as _____

B Listen to the second part of the recording again. Kathy Manchester talks about how men and women behave on the programme 'Just for Fun'. Answer these questions by writing M (men) or W (women).

1 On 'Just for Fun' who have more confidence? _____
2 Who get more problems right on the programme? _____
3 Who try to answer the questions more quickly in the first place? _____
4 Who panic when they're being watched? _____
5 Who don't like taking risks? _____
6 Who take longer to answer the questions? _____
7 Who are probably naturally better at maths? _____

4 Vocabulary

A Guess or work out the meanings of the words or phrases in *italics* in these extracts from the recording. Then answer any questions that follow.

1 'On 'Just for Fun' we're trying to bring maths to a *non-specialist audience*.'
What other kinds of audience could there be?
2 'The strange thing is that, on public display, the *macho image* begins to *crack*.'
How do men with a *macho image* behave? Think of some examples of typical *macho* behaviour.
3 '*In the limelight* the men become so nervous: *blind panic* crosses their faces and their minds seem to turn *blank*.'
What kinds of people spend most of their life *in the limelight*?
On what occasions do people's minds *turn blank*?
4 The old saying *behind every successful man there's a successful woman* may have taken on a new meaning.
Can you think of any real-life couples who illustrate this saying?
Can you think of any situations where the opposite is true?

B Fill the spaces in these sentences with suitable prepositions. They are similar sentences to some in the recording you have just heard.

1 When I was 21 I was better _____ driving than I am now.
2 _____ some cases, people's driving improves as they get older.
3 _____ my experience, women are better drivers than men.
4 A lot of men just don't seem capable _____ driving slowly.
5 It's something to do with the fact that they feel they are _____ display.
6 _____ the other hand, men tend to know about how car engines work.

5 Over to you

1 At what age are the abilities of men and women, or of boys and girls, the most similar? At what age are they the most different? Why?
2 Are there any skills or abilities that men or women are particularly good at? Think of as many different skills as possible. Here are some ideas:
music, sports, science, politics, languages, cookery, economics, child-rearing, teaching, painting.

Vocabulary

1 Family Relationships
Vocabulary reference p 215

A Go through the members of the British Royal Family in turn and say what relation they are to Prince Charles.

Example   *Captain Mark Phillips is his **ex-brother-in-law**.*

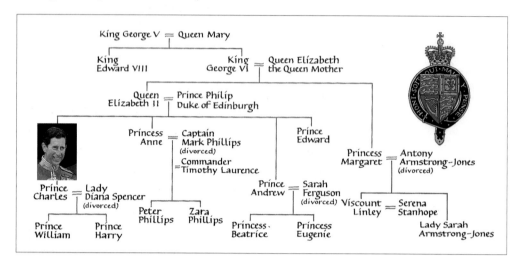

B Now say what relationship these pairs of people are or were to each other.

Example   King George VI and Queen Elizabeth the Queen Mother
*They were **husband** and **wife**. Now she is his **widow**.*

a   Mark Phillips and Princess Anne
b   Queen Elizabeth and Prince William
c   The Duke of Edinburgh and Princess Diana
d   Princess Diana and Princess Anne
e   Queen Elizabeth the Queen Mother and Princess Eugenie

C Work in pairs or small groups. Find out about each other's families.

a   brothers and sisters   How many? How old?
b   cousins   How many? How old? Boys or girls?
c   grandparents   How many? How old?

2 Jobs
Vocabulary reference p 216

A Who's who?

The answers to all these questions are words for people's jobs. There is a list of jobs to help you on page 216.
What do you call someone who . . .

1   plays a part in a play or a film?
2   works underground digging coal?
3   is elected to be part of a government?
4   constructs houses and other buildings?
5   collects rubbish from people's houses?
6   designs or builds bridges, etc.?
7   cooks meals in a restaurant?
8   makes bread?
9   sells meat?
10 teaches at a university?

B Job endings

Here are five common endings for the names of occupations: *-ist, -er, -or, -ian, -ant*. Choose one of them to form the occupation associated with each of these subjects.

1   electricity
2   law
3   journalism
4   music
5   economics
6   sailing
7   jewellery
8   civil service

3 Word building

A Use of English

Read this text and fill the gap in each line with a word formed from the word in capital letters.

I met Sue at work five years ago. In fact she was the (1) _____ of the	MANAGE
department I worked in. For a couple of years, we were what I'd call (2) _____ .	ACQUAINT
Our really close (3) _____ began after we had spent an evening together	FRIEND
at the (4) _____ party of a mutual friend. From then on, our	ENGAGE
(5) _____ grew stronger and stronger, and it wasn't long before we fell in love.	RELATION
Until that time the idea of (6) _____ had not really occurred to either of us.	MARRY

B Compound nouns

In English, compound nouns can be made from various word combinations. Some are written as single words, some are joined by hyphens, and some are separate words. You will need to check them in a dictionary.

Examples   single words: *birthday, weekend*
two words joined by a hyphen: *round-up, half-time, self-confidence*
two separate words: *video recorder, soap opera , power game*

1 What are the compound nouns (single words) which match these definitions?
   a schedule telling you when a train leaves or arrives
   b safety strap worn in a car or aircraft to prevent passengers being thrown forward
   c amount of rain which has fallen in a particular area over a particular time
   d road junction in the form of a circle
   e part of a radio, CD player, etc. which changes electrical impulses into sounds

2 Think of more two-word compound nouns joined by hyphens in these categories.
   a nouns from phrasal verbs, e.g. *round-up*
   b words starting with *half,* e.g. *half-time*
   c words starting with *self,* e.g. *self-confidence*

3 How many compound nouns can you think of using these words?

   hand   foot   day   night   sun   star   head   heart   water   air

4 Phrasal verbs

Read this sentence from the listening. 'The old saying "behind every successful man there is a successful woman" may have taken on a new meaning.' Here *take on* means *assume* or *develop. Take* can be used with other particles to express different meanings.
Replace the verbs in *italics* in these sentences with the correct form of *take* and one of the particles from this list.

after   back   down   over   to   up

1 Within the last year Japanese corporations *have gained control of* more than a hundred European companies.
2 I *retracted* everything I said as soon as I realized that none of it was true.
3 The reporter *wrote* everything I said in his notebook.
4 I didn't start playing basketball until I was 15, but I *liked* it immediately.
5 When my father retired he *started* painting.
6 He's very quick to lose his temper. In that respect he *resembles* his father.

Exam techniques

Speaking Paper 5 Parts 1 and 2

1 Guidelines for Part 1 – Personal information

Do	Don't
• Be prepared to talk naturally for about 2 minutes about yourself. You may be asked about your present or past life, or about plans for the future.	➡ Don't prepare a long speech before the exam. If you recite something you have learnt by heart, it will sound very unnatural.
• Listen to the interviewer's questions and answer them as fully as possible.	➡ Don't just give short answers and then wait for the next question.
• Talk as confidently as you can.	➡ Don't be shy – the interviewer wants you to relax and speak English.

2 Model

You are going to hear the first part of a Paper 5 Speaking test. As you listen, imagine how you would answer the interviewer's questions.

3 Practice

A Work with a partner.
Student A: the interviewer
Think of three questions to ask your partner about himself or herself. Try to ask questions about the past, present and future.
Student B: the FCE candidate
Be prepared to answer your partner's questions. Try to use a range of verb tenses in your answers.

B Now reverse roles.
Student B should not ask Student A the same questions that he or she was asked.

4 Guidelines for Part 2 – Talking about photos

Do	Don't
• Listen to the interviewer, who will tell you what the subject of the photos is.	➡ Don't panic if you don't fully understand what is going on in the photos. The general subject is more important than the details.
• Look at the photos and think about the subject in relation to yourself.	➡ Don't stop talking unless the interviewer wants to ask you a question.
• Talk naturally for about a minute about your photos.	
• Listen to your partner talking. Are his or her photos on the same subject?	
• Discuss the subject with your partner. Try to ignore the interviewer and make sure you talk the same amount as each other.	➡ Don't wait to be asked questions by the interviewer – keep talking with your partner.

5 Model

You are going to hear a recording of the second part of the test. Before you listen, imagine what you would say about these two pictures of weddings.

6 Practice

A First turn
Student A: the interviewer
Turn to page 197 and read the part of the interviewer.
Student B: the candidate
Look at the pictures below. Listen to your partner and follow his or her instructions.

B Second turn
Student B: the interviewer
Turn to page 198 and read the part of the interviewer.
Student A: the candidate
Look at the pictures on page 197. Listen to your partner and follow his or her instructions.

Writing

Describing objects

1 Theft!

Read this newspaper report of a theft.

The police were called and after they had arrived, some of the guests were asked to write descriptions

Thieves strike while bride dances

Two men posing as wedding guests strolled into the Mill Hotel last Saturday and stole items from a display of wedding presents.

The theft occurred while the bride and groom were dancing and chatting to guests. No one realized that anything was wrong until the end of the evening when the bride's mother, Mrs Pamela Hill, found a number of empty boxes.

of their wedding gifts. Read these descriptions of three of the missing presents.

They're a matching pair of candlesticks – about two hundred years old, according to the dealer I bought them from. They're solid silver and extremely heavy. The main part – the stem – is made of three pieces of metal woven together. The two arms each have a candle holder at the end. They were very expensive.

It's quite a small travel alarm clock — about eight centimetres high and six wide. The knobs are all on the back, which is round. It's made of black plastic but, of course, the face is clear. The numbers and the two hands are white and the alarm hand is black. All the hands have luminous green tips which glow in the dark. It cost about £10, as far as I can remember.

It's a medium-sized table lamp, about 50 centimetres tall, I suppose. It's got a plain blue pottery base and a wide shade, which is dark blue with a pretty flowery pattern. It hasn't got a plug on the end or a bulb in it. The on-off switch is just below the bulb holder. I can't remember exactly how much it cost, but I know it was more than £40.

2 What to include in a description

A Look at the descriptions again and for each present. Find the words or phrases which describe the features listed below.

Size/measurements   Shape   Weight   Colour   Material
Position of parts in relation to each other   Purpose   Price/value

B Now add other words which you might use in a description.

3 Expanding notes

Write a description of a personal stereo using these notes.

14 cm x 8 cm, lightweight, black metal and plastic, buttons on long edge, microphone at end, headphone socket and volume on short edge.

4 Writing

Write your own description of something that is of great value to you. Include the features listed in 2A above. There are notes on the order of adjectives which come in front of the nouns they describe on page 211 of the Grammar reference.

5 Narrative

It happened to me

Introduction

Describe what is happening in these pictures. Has anything similar happened to you while travelling? Or to someone you know? What other things can go wrong? Make lists for air, sea, road and rail travel, and discuss your ideas with another student.

Reading

1 Think ahead

You are going to read the true story of how Nigel Hughes flew to Brazil by accident. How do you think this could have happened?

2 Reading

Read the text through and check whether your prediction was right. Don't worry about the missing paragraphs yet. As you read, pay attention to the order in which things happen.

I FLEW TO BRAZIL BY ACCIDENT

Settling into my seat on the plane, I felt tired, ready for a drink and looking forward to getting home. As I sipped a gin and tonic and pushed my seat back, I remember thinking, 'Only a couple of hours and I'll be home.'

1

After another drink, I snoozed until I heard a flight attendant announce, 'We will shortly be landing at Heathrow.' 'Better get my things together,' I thought. And that was it. I honestly don't remember another thing until I woke up again later on.

2

Slowly it began to dawn on me what had happened. I simply couldn't believe it and felt increasingly horrified. The plane must have landed at Heathrow, let off some passengers, taken on others and set off on the next part of its journey. And I knew where that was to – Rio de Janeiro, in Brazil.

3

Not knowing what else to do, I went to look for a flight attendant and told her what had happened. I found out it was about 3 a.m. and we were several hours into the 11-hour flight to Brazil. The flight attendant thought it was very funny and told me not to worry. There wasn't much anyone could do, anyway.

4

The first thing I did was call Georgina. She was furious because she had convinced herself that I'd been in a plane crash which she'd heard about on the news. Once I'd made the call, I decided it would be a shame to be in Rio and not see any of it. So, I slipped out of the airport and jumped into a passing taxi. It was surprisingly easy!

5

In the late afternoon I headed back to the airport. I had to confess that I'd sneaked out. The airline staff were not at all pleased and gave me an escort to watch my every move. However, I wasn't planning on going anywhere else – I wasn't going to miss that plane home.

6

Georgina recovered from the shock and was able to see the funny side of it, eventually. As for me, I still haven't worked out how I slept through a whole landing and take-off.

3 Comprehension

A Now read paragraphs A–G and decide which one fits each gap in the text. There is one extra paragraph which you do not need to use. When you have finished, check that this paragraph does not fit anywhere.

A The driver took me round Rio and down to Copacabana beach. It was great! There I was, sitting on one of the most exotic beaches in the world instead of being back in gloomy England, hard at work. The thought of work and the valuable contract I knew I had now lost depressed me for a moment. But then I decided that since I couldn't do a thing about it, I might as well take in the sights.

B For a couple of minutes I sat wondering sleepily if we were still on our way down to Heathrow. Then I began to realize something funny was going on. The two seats next to me had been empty when I fell asleep. Now a man was lying across them sleeping. There'd been a little girl in front, who'd kept grinning at me over the back of her seat. She had gone. And weirdest of all, all the lights were off and everyone seemed to be asleep.

C I'd phoned my girlfriend, Georgina, from Copenhagen before the plane took off, to tell her I was on my way. She'd said she'd pick me up at Heathrow Airport but I told her not to bother. I'd make my own way home.

D I couldn't believe my luck! I'd always wanted to go to Brazil and now my dream was coming true. Pictures of sun-kissed beaches flashed through my mind. Closing my eyes, I settled back in my seat again, smiling in anticipation.

E Fortunately, there were no problems or delays and we landed at Heathrow at lunchtime on the Sunday. I'd set off from Denmark 48 hours earlier and had spent most of that time in the air. I'd travelled an unbelievable 11,000 miles across the world and back, had a quick paddle in Brazil and landed back home again, tired, fed up but none the worse for the experience.

F We landed in Rio at lunchtime on the Saturday. I was slightly worried that I might be hauled off the plane and locked up as an illegal immigrant. In fact, they took me straight to the departure lounge and told me that I had to sit and wait for the next flight to London, which was at 10 o'clock.

G What on earth was I going to do? Poor Georgina would be wondering what had happened to me, and by now she was probably frantic with worry. And I was stuck on the plane with no ticket. Would they believe it was an accident? Had I really fallen so deeply asleep that I'd completely missed the plane landing and taking off again? I'd certainly been tired but this was ridiculous!

B Vocabulary

Find words or phrases in paragraphs A–G which have these meanings. The paragraph letter is in brackets.

1 dark and depressing (A)
2 smiling from ear to ear (B)
3 strangest (B)
4 start a journey (E)
5 walk in shallow water with bare feet (E)
6 extremely anxious (G)

C Reading between the lines

1 What had probably happened to the little girl who had been sitting in front of him?
2 Why did he have to confess that he'd sneaked out?
3 Why do you think the airline staff 'were not at all pleased' he had left the airport?

4 Over to you

Discuss this statement.

All barriers between countries should be lifted, allowing people to live and work wherever they like.

Grammar and practice

1 The past

A Form and use of tenses

The following four sentences from the reading text contain examples of the past simple, past continuous, present perfect and past perfect. Name the tenses in each sentence.

1 I*'d phoned* my girlfriend, Georgina, from Copenhagen before the plane took off.
2 Now a man *was lying* across the seats, sleeping.
3 We *landed* in Rio at lunchtime on the Saturday.
4 I still *haven't worked out* how I slept through a whole landing and take-off.

Which of the above verb tenses is used to describe a past event or situation that:

a happened before another past event or situation?
b happened at an unspecified time and is relevant to the present?
c happened at a specific time in the past? A time reference is given or understood from the context.
d continued over a period of time?

B Differences in meaning

Name the verb tenses in the following pairs of sentences. What is the difference in meaning between the sentences in each pair?

1 a When Dave arrived, Emma left.
　b When Dave arrived, Emma had left.
2 a I've decorated the hall.
　b I've been decorating the hall.
3 a I was crossing the road when I saw Michelle.
　b I crossed the road when I saw Michelle.
4 a Linda did her homework last night.
　b Linda was doing her homework last night.
5 a He played for Arsenal for two seasons.
　b He's played for Arsenal for two seasons.
6 a When they arrived, we had dinner.
　b When they arrived, we had had dinner.

C Before going on to the following practice exercises, check your understanding of past verb forms in the Grammar reference on page 204.

2 Practice

A Read the newspaper article. Then fill the gaps with an appropriate verb from the ones below in the correct past tense. There are two extra verbs.

arrive brake carry charge drive
happen hold skid slip take.

Three hurt in crash

Three people were injured in a crash involving two lorries and a van on the A14 near Bury St Edmunds on Saturday. The accident (1)_____ in heavy rain at approximately 2.45 p.m. when a lorry, which (2)_____ grain, (3)_____ on the wet surface of the dual carriageway, spilling its load across both lanes. According to a police spokesperson, the driver of the lorry (4)_____ suddenly to avoid hitting a dog, which had run out into the road in front of him. The drivers of the two other vehicles involved, Darren Holmes, aged 21, and Brendan Murphy, aged 37, (5)_____ too close behind to be able to stop in time. Ambulances, which (6)_____ on the scene within minutes, (7)_____ the injured to the nearby Royal Infirmary. Holmes, of Stanway near Colchester, has three broken ribs and is still under observation. The drivers of the lorries, John Peters, 52, of Ipswich, and Brendan Murphy, of Clacton-on-Sea, were treated for minor injuries and later sent home. The police (8)_____ all three drivers with dangerous driving.

B Use of English

Complete the second sentence so that it has a similar meaning to the first sentence. Use up to five words including the word you are given. Do not change this word.

1 The moment he realized his mistake, he apologized. **soon**
He apologized _____ his mistake.
2 Whenever Barbara saw Mick, she crossed the street to avoid having to speak to him. **every**
Barbara crossed the street _____ to avoid having to speak to him.
3 It is ages since I saw Andy. **for**
I _____ a long time.
4 Emily's cousin lost his job two years ago. **unemployed**
Emily's cousin _____ two years.
5 After locking up, she left. **until**
She didn't _____ up.

> 6 Having peeled the onions, he added them to the soup. **when**
>
> He added the onions to the soup _____ them.

C Fill in the gaps with one of the following time expressions and put the verbs in *italics* in an appropriate past tense form, making any other necessary changes. Try to use all the time expressions.

after   as   as soon as   before
then   when   whenever

I travel all over the country in my job and (1)_____ I take the train to Scotland, I remember the story about the man whose wife just *have* (2) a baby. He *work* (3) in London at the time but he *live* (4) in Newcastle, which is in the north-east of England, not far from the Scottish border. (5)_____ he *hear* (6) the news, he *rush* (7) to King's Cross Station. He bought his ticket and (8)_____, just (9)_____ he *jump* (10) on the first train north, he *ring* (11) his wife to say he would soon be with her. He *be* (12) so excited at the news that he *tell* (13) the woman who *sit* (14) in the same compartment. She *ask* (15) him if he lived in Edinburgh, as that was where the train *go* (16), and was surprised to hear that he lived in Newcastle. 'But this train doesn't stop at Newcastle,' she *reply* (17). 'It goes straight to Edinburgh.' (18)_____ the man *hear* (19) this, he *run* (20) to the front of the train to speak to the driver. (21)_____ telling him his story, he *beg* (22) him to stop the train at Newcastle. He even *offer* (23) him money, but the driver still *refuse* (24). However, he *agree* (25) to slow the train down to 15 m.p.h. so that the man could jump off. An hour later, (26)_____ the train *approach* (27) Newcastle Station, the ticket-collector *hold* (28) the man out of the window and he *begin* (29) running in mid-air. (30)_____ they *reach* (31) the station, the ticket-collector gently *drop* (32) the man onto the platform and he *run* (33) very fast along it. The guard, at the back of the train, *see* (34) a man running along the platform. He *put out* (35) his hand and *pull* (36) the man onto the train. 'Lucky I *see* (37) you,' *say* (38) the guard. 'You almost *miss* (39) the train.'

3 Pronunciation of regular verbs 📼

The *-ed* ending of past tense regular verbs can be pronounced in three different ways:
* /d/ after a voiced sound, e.g. *b, n*.
* /t/ after a voiceless sound, e.g. *p, s*.
* /ɪd/ after *t* or *d*.

A Look back at the regular verbs in exercise 2C and decide how they are pronounced in the past simple. Write them in the order in which they occur in the text under the headings /d/, /t/, /ɪd/. Listen to the cassette to check your pronunciation.

B Do the same with *wash, shave, brush, cook, wait, push, arrive, shout*. Listen to the cassette to check your pronunciation.

C Now make up a story starting with the words *It was eight o'clock when Ian woke up. He was late as usual. He quickly washed his face . . .*
Try to use ten regular verbs. Read your story aloud, paying particular attention to your pronunciation.

4 Fluency 📼

A Listen to Michael talking about something that happened to him when he was in Germany. During the recording there will be two pauses. Try to guess the next part of the story.

B Tell your partner or your group about something that has happened to you or to someone you know. Choose something sad, funny, embarrassing or exciting. As you listen, ask questions to encourage the story-teller to give more details. Interrupt if you think you can guess what happened.

Writing

Exam training: Stories 1 Paper 2 Part 2

1 Introduction

A story describes a series of real or imaginary events and can be written in the first or third person. It should entertain the reader in some way, for example by being funny or sad or strange.

2 Model

A You are going to read a story which ends with these words:

> 'What are we going to do now?' Lisa said.

First look at the picture of an event in the story. Working with a partner, decide who the main characters are, what the situation is, and what might happen next.

B Now read the text to see if you were right.

Alex dropped Lisa outside her house at eight. They had spent the day at the beach and Lisa wanted a quick shower before they went out again for the evening.

However, as she walked towards the front door, she realized with horror that she had left her keys inside. Her parents had gone to visit her aunt and would not be back for days. What was she going to do? Alex told her not to worry. 'I can climb up the ladder and get in that way,' he suggested, pointing to the open bathroom window.

Unfortunately, just as he was disappearing inside, a policeman appeared. Given the circumstances, it understandably took some time to convince him that Alex was not a burglar, but finally they did and he left.

Lisa said goodbye to Alex again and was walking towards the door when suddenly the wind blew it shut. Alex had to tell her there was a minor problem. He had closed the bathroom window before coming out. 'What are we going to do now?' Lisa said.

3 Analysis

A What is the purpose of the first and last paragraphs of the story?

B Number the following events in the order in which they occur in the story. The first one has been done for you. How does the writer indicate the order of events?
a Alex brought Lisa home. ____
b Alex closed the bathroom window. ____
c Lisa's parents went to visit her aunt. __1__
d Alex climbed in through the bathroom window. ____
e Lisa and Alex convinced the policeman they weren't burglars. ____
f Lisa left her keys in the house. ____
g Lisa got out of the car and walked towards the door. ____
h Lisa and Alex went to the beach. ____

C Which three pairs of events happened at the same time? Which verb tenses and words are used by the writer to indicate this?

4 Sequence words

Choose an appropriate word or phrase to complete the sentences below. Use each word or phrase once only.

after   as   as soon as   by the time   just before   while

1 _____ Lisa reached the front door, she realized that she didn't have her keys.
2 _____ Alex climbed the ladder, Lisa held it steady.
3 Alex went downstairs _____ carefully closing the bathroom window.
4 _____ the policeman was satisfied that they were not burglars, he left.
5 Alex's face got redder and redder _____ he told Lisa about the problem.
6 The door blew shut _____ Lisa reached it.

5 Think, plan, write

A Read this exam question.

> You have decided to enter a short-story competition. Write a story which begins with these words:
>
> It was the worst holiday Monika had ever had. She had never ...

Using the pictures and your own experience, think about the kind of things that can spoil a holiday. How would someone on holiday feel if things went wrong?

B Make some notes for your story following this plan.

Paragraph 1   Set the scene
Where did the story take place? When did it happen? What is Monika's character? Add any other important details – for example, it was Monika's first holiday in two years.

Paragraph 2   Tell the story
Choose two or three of your best ideas and list them in the order that they happened. Think of time sequence words you can use to link the ideas. Be careful to use the right tenses. (Check the Grammar reference on page 204.)

Paragraph 3   Conclude the story
Summarize what happened and how Monika felt.

C Now write your story, beginning with the words given. Write 120–180 words – but not more! Finally, check grammar, spelling and punctuation.

Stories 1

Beginning a story Set the scene by giving some details about the main characters and saying where and when the story takes place. You may have to begin with the words given.

Developing a story Describe what happens. Don't write about too many events – it is better to describe fewer things in more detail.

Ending a story Bring the story to a definite conclusion. You may have to end with the words given.

Sequencing Use a variety of past tenses and link the events with suitable sequence words.

Stories 2 covers descriptive narrative.   p 193

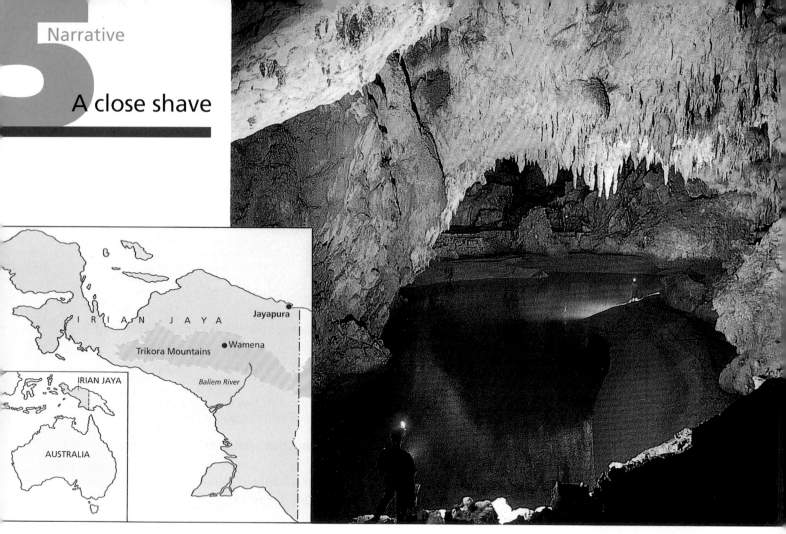

Introduction

These people are cavers. They explore underground caves as a sport. What sort of people go caving? What things can go wrong? What precautions should cavers take?

Listening

1 Think ahead

You are going to hear a news report about a caving expedition to the Baliem River caves. The caves are in the Trikora Mountains of Irian Jaya, New Guinea. Before you listen, study the three diagrams below carefully.

2 Listening

As you listen for the first time, decide which diagram best represents the place and the incident you hear about. Put a tick (✔) in the appropriate box.

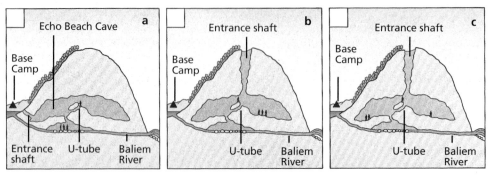

3 Comprehension

A True or false?

As you listen for the second time, decide if the following information is true or false. Write T or F in the box next to each statement.

1 ☐ The area is difficult to reach.
2 ☐ This was the group's second visit to the area.
3 ☐ The team are all shocked by the incident.
4 ☐ The cavers explored together.
5 ☐ They were expecting it to rain.
6 ☐ Tony realized the danger before the others.
7 ☐ The team are impatient to continue the expedition.

B Listening between the lines

1 Why do you think these caves haven't been explored before?
2 The reporter says, 'They've all gone back to the base camp to check their equipment and see what the situation is.' What situation is he referring to? How can they check the situation from the base camp?

4 Over to you

1 Have you ever been caving or done any other sport which involves taking risks, like parachuting, mountaineering or hang-gliding? What do you like about the sport? Have you ever been in a dangerous situation? What happened?
2 Would you like to do one of these sports or a similar one? Why? Why not?

Grammar and practice

Participle clauses

A Form and use

Here are some sentences which contain participle clauses. Read them and note how the participle clauses in *italics* have been reworded using a reason clause or a time clause. Identify the two types.

1 *Travelling on the bus the other day,* I bumped into Jill.
When/while I was travelling on the bus the other day, I bumped into Jill.

2 *Not knowing what else to do,* I went to look for a flight attendant.
Because I didn't know what else to do, I went to look for a flight attendant.

3 *Settling into my seat,* I felt tired.
As I settled into my seat, I felt tired.

4 *Having spent so much time getting the trip under way,* they don't want it all to go to waste.
Since they have spent so much time getting the trip under way, they don't want it all to go to waste.

Why is the present participle used in 2 but the perfect participle used in 4?

B Read the Grammar reference on page 205 before you do the practice exercise.

C Practice

Rewrite every sentence in this story in an alternative way, as in the examples above, making all necessary changes. The first sentence has been done for you.

Opening the living room door, Michael went inside.
Michael opened the living room door and went inside.

But because he didn't recollect the man's face immediately, he said nothing. Then, opening his mouth to ask him what he wanted, Michael realized who the man was. Since he hadn't seen him for over twenty years, he hadn't recognized him earlier. His brother, having grown a beard, looked quite different. Michael threw his arms around him and hugged him tightly.

Now finish the story in your own words. Try to use some participle clauses.

Exam techniques

Reading: Matching headings Paper 1 Part 1

1 Guidelines

Do	Don't
• Read the instructions carefully. They include some information about the text.	➡ Don't start reading until you know what you have to do.
• Skim the text quickly for its general meaning.	➡ Don't read the text word for word.
• Read the list of possible headings for each section of the text.	➡ Don't omit this stage. It is important to know what you're looking for before you start working through the text.
• Read the text section by section and underline any words which go with a heading.	➡ Don't spend too long doing this and don't worry if you don't understand every word.
• Check that each heading fits before you make a final choice of answer. You may need to read some sections more carefully.	➡ Don't leave any answers blank – if you don't know, make a sensible guess.

2 Practice

A Now try out the guidelines on the text which follows. There are some questions and clues below the headings to help you.

B You are going to read an article about some people who want to join an expedition. Choose from A–I the best heading for each section (1–7) of the text. There is an extra heading which you do not need to use. You are given an example (0).

A Things get better but not for long
B Suffering but not giving up
C Safety is all that matters
D A helping hand
E Early drop out

F It's good to know your limitations
G At last it's over
H Warning: take note
I The chosen few

Questions and clues

A Look for an improvement which doesn't last long.
B There is a lot of evidence of suffering in the text but in this section, unlike in several others, no one decides to leave.
C Look for a similar word to *safety* in the text. What does *matter* mean?
D In which section does someone help someone?
E What does *drop out* mean? If it's *early*, where in the report is it likely to be? Remember that this is a day-to-day report: you can expect the events to be told in the order in which they happened.
F What do you know if you *know your limitations*? Look for a word which expresses the writer's positive opinion of someone who knows their limitations.
G What does *it* refer to? When would someone use this expression – at the beginning of something or at the end?
H Look for references to danger or strong advice.
I When are the people chosen – at the beginning of the selection procedure or at the end ? How many is *a few*?

Torture, but it's worth it

THE PHOTO shows one of the many gruelling tasks faced by a group of young adventurers, who are competing against themselves and nature to win the chance to join a Himalayan expedition. **Ruth Fisher** records their day to day progress over three days in this report.

0 *H*

A notice on the wall just inside the front door reads: 'Be clear. On the expedition there will be NO DOCTOR, NO SUPPORT, NO HOSPITALS AND NO EXTRA SUPPLIES. Five minutes in intense pain is a very long time, so any group must be self-sufficient and able to cope in an emergency.' When the eleven determined young people hoping to be selected by the Dorset Expeditionary Society for next summer's journey to the Tibetan Moonlands arrive in Ystradfellte, South Wales, it is made quite clear to them that going on the expedition means putting their lives at risk.

1

The would-be adventurers have only to be in good physical condition, young and enthusiastic. The first is especially important. But hiking 16 kilometres through the pitch-black countryside with 17 kilos of rucksack rescued from an icy stream proves too much for one girl. Her rucksack was thrown in to test whether it was water-tight. She decides she's had enough and quits. Those remaining spend a cold night in shelters they have made from branches and plastic dustbin liners.

2

The next day ten determined young people come out of the forest and run uphill for the next round of torture – a swimming test in water cold enough to chill champagne. No one refuses but a sensible young man realizes his swimming is not quite of the standard required for the upper reaches of the River Indus.

3

Breakfast. But only bowls of cold peas floating in a sea of soya milk. Although Sarah swallows hers in rapid spoonfuls, Claire has difficulty eating hers, while Jo weeps silently. But no one refuses. Later in the day Simon injures his knee and Bobby slips and bruises his spine during a long hike but they carry on all the same. No one refuses to climb down a 20 metre rock face though it's a terrifying experience for some.

4

The first hot meal in more than 24 hours. But, in case the group starts to feel spoilt, the meal is followed by making a stretcher from rope and carrying Charles over two kilometres down the hill on it in the dark. Before bedtime there are lots of silly games and songs. Two more have quit today.

5

The last day and the ones who are left set out to climb Pen y Fan, the highest peak in South Wales. It's steep and painful. Cathy drops behind with breathing problems. The weight of her pack is too much for her. She gives up, but only because she is made to. Jo has similar problems but the others, feeling guilty about letting Cathy struggle alone, distribute the weight of her pack between them. Simon insists he can finish the course but he's hurt his foot and is limping badly. He's excused but not disqualified.

6

Seven descend the mountain the worse for wear but still determined. Five are offered unconditional places on the Moonlands expedition. One is told there is a place for him but only if he gets fit by Christmas. At least one member of the group spends the next 24 hours unable to move from her bed. That was after only 36 hours in South Wales; the Himalayas expedition will last 30 days.

7

'No problem,' says selector David Akers:'If they can survive this, they can survive anything.' John Hegarty looks at it another way. 'If I take 30 kids to Delhi, lock them in a hotel for a month and bring them all safely home then I'm a hero. I take 30 kids climbing and lose one and I'm in big trouble. Getting everyone back in one piece is the number one priority. Everything else is irrelevant.'

Vocabulary

1 Sports

Vocabulary reference p 216

a

b

c

d

e

f

g

h

i

j

k

l

m

A Sports and personalities

1 Name each sport. Use the Vocabulary reference on page 216 to help you.
2 Can you think of a famous personality in each of these sports?
3 What is the name for the person who does each of the sports, e.g. athletics, *athlete*?
4 Which are the most popular sports in your country? Which sports are not very popular? Why? Who are your favourite sports personalities? Why?

B What do you know?

1 Where do sporting activities take place?
   Example   motor-racing, *on a circuit* or *race-track*
   Fill in the missing letters to give you the names of the places where the following activities take place. You can use a dictionary and the Vocabulary reference on page 216 to help you.

football	p _ _ _ h	diving	_ _ _ _
tennis	_ _ _ r t	gymnastics	_ _ m
ice-skating	r _ _ _	horse-racing	c _ _ r _ _

2 What other sports do you know which take place in or on each of these places? Make a list.

C
Choose three sports you have either played or watched. Working with two or three other students, compare the sports on your lists from these points of view.
- How dangerous are they?
- How energetic do you have to be?
- Are they expensive to play?
- How competitive are they?

D Use of English

Read this text and choose the best alternative from the four choices given to fill each gap.

To be good at whatever sport you (1)_____ , you need to (2)_____ a lot of time and energy on it. Professional footballers, for example, need to develop particular (3)_____ , like passing the ball and tackling, but they also need to improve their stamina and general (4)_____ . They (5)_____ most days. This usually involves running round the (6)_____ and doing lots of exercises.

1	A	do	B	make	C	practise	D	take
2	A	dedicate	B	devote	C	give	D	spend
3	A	talents	B	qualities	C	skills	D	abilities
4	A	state	B	fitness	C	shape	D	form
5	A	prepare	B	train	C	perform	D	rehearse
6	A	pitch	B	grass	C	circuit	D	course

E Over to you

What is your least favourite sport? Why do you dislike it so much?

2 Compound adjectives

Compound adjectives are often joined by hyphens. One of the commonest types is formed with a number and a singular noun. 'I found out it was about 3 a.m. and we were several hours into the *11-hour flight* to Brazil.' This kind of compound adjective gives information about age, weight, duration, etc.

Match the compound adjectives in Box A with the nouns in Box B. Then Fill in the gaps in the following sentences with an appropriate adjective + noun combination from the ones you have just matched.

> **Box A**
>
> one-egg   one-litre   three-course   five-minute
> ten-ton   twelve-man   fifteen-piece   thirty-five-hour
> ninety-year-old   2,000-word

> **Box B**
>
> bottle of whisky   essay   grandmother   jury   lorry
> meal   omelette   orchestra   walk   week

1 It's excellent value for money. You get a _____ and coffee for under £10 per person.
2 A_____ is getting married for the fourth time.
3 He was convicted of murder by the _____ .
4 They are on strike for better pay and a _____ .
5 Their new house is very handy for the shops and only a _____ from Lisa's school.
6 Joe's cat was run over by a _____ .
7 I didn't have a big lunch. Just a _____ and some salad.
8 The price of a _____ has gone up by 60p.
9 I can't go out. I have to write a _____ by tomorrow.
10 The concert was performed by a _____.

3 Phrasal verbs

The phrasal verbs which fill the gaps in the following sentences mean the opposite of the verbs in *italics*. Put the missing verb in the correct tense and make any other necessary changes.
1 The plane _____ on time but *landed* 20 minutes late.
2 I _____ the end of term but I *dread* the end-of-term exams.
3 Simon always _____ on his way to work and *drops* me *off* outside my office.
4 Although they _____ in the early morning, they didn't *get to* Manchester until almost midnight.
5 She *fell asleep* immediately but _____ shortly afterwards by the sound of someone knocking at the door.
6 Sally _____ every single letter Bill ever wrote to her. She hasn't *kept* one.

Exam techniques

Use of English: Word formation Paper 3 Part 5

1 Guidelines

Do	Don't
• Read the text quickly to see what it is about.	◆ Don't worry about understanding all the words.
• Look for clues which tell you what kind of word is missing (adjective, noun, verb, adverb).	◆ Don't just write the first thing that comes into your head.
• Complete the answers you know first.	◆ Don't panic about the ones you don't know.
• Make a sensible guess if you don't know the answer. For example, if the missing word is a noun, think of some typical noun endings and choose the one that sounds best.	◆ Don't leave any answers blank. Your guess could be correct.
• Read through the completed text to check it makes sense. Remember, you may need to make some words negative.	

2 Practice

A Read the text quickly. What's the problem? How has it been solved?

New signings for football club

The local pigeons haven't been on the (0) _winning_ side since the (1)_____ of a team of cardboard cats at Torquay United football club.   WIN   ARRIVE

Torquay had already tried a (2)_____ of methods to stop the birds from eating the (3)_____ seeded pitch, but they were all (4)_____ or, in the case of shooting or poisoning, considered (5)_____ alternatives.   VARIOUS   RECENT   SUCCESS   ACCEPT

The cats, a club official's idea, proved to be the (6)_____ . They have been (7)_____ effective in the goalmouths, where the (8)_____ of seed is most tempting.   SOLVE   SPECIAL   CONCENTRATE

The (9)_____ of the lifelike models, which have shiny marbles for eyes, has certainly made the pigeons keep their (10)_____ . The cats have turned out to be bargain signings.   PRESENT   DISTANT

B Now use the word given in capitals at the end of each line to form a word that fits in the space in the same line. There is an example at the beginning (0). Use the guidelines and the questions and clues below to help you form the missing words.

Questions and clues
• Six of the missing words are nouns; two are adjectives; two are adverbs. Can you spot which is which? What clues did you use to decide?
• Two of the words are negative. How many negative prefixes do you know? You can check your ideas on page 102.

Common noun formations	Common adjective formations
Verb + -ment / -ion; -sion; -tion / -ence / -ance / -al	Noun + -y /-ful; -less / -ous / -al
Adjective + -ence; -ance / -ness / -ity; -ety	Verb + -ing / -ed / -ive / -ent / -able

6 Conditions

Cause for concern

a

b

c

d

e

f

Introduction

A Look at these photographs which illustrate various twentieth century problems and match them with an appropriate sentence.

1 Poverty is a problem in all parts of the world.
2 Air pollution has reached danger levels in some countries.
3 Unemployment is hitting some industrialized countries badly.
4 Wildlife is under threat from human activity.
5 Green belt areas are being destroyed at an alarming rate.
6 Cars are bringing the big cities of the world to a standstill.

B Are the problems shown in the photos mainly economic, political or environmental?

C In your opinion, which is the most serious problem shown here?
If you were in a position of power, what would you do to help solve this problem?

D Can you think of any other serious twentieth century problems which should be added to this list?

Reading

1 Think ahead

Imagine you had agreed to take part in an opinion survey. How would you answer these questions?

1 What are your main leisure activities?
2 What do you think is the most important political issue at the moment?
3 What environmental issue is of greatest concern to you?

2 Reading

Read the article, which summarizes the views of five British students. Which of the five students share your views about politics and the environment?

3 Points of view

How do you react to these statements from the article?

1 '. . . all politicians are basically the same.' (T)
2 '. . . animals should have the same right to live on the planet as humans.' (C)
3 'I only came to college because my Mum and Dad wanted me to.' (C)

4 Comprehension

A Read the text again and answer these questions, by writing a student's initial in 1–11. Sometimes there are two answers.

J-John **C**-Catherine **R**-Robert
P-Paul **T**-Teresa

Which speaker or speakers

• are hoping to get a job directly related to the course they are following? [1] [2]
• expresses concern about their own future economic situation? [3]
• has a leisure interest which is closely related to the subject they are studying? [4]
• express concern about the problem of unemployment? [5] [6]
• is most concerned about the situation of students? [7]
• are concerned about the protection of non-human life? [8] [9]
• regards education as a means of achieving their career ambitions? [10]
• has definitely decided on the kind of job they want to do after they have finished their course? [11]

B Text references

What do the words and phrases in *italics* in these extracts from the article refer to?

1 '*We* play at local clubs and occasionally at festivals.' (J – Leisure)
2 'I try and combine *the two*.' (T – Leisure)
3 '. . . *we* wouldn't have so many problems.' (T – Politics)
4 '. . . *he's* only forty-three – *it's* tragic.' (C – Politics)

The Shape

John
is 19 years old and is a student of Physics.

Robert
is 18 years old and has just started his first year at university studying Politics and Economics.

Teresa
is a 19-year-old Music student who has just finished the first year of a degree course.

Catherine
is 17 years old and is doing a course in Hotel and Catering.

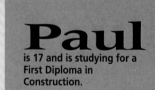

Paul
is 17 and is studying for a First Diploma in Construction.

It is the young of today who will play a key role in deciding the direction of our society in future. Their views will shape services, leisure, central and local government and the environment. Below are extracts from interviews with five college and university students.

.... of things to come

LEISURE What are your main leisure activities?	THE ENVIRONMENT What environmental issue is of greatest concern to you?	POLITICS What do you think is the most important political issue at the moment?	EDUCATION Why did you choose to continue your education?	CAREERS Have you decided what you want to do after college?
Playing jazz on the saxophone. I'm in a semi-professional modern jazz group. We play at local clubs and occasionally at festivals.	Houses being built on green belt areas just outside towns and cities. Personally, I hate going into the countryside and seeing more and more concrete where there should be trees and fields.	Taxes. I'm worried that if I have to pay too much income tax, I won't be able to afford a reasonable standard of living. I'll always vote for the party which promises the lowest taxation.	I wanted to give myself as much chance as possible to have a decent career later on in life. These days you've got to do everything you can to help yourself. If you don't look after yourself, no-one else will.	Ideally, I'd like to run my own business involving computers.
Going out with my friends to clubs and discos. And swimming. If I get up in time, I go swimming in the morning before classes start.	The hole in the ozone layer is the issue which concerns me most. Future generations will suffer if we don't do something about it now.	The economy, definitely, because if the country as a whole is wealthy, businesses do well, and if the economy's healthy, there are more jobs and therefore fewer people out of work.	To further my education, that's obvious, and I suppose, if I am honest, to save myself from having to get a job.	When I leave college I don't plan to get a job straight away. I'd like to travel for a couple of years.
Opera and travelling. If it's possible, I try and combine the two. So, for example this summer, I'm going to an opera festival in Berlin.	Inner city pollution. What gives us the right to ruin the places future generations are going to have to live in?	I'm not interested in politics. As far as I can see, all politicians are basically the same. I mean, if the parties all worked together, instead of arguing with each other all the time, we wouldn't have so many problems.	Because I'd finished school and the music course here appealed to me.	I haven't decided yet, but I want to do something connected with music – maybe teaching or music therapy.
Socializing with my friends, which I find really relaxing.	Animal Rights. I believe animals should have the same right to live on the planet as humans. What harm have they done to anyone?	Employment is important. In the last ten years, more and more people have been affected by the recession. My Dad was made redundant three years ago, and he's almost given up hope of ever working again. And he's only forty-three – it's tragic.	I only came to college because my Mum and Dad wanted me to. They've always wanted me to have a better education than they had themselves – I couldn't let them down.	I know what I want and that's a job in a hotel in the town. I've done some temporary work in the George Hotel, and they're quite keen to take me on when I finish my course.
I like football, rugby and all sport. I play the guitar and enjoy dancing – I take my dancing very seriously.	The threat to the survival of dolphins – I think it's something the whole world should be talking about. If they actually died out, our grandchildren would never know what graceful creatures they were.	Student grants and housing benefits, because they affect me personally.	Because I want to be a civil engineer and I need to pass the right exams.	I have four more years to do, after which I'll get a job – possibly in the north of England.

5 'If *we* don't do something about *it* . . .' (R – Environment)

6 'What harm have *they* done to anyone?' (C – Environment)

7 '. . . a better education than *they* had *themselves*.' (C – Education)

8 '. . . *they're* quite keen to employ me.' (C – Careers)

5 Over to you

1 Robert says that, after he finishes at university, he's going to *'travel for a couple of years.'* If you could travel for a couple of years, where would you go and what would you do? Compare ideas with a partner.

2 Write a paragraph of 60–80 words describing how you would spend your two years.

Grammar and practice

1 Conditional sentences, types 0, 1 and 2

A In what ways are these three conditional sentences different?

1 *If I* **get** *up in time, I* **go** *swimming.* (0)
2 *If I* **get** *up in time, I'll* **go** *swimming.* (1)
3 *If I* **got** *up in time, I'd* **go** *swimming.* (2)

Which verb tenses are used in the two parts of each of these sentences?

B How do these tense differences affect meaning? Which sentence refers to:

a an imaginary or unreal event or situation?
b a general rule that's always true?
c a possible or likely future event or situation?

C Here are some more conditional sentences. Which type are they: 0, 1 or 2?

1 If it's possible, I try and combine the two.
2 If the country is wealthy, businesses do well.
3 If the parties all worked together, we wouldn't have so many problems.
4 Future generations will suffer if we don't do something about it now.
5 If they became extinct, our grandchildren would never know what graceful creatures they were.
6 If you don't look after yourself, no-one else will.

D What is the difference in meaning between these pairs of sentences?

1 a *If I have to pay too much income tax, I* **won't** *be able to afford a reasonable standard of living.*
  b *If I have to pay too much income tax, I* **may not** *be able to afford a reasonable standard of living.*
2 a *If the parties all worked together, we* **wouldn't** *have so many problems.*
  b *If the parties all worked together, we* **might not** *have so many problems.*
3 a *Future generations* **will** *suffer if we don't do something about it now.*
  b *Future generations* **could** *suffer if we don't do something about it now.*

E How could this sentence be rewritten using the word *unless*:

Future generations will suffer if we don't do something about it now.

F Before continuing with the practice exercises, read the Grammar reference on page 205.

2 Practice

A What do you do?

People have their own cures for minor problems, such as headaches, colds, etc. Finish these conditional sentences (type 0) with your own favourite cures. The first one has been done as an example.

1 If I have a headache, *I go to bed and sleep for an hour.*
2 If I have hiccups,   4 If I catch a cold,
3 If my nose bleeds,   5 If I can't get to sleep,

B Type 1 conditional sentences are often used to persuade or warn. Here are the first parts of sentences spoken by adults trying to persuade or warn children. Finish each of these sentences in different ways.

1 If you watch too much television,
2 If you don't go to bed earlier,
3 Unless you tidy your room this weekend,

Make up some more sentences of your own like these.

C Types 1 and 2 conditional sentences can also be used in bargaining or negotiating situations. For example, children might say to their mother or father: 'I'll do the washing up if you let me watch the late film.' Make up some more sentences of your own like these.

D *As long as, provided (that), unless*

1 Match a beginning a–c with an ending d–f and join the two with *as long as, provided (that),* or *unless*.
  a You can come to my party . . .
  b You mustn't telephone me . . .
  c You'll pass your driving test . . .
  d . . . you have some important news.
  e . . . you spend enough time practising.
  f . . . you don't eat too much.

2 Now finish these sentences in several different ways. Two possible answers are given for the first one.
  a I'll come on holiday with you provided that . . .
    . . . *you don't smoke in the car.*
    . . . *you do your share of the cooking.*
  b I won't speak you again unless . . .
  c I'll lend you the money you need as long as . . .

3 What would you do if...?

What would you do if the building you are in now caught fire? How would you escape from the fire? Work out a route. What things would you try to take with you?

Exam techniques

Listening: Note-taking and blank-filling Paper 4 Part 2

1 Guidelines

Do	Don't
• Read the sentences or notes you have to complete.	➡ Don't waste the time before you hear the recording.
• Work out the kind of information you need to listen for.	➡ Don't try to predict actual words or phrases yet.
• Listen to the recording and complete any sentences you can.	➡ Don't panic if you can't complete many sentences at this stage.
• Listen again. Complete the remaining ones and check the sentences you have already completed.	➡ Don't leave any unfinished sentences. If necessary, make sensible guesses.
• Check all your answers make grammatical sense.	

2 Practice

Follow the guidelines as and use the clues in *italics* to help you.

You will hear a discussion about air pollution. For 1-10 complete the sentences, which summarize what the two speakers say.

The people of Wivensea think that their breathing problems may be caused by dust from **1**

What kind of a place is Wivensea?

People are particularly worried because many of the new cases of asthma are among **2**

What groups of people might be particularly at risk from the effects of asthma?

The people of Wivensea think that eventually someone may **3**

What is the worst thing that could happen to someone suffering from breathing problems?

Six months ago, Dr Edwards was asked by Wivensea council to do **4**

What could a council ask a doctor to do in relation to a public health problem?

The doctor says that two other possible causes of the breathing problems could be **5**

Think of two common causes of breathing problems

The survey will collect evidence by studying **6**   living in different **7**

Surveys need the right kind of evidence, so who would researchers choose to study?

If it was shown that people did not react to other dusts, like pollen, it would suggest that the dock was **8**

Why might the doctor test people's reactions to pollen?

After all the evidence has been collected, the results have **9**

What is done with evidence before it can be made public?

The doctor thinks that all the research will have been finished by **10**

*What kind of word or expression could follow the word **by**?*

Writing

Exam training: Reports 1 Paper 2 Part 2

1 Introduction

A report is a piece of factual writing, often based on research of some kind. The style is usually formal and impersonal, so the writer's opinions are not necessarily included. Reports should have a clear layout. An informative title is useful, and sub-headings can be used to mark the beginning of each new section.

2 Sample question and model answer

A Look at this exam task.

> You have a part-time job at the local zoo. As the council is threatening to close the zoo, you have recently conducted a survey among people in your area, to find out their views. Write a report on the results of your survey to send to the council.

B Now read the model report and decide which of the five sub-headings is written in an unsuitable style.

ATTITUDES TO THE LOCAL ZOO

Introduction
The aim of this report is to summarize the results of a survey about our zoo, which is being threatened with closure. The report is based on a sample of over 200 local people.

Visiting patterns
A total of 62 per cent of those questioned had visited the zoo during the last year. Half said they had gone for 'a day out'. Interestingly, although only about 10 per cent went to learn about animals, 88 per cent thought that 'animal conservation' was the zoo's main function.

What people really hate opions
Not surprisingly, what annoyed most people

(nearly 90 per cent) was the lack of space for animals. 8 per cent complained that animals seemed unhappy or restless.

The future
When asked whether they thought the zoo should stay open at public expense, a large majority (70 per cent), 'said 'Yes'. In general, men felt more strongly about this than women.

Conclusion
To sum up, it is clear that the zoo is popular. On the whole, local people see it as a valuable facility and would regard its closure as a great loss.

C Think of a more appropriate sub-heading to replace the unsuitable one.

3 Analysis

A Now study the report more carefully and answer these questions.

1 How do the sub-headings help the reader?
2 What questions were people asked in the survey?
3 How is a factual and impersonal style achieved?

B Make a list of number phrases.   Example *over 200 people*

C Make a list of any other words or phrases that you might find useful when writing a report. Look for language with these functions: *= The aim of this report.*
- to introduce   Example *The purpose of this report : ...*   *= on the whole*
- to generalize   Example *By and large : ...*   *In general*
- to comment on a fact   Example *As might be expected . . .*   *not surprise*
- to conclude or summarize   Example *In conclusion . . .*   *=to sum up.*

4 Practice   *1/3*   *homework*

A Here is an extra paragraph for the same report. Think of a suitable sub-heading for it.

> *People often think that of all the animals that can be seen, apes and monkeys are the main attraction during a day out at the zoo, but the survey showed that big cats are actually the most popular animals, with one-third of those asked choosing lions and tigers as their favourites. 23 per cent chose apes and monkeys, while penguins and seals were the first choice for just 12 per cent. Elephants (9 per cent) and pandas and bears (8 per cent), made up the numbers.*

B This paragraph has 87 words. Re-write it in about 40 words, keeping only the most important points. Try to re-write it in the style of the model.

5 Think, plan, write

A You are now going to write a report in answer to this question.

> You do unpaid voluntary work for an animal welfare organization. This organization is investigating the growing popularity of keeping pets and has asked you to conduct a survey on this topic among students at your school. Write a report for the organization, summarizing your survey results.

B Working in pairs, discuss the kind of information you want to find out from your survey. Make a list of five or six questions you could ask other students.

Examples   *Do you or does anyone in your family own a pet? What kind?*
          What is your main reason for having a pet?
Do the survey and base your report on the most interesting questions.

C Plan your report, making use of the model report opposite; the words and phrases from 3D and 3E; the information and ideas you have worked out in 5B above. Think of a suitable title for the whole report and suitable sub-headings for the main sections.

homework Monday 2

D Write your report in 120–180 words. Then check spelling, grammar and punctuation.

Reports 1

Content   Concentrate on factual information which is relevant to the topic. If the report is based on a survey, include number language.

Title   Choose an informative title.

Layout   Use sub-headings to emphasize the different sections of the report.

Style   This should be impersonal. Comment on facts briefly, but do not express strong personal opinions.

Reports 2 covers the formal language of reports.   **p 169**

If only . . .

Introduction

How would you react in these situations?

1 A friend gives you an expensive present. Unfortunately, you have recently bought the same thing for yourself. Your friend asks you if you like it. What do you say?

2 Which of these quotations about lies do you agree with? Discuss your ideas in pairs or groups.

   a The moment a man talks to his fellows he begins to lie.

   b Unless a man feels he has a good enough memory, he should never lie.

   c The greater the lie, the greater the chance that it will be believed.

   d The cruellest lies are often told in silence.

Listening

1 Think ahead

Can you remember an occasion when you told a deliberate lie? If you can, answer these questions.

1 Was it a serious lie, or just a bit of fun?

2 Did you lie for your own benefit or for someone else's?

3 Did anyone find out about the lie?

2 Listening

A You are going to hear five young women talking about occasions on which they told a deliberate lie. Decide which of the occasions is most like the one you have just thought about.

B Listen again and match Speakers 1–5 with their reasons for lying A–F. There is an extra reason that you do not need to use.

Reasons	Speakers
A to avoid embarrassment to herself	1
B to do someone a favour	2
C to avoid offending another person	3
D to prevent someone's enjoyment from being spoilt	4
E to protect another person's privacy	5
F to watch other people's reactions	

3 Comprehension

A Multiple choice

Listen to the five speakers again and choose the best answers to these questions.

1 What was Speaker 1's excuse for not staying for lunch?
  A She said she had arranged to eat at home.
  B She said she hadn't expected to stay for lunch.
  C She said she didn't like his mother's cooking.

2 Why didn't Speaker 2 tell her neighbour anything about her sister?
  A The rumour about her sister was not true, so there was nothing to tell.
  B She didn't want the neighbour to tell other people about her sister.
  C She didn't know anything about her sister's situation.

3 Why did Speaker 3 tell the man she was talking to that her cousin was a famous footballer?
  A She wanted to see the man's reaction.
  B She wanted to impress the man.
  C She wanted to continue talking to the man.

4 Why was Speaker 4's brother angry?
  A He had wanted to speak to Annie.
  B He had wanted to answer the phone himself.
  C He had wanted to speak to Barbara.

5 Why didn't Speaker 5 tell her sister her exam results?
  A She didn't want her to know she had opened her letter.
  B She didn't want to spoil her sister's holiday.
  C She didn't know how to contact her sister.

B Vocabulary

Match the words and phrases in *italics* with the correct meanings.

1 I was in town the other day and I *bumped into* one of my neighbours.
2 She's a well-known local *busy-body*.
3 She'd heard that my sister and her husband had *split up*.
4 It was a *blatant* lie, of course.
5 Not *wicked* ones, you know, just white lies . . .
6 I *got stuck* with this really boring boy . . .
7 I thought he was going to *pass out* with excitement.
8 I just *ripped* the letter open without thinking.

a became trapped
b separated
c obvious, unashamed
d faint, lose consciousness
e met by chance
f tore quickly and roughly
g very bad
h person who interferes in other people's affairs

4 Over to you

Have you ever known a compulsive liar or someone, like the third speaker, who lies for fun? How do you react to people like this?

Grammar and practice

1 Conditional sentences type 3

A Form and use

1 What verb forms are used in the two parts of these sentences from the listening?

If I'd known it was Annie, I'd have spoken to her.

If I'd told her the result, it would have ruined her holiday.

2 What is the difference in meaning between type 3 conditional sentences and the three types introduced earlier in the unit? Think about these examples:

My life is pretty dull if I don't tell lies. (0)

My life will be pretty dull if I don't tell lies. (1)

My life would be pretty dull if I didn't tell lies. (2)

My life would have been pretty dull if I hadn't told lies. (3)

B Before going on with the practice exercises, read section 4 in the Grammar reference on page 205.

C Making excuses

Complete the second sentence so that it has a similar meaning to the first sentence. Use up to five words including the word you are given. Do not change this word.

1 I didn't answer the phone because I didn't know it was you.   **had**
   If I _____ , I would have answered the phone.

2 I didn't know you were back from your holiday, so I didn't phone you.   **if**
   I would have phoned you _____ you were back from your holiday.

3 If she'd had my address with her, she'd have sent me a postcard.   **because**
   She didn't send me a postcard _____ my address with her.

4 He forgot to put his watch on – that's why he was late.   **been**
   He wouldn't _____ he hadn't forgotten to put his watch on.

5 I'd have bought you a present, but I forgot when your birthday was.   **if**
   I'd have bought you a present _____ when your birthday was.

6 We got in from work really late – that's why we didn't come to your party.   **would**
   If we hadn't got in from work so late,
   _____ to your party.

2 Moments of decision

What would you have done in these situations?

Motorway nightmare

When Jill Frame broke down on the M1 at 2 a.m. last Tuesday, she got out of her Mini and went to find a telephone. The nearest one was on the opposite side of the six-lane motorway.

Supermarket Mum

Mother-to-be Sheila Sutton and her friend, Liz Curry, were doing their shopping in the local supermarket. It was a Friday evening and the shop was very busy. Suddenly Sheila realized that her baby was on its way.

3 On the spot

Have you ever been in a difficult situation where you had to make an important decision very quickly? What happened as a result of your quick decision? Think about what would and would not have happened if you had made a different decision. Write three paragraphs following this plan.

Paragraph 1   a brief description of the situation and your decision

Paragraph 2   what the result of your decision was

Paragraph 3   what would or would not have happened if you had made a different decision

4 Mixed conditionals

What is the difference in meaning between these two sentences?

*If I hadn't broken my leg, I **would have gone** on holiday with you.*

*If I hadn't broken my leg, I **would go** on holiday with you.*

The second sentence is an example of a mixed conditional. It refers to the present result of a completed past action.

Finish these sentences with appropriate *present results*. Use your imagination.

1 If I hadn't learned to read, . . .

2 If I'd won the lottery at the weekend, . . .

3 If I'd saved all my money for the last year, . . .

4 If I hadn't had such a good education, . . .

5 If I'd been born into a very rich family, . . .

6 If my mother hadn't met my father, . . .

Vocabulary

1 Body language

Vocabulary reference p 216

A Reactions

In the listening about lying, one of the speakers said 'His eyes <u>nearly popped</u> <u>out</u> of his head.' *almost come out* This is a description of how people react when they feel very surprised. How do people react when they are in these situations?

1 afraid, e.g. *they turn pale*
2 cold
3 angry
4 embarrassed

B Parts of the body

Label the parts of the body shown in these photos.

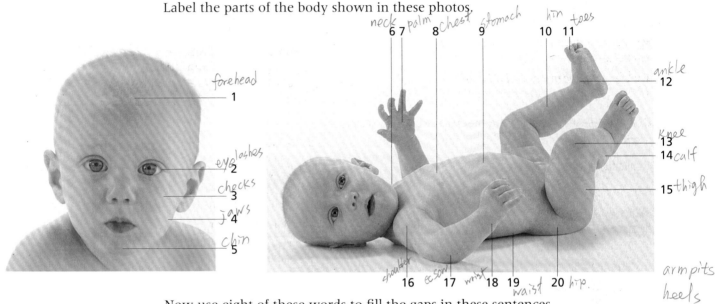

forehead 1
eyelashes 2
cheeks 3
jaws 4
chin 5
neck 6 7 *palm* 8 *chest* 9 *stomach* 10 *hip* 11 *toes*
ankle 12
knee 13 14 *calf* 15 *thigh*
shoulder 16 *elbow* 17 *wrist* 18 19 *waist* 20 *hip*
armpits
heels

Now use eight of these words to fill the gaps in these sentences.

1 When I asked her the time, she just shrugged her *shoulder* and said she didn't know.
2 As I went upstairs to bed last night, I stubbed my *toes* on one of the stairs.
3 Some fortune-tellers read people's *palm*.
4 I saw this really pretty girl at the party. I think she liked me because she fluttered her _____ at me.
5 I always wear my watch on my left *wrist*.
6 It was easy to see who the boss was – the woman standing with her hands on her *hips*
7 Babies crawl around on their hands and *knees*.
8 He sat with his *elbows* on the table and his head in his hands.

2 Compound adjectives

We often use compound adjectives to describe people. They are formed by joining an adjective and a 'body noun' which looks like a past participle, e.g. *red-faced, long-haired*.

Think of famous people who are

1 pale-skinned
2 long-legged
3 square-faced
4 green-eyed
5 square-shouldered
6 left-handed
7 blond-haired

Exam techniques

Reading: Gapped text (missing paragraphs) Paper 1 Part 3

1 Guidelines

Do	Don't
• Read through the gapped text quickly. Think about what information might be missing.	➡ Don't try to fill any gaps until you have understood what the text is about.
• Read the missing paragraphs. Remember, there is one more than you need.	
• Try to fit the paragraphs into the gaps, thinking about the order of events or a logical sequence of ideas.	➡ Don't worry about changing your mind several times at this stage.
• Check your guesses by looking for language connections between paragraphs, e.g. reference words and phrases *It is for these reasons . . .*; linkers and sequencers *On the other hand . . . .*	➡ Don't worry if you can't always find a language connection. Appropriate text development is what matters most.
• Read the text with the missing paragraphs you have chosen, to check it makes sense.	➡ Don't forget to check that the extra paragraph does not fit in any of the gaps.

2 Practice

A As you read this gapped text for the first time, try to answer the clue questions in *italics* between the paragraphs, which are intended to help you to think about the missing information.

Nature's cheats

Anna is happily digging in the ground for a potato, when along comes nasty little Paul. Seeing that there is no-one in sight, he checks what Anna's doing, and then starts to scream as loud as he can. Paul's angry mother rushes over and chases Anna away. Once his Mum has gone again, Paul walks over and helps himself to Anna's tasty potato.

1   *Who or what do you think Anna and Paul are?*

Throughout nature, tricks like this are common – they are part of daily survival. There are insects that hide from their enemies by looking like leaves or stones and harmless snakes that imitate poisonous ones. Such behaviour, which has developed over hundreds of thousands of years, is instinctive and completely natural.

2   *What is the main feature of **instinctive** behaviour? What other kinds of behaviour are there?*

What about Paul the baboon? Two psychologists who saw the incident are sure that he intended to get the potato. Paul's scream and his mother's attack on Anna could have been a matter of chance, but Paul was later seen playing the same trick on others. This use of a third individual to achieve a goal is only one of the tricks commonly used by apes.

3   *What does **only one of the tricks** suggest about the next paragraph?*

Studying behaviour like this is complicated, because it is difficult to do laboratory experiments to test whether behaviour is intentional. It would be easy to suggest that these cases mean the baboons were deliberately tricking other animals; but they might have learnt the behaviour without understanding how it worked.

4   *What other ways could scientists have of doing research apart from **laboratory** experiments?*

An amusing example of this comes from a psychologist working in Tanzania. A young chimp was annoying him, so he tricked her into going away by pretending he had seen something interesting in the distance. When the chimp looked and found nothing, she 'walked back, hit me over the head with her hand and ignored me for the rest of the day'.

5 *Is this chimp story an example of instinctive or deliberate behaviour?*

Of course it's possible that the gorilla could have learnt from humans that such behaviour works, without understanding why. But looking at the many cases of deliberate deception in apes, it is impossible to explain them all as simple imitation.

6 *How would you summarize what you have learnt from this text?*

The ability of animals to deceive and cheat may be a better measure of their intelligence than their use of tools. Studying the intelligence of our closest relatives could be the way to understand the development of human intelligence.

C G A F E D

B Read through the missing paragraphs A–G. Do any of them fit naturally into the main text? Make your first guesses.

A Another tactic that the psychologists came across was the 'Look behind you!' trick. When one young male baboon was attacked by several others, he stood on his back legs and looked into the distance, as if there was an enemy there. The attackers turned to look behind them, and lost interest in their victim. In fact there was no enemy. To discover whether this tactic was genuine the researchers needed more evidence.

B To show such intelligence and to be able to work out this scheme, Anna must have been able to read Paul's mind and see the world from his point of view.

C Does this sound familiar? We've all experienced annoying tricks when we were young – the brother who stole your toys and then got *you* into trouble by telling your parents you had hit him. But Anna and Paul are not humans; they're African baboons, and playing tricks is as much part of monkeys' behaviour as it is of humans'.

D Taking all the evidence into account, it seems that deception does play an important part in ape societies where there are complex social rules and relationships, and where problems are better solved by social pressure than by physical conflict.

E Another way to decide whether an animal's behaviour is deliberate is to look for actions that are not normal for that animal. For example, a zoo worker describes how a gorilla dealt with an enemy. 'He slowly crept up behind the other gorilla, putting his feet down carefully, with his whole body tense. He walked on tiptoes, lifting his legs quite high. When he got close to his enemy he pushed him violently in the back, then ran indoors.' Wild gorillas do not normally walk on tiptoes.

F So the psychologists talked to colleagues who studied apes and asked them if they had noticed this kind of deception. They discovered many liars and cheats, but the cleverest were apes who clearly showed that they intended to deceive and that they knew when they themselves had been deceived.

G Some animals, however, go further and use a more deliberate kind of deception: they use normal behaviour to trick other animals. In most cases the animal probably doesn't know it is deceiving, only that certain actions give it an advantage. But in apes and some monkeys, the behaviour seems much more like that of humans.

C Check your guesses by looking for language connections between the missing paragraphs and the main text. Here are some questions to start you thinking.

Paragraph A	What does **another** tactic suggest?
Paragraph B	What does **such** intelligence refer to?
Paragraph C	What is *this* in Does **this** sound familiar?
Paragraph D	Is the phrase *Taking all the evidence into account* more likely to occur at the beginning or the end of a text?
Paragraph E	What does **another** way to decide suggest?
Paragraph F	What is the purpose and meaning of the word **So** at the beginning of this paragraph?
Paragraph G	What does the word **however** tell you about the link between this paragraph and the preceding one?

Vocabulary

1 Word combinations

Say, speak, talk, tell

The verbs *say, speak, talk* and *tell* have similar and related meanings, but they are not interchangeable. So, for example, you can say **tell** *a lie*, but not **talk** *a lie*. Complete these phrases with the correct verbs. Occasionally more than one combination is possible.

tell
say
talk

someone's fortune	*say* your name	*speak* a language	*tell* a lie	*tell* the time
hello and goodbye	*speak* your mind	*say* a prayer	*tell* a joke	*tell* the truth
sense or nonsense	*say* 'yes' and 'no'	rubbish *talk*	*tell* a story	

2 Colours

Vocabulary reference p 216

One of the speakers who talked about lying described the lies she told as 'white' lies. What does this mean?

A What qualities, moods or feelings do you associate with these colours?

black   blue   green   red   white

B Fill the gaps in this story with one of these five colour words.

Last night, I dreamt I was at a party. As I went into the room everyone's eyes turned towards me. I could feel myself going (1)_____ with embarrassment. Some of the women gave me really (2)_____ looks, as if I'd seriously offended them. I got a drink and looked for someone to talk to. Everyone had their backs towards me, then, quite out of the (3)_____, my grandfather walked into the room and came over to me. I told him what had happened, and he tried to reassure me. 'I expect those women are admiring your dress', he said. 'They're probably (4)_____ with envy.' I relaxed and we chatted about this and that. Then suddenly, my grandfather stopped talking and went as (5)_____ as a sheet.

'What's the matter?' I asked

'You shouldn't really be here,' he whispered. 'You've had a (6)_____ mark against your name ever since you admitted you couldn't swim.'

Suddenly I saw (7)_____ . 'I've had enough of this,' I screamed angrily. Again everyone looked at me. 'This is my party and if you can't be nicer to me, you can all leave now!'

I woke up feeling anxious. The phone was ringing. It was my grandfather. That was strange enough because he only rings me once in a (8)_____ moon, but what he said was even stranger: 'I'm having a party next Friday,' he said. 'Can you come?'

3 Phrasal verbs

It is often possible to form nouns from phrasal verbs. For example, in the story 'Motorway nightmare' on page 86, the first sentence 'Jill Frame *broke down* on the M1' could be rewritten as 'Jill Frame had a *breakdown* on the M1'.

A Fill the gaps in these sentences with phrasal verbs related to these nouns.

break-out   give-away   hold-up   let-down   turn-out

1 Three armed men _____ the main branch of Barclays Bank in Swindon last Tuesday morning.
2 Nearly 50,000 people _____ to see their team win the cup.
3 We tried to find out the exam results but our teacher _____ nothing.
4 Six prisoners _____ of the high security prison last night.
5 You can rely on Paula. She'll never _____ you _____ .

B Now guess or work out the meanings of these nouns related to phrasal verbs.

1 a scientific *breakthrough*
2 children and *grown-ups*
3 a Chinese *takeaway*
4 my car was a *write-off*
5 a supermarket *checkout*
6 a *workout* in the gym
7 an *outbreak* of flu
8 a medical *check-up*

7 Description

A woman's place

Introduction

A What occupations are shown above?

B The following adjectives can be used to describe a person's character or physical condition.

brave	✓creative	fair	hard-working	sociable
✓caring	✓energetic	fit	organized	✓strong
cheerful	enthusiastic	✓patient	✓well-educated	

Match each adjective with its definition and write it in the space provided. The first one has been done for you.

A person who is

a *well-educated* has had a good education.

b _energetic_ is always lively and doesn't tire easily.

c _creative_ is original, artistic and imaginative.

d _strong_ has well-developed muscles and can do hard, physical work.

e _patient_ is calm and does not get annoyed or frustrated.

f _caring_ is helpful and sympathetic to other people.

g _brave_ is not afraid of frightening or dangerous situations.

h _sociable_ is friendly and enjoys being with other people.

i _fair_ treats everyone equally and is not influenced by personal feelings.

j _organizer_ is efficient, and good at making and carrying out plans.

k _fit_ is healthy and in good physical condition.

l _Enthusiastic_ is interested in and excited about something.

m _hard-working_ is not at all lazy.

n _cheerful_ is always happy and optimistic.

C With a partner, choose two of the jobs shown in the photos above. Decide on your own what qualities you think people need to do these jobs well, and why they need these particular qualities. Choose from the adjectives listed in B and add any other adjectives of your own. Then compare your ideas with your partner. Did you agree or disagree about the qualities needed?

Reading

1 Picture discussion

Study both pictures of this woman carefully and look for clues to the following questions.
1 What do you think she does for a living?
2 What kind of person do you think she is?
Discuss your ideas with a partner.

2 Reading

Read the article quickly. Did you guess her job correctly?

Living Dangerously

There's a joke going round at the moment: 'War's about to break out in Britain.' 'How do you know?' 'Because Kate Adie flew into Heathrow this morning.' No one's suggesting she's a trouble-maker. But it seems that no disaster, in any part of the world, is complete without the distinctive voice of the BBC's star reporter bringing the news to us from the middle of a danger zone.

Beirut, Libya – wherever the bombs fall and the bullets fly is where you'll find Kate Adie. And nearer home too, covering national tragedies such as the Zeebrugge and Hillsborough disasters. But it's her cool, objective reporting that people most praise.

She's received many honours for her work, but replies, 'It wasn't just me. Don't forget the camera crew.' It's unusual to find this attitude these days, but typical of Kate Adie.

The reporter, whose sensible haircut and pearl ear-rings make her look more like a school prefect than a war correspondent, admits that her job rules her life. She's never off-duty. She recalls the time when the telephone rang in the middle of a dinner party. 'I had to turn to everyone and say, "Does anyone know how to cook trout?"' And she ran off to cover the Brixton riots.

There's a price to pay of course. Still single and in her forties, she's described as being married to the BBC. Certainly, it would be a very tolerant man who would stay at home while Kate rushed off on an assignment. It's not a life that most people would choose. And it's one where you find few women. 'But,' says Kate, 'I think it's important that a woman is seen to do it, particularly in areas of combat. I find it insulting that people see it as exclusively somewhere where men can operate.'

Being the first woman to make it as a front-line TV reporter has its own problems, however. When she got her first foreign assignment she was terrified that the camera crew would think she was a 'silly, frilly girl'. That's the reason why she crammed everything she needed into a tiny bag which would fit underneath her plane seat. She was then amazed to see the cameraman stagger into the airport with a trunk. Now she knows that it's her appearance as well as her words that matter.

She used to get letters from viewers saying, 'You look a real mess. Haven't you got a hair-dresser?' So she decided to include a pair of curling tongs in a holdall that she now takes everywhere. But as she said, 'Can you imagine getting out a hairbrush when someone's pointing a rifle at you?'

She's often worked in dangerous situations but she says she's not a heroine. 'I don't get a buzz or wonderful feeling when I go into danger,' she says. 'I'm a 5'7" chicken and I run fast. You're not there to fight. You're there to report. But there's a great human desire to push sadness, misery and cruelty out of sight, and people often turn away from the sort of reporting I do. My reply to them is: you may not want to know but you should know.'

However, despite all the drawbacks, she wouldn't change her life for the world. 'It's an incredible job. You go to places you'd never dream of going to.' So could she ever give it up? 'I tend not to plan ahead,' she says. 'I just bump along from one story to another. But I suppose one of these days I'll have to stop climbing over walls when arthritis sets in,' she joked.

Heathrow – London's main airport.
Zeebrugge – A port in Belgium where 193 people, mainly British, were drowned when a ferry overturned in March 1987.
Hillsborough – The football ground of Sheffield Wednesday, where 95 Liverpool supporters were crushed to death in April 1989.
The Brixton Riots – Brixton is a district of London with heavy unemployment. The riots occurred in April 1981 and lasted 4 days.
5'7" – five feet and seven inches is about 1.70 m.
arthritis – swelling of the joints, which makes movement difficult and painful.

3 Points of view

1 Would you do a job that took up as much of your life as Kate Adie's job does?
2 Who does a more valuable job? Someone who works in the emergency services, such as a firefighter, or a war reporter like Kate Adie?

4 Comprehension

A Read the questions below, then read the article again carefully and choose the best answer.

1   What people especially admire about Kate Adie is

    A   her capacity for hard work.   B   her courage and independence.
    C   the way she reports events.   D   her clear way of speaking.

2   The writer thinks Kate Adie is unlikely to get married because

    A   she cannot cook well.   B   she is too independent.
    C   she likes being single.   D   she puts her job first.

3   She only took a small bag with her on her first foreign assignment because

    A   she wanted to be able to keep her luggage with her.
    B   she didn't think she would need a lot of things.
    C   she wanted her colleagues to take her seriously.
    D   she thought there were luggage restrictions.

4   What does the writer say about Kate and her appearance?

    A   She has changed her attitude to her appearance.
    B   She has become obsessed with her appearance.
    C   She doesn't think her appearance is important.
    D   She spends less time on her appearance than she used to.

5   How does Kate summarize her attitude towards her job?

    A   She loves her job even though it has some disadvantages.
    B   She likes being able to visit places she has always wanted to.
    C   She would only give up her job if her arthritis got worse.
    D   She wouldn't want to do the same job for the rest of her life.

6   The writer describes Kate Adie as

    A   silly.   B   vain.   C   modest.   D   caring.

B Reading between the lines

1 How important is Kate Adie's job to her? Find evidence to support your answer.
2 'She recalls the time when the telephone rang in the middle of a dinner party.' (line 29). Who do you think phoned her? What do you think they said?
3 'There's a price to pay, of course.' (line 34) What is the price she has to pay?

5 Over to you

'It's not enough to *read* about natural or man-made disasters. It's important to be able to *see* them too.' Do you agree or disagree?
Before beginning your discussion, think about some events you have seen reported on TV. Then answer these questions.
1 Did you learn anything that you could not have learnt from just reading about the event?
2 Did the report affect you in any way? Did you do anything as a result?

Grammar and practice

1 Relative clauses

Form and Use

Relative clauses can be introduced by the relative pronouns *who, which, that, whose* or no relative pronoun (Ø).

Look at the following sentences from the article. Fill in the gaps with relative pronouns, giving as many alternatives for each answer as you can. Then check your answers with the article.

1 The reporter, _whose_ sensible haircut and pearl ear-rings make her look more like a school prefect than a war correspondent, admits that her job rules her life. (line 24)

2 It would be a very tolerant man _who_ would stay at home while Kate rushed off on an assignment. (line 37)

3 It's not a life _that_ most people would choose. (line 39)

2 Defining and non-defining clauses

A Difference in meaning

Look at these two sentences. How do the commas change the meaning?

1 My sister who lives in Melbourne has two children.

one
sister 2 My sister, who lives in Melbourne, has two children.

How many sisters have I got in each case?

B Practice

Decide whether the clauses in the following sentences are defining (they contain essential information) or non-defining (they contain non-essential information). If the clause is non-defining, add commas. Can you replace any of these relative pronouns by other relative pronouns?

1 I received six letters yesterday. The letter which included an invitation to their wedding arrived by the first post.

2 The groom, who is Erica's cousin, is much older than the bride.

3 The bride, whose family is quite well-off *rich* has just celebrated her 21st birthday.

4 The man who is going to play the organ played at my wedding too.

5 The reception which will be held at the Crown Hotel is for invited guests only.

C Find more examples of relative pronouns in the text and underline them. What other relative pronouns could be used in their place?

D Check your answers with sections 2 and 3 in the Grammar reference on page 206.

3 Relative pronouns and prepositions

A What changes need to be made to each of these sentences to make them less formal?

1 Mr Walker, ~~with whom~~ I have worked closely for years, is an excellent colleague.

2 The man ~~to whom~~ I complained was extremely rude.

In which of your sentences can you leave out the relative pronoun?

B Check your answers with section 5 in the Grammar reference on page 207.

4 Other relative pronouns

A The relative pronouns *where, why* and *when* have been removed from these sentences from the article on Kate Adie. Without looking back at the article, fill each gap with the appropriate pronoun. Then check to see if you were right.

1 She recalls the time _when_ the telephone rang in the middle of a dinner party. (line 29)

2 Wherever the bombs fall and the bullets fly is _where_ you'll find Kate Adie. (line 12)

3 That's the reason _why_ she crammed everything she needed into a tiny bag. (line 53)

In which sentences can the relative pronoun be left out?

B Rephrase the clause in italics in this sentence in four different ways. *in which*

We visited the house *where Shakespeare was born*.

C Before you do the following exercise, read section 4 in the Grammar reference on page 206.

5 Practice

Fill in the gaps in the following sentences with an appropriate relative pronoun. Indicate where there is more than one possibility and add commas if necessary.

重要的代名詞句子不要去掉
common 分開,要跟著
主要句子,

1 I don't like people *who* are big-headed.
2 Have you seen the awful hat *which* Mary's bought?
  that; ∅;
3 She wanted to know the reason *why* I had turned down her invitation.
4 We were unable to get tickets for Madonna's Wembley concert, *which* was a sell-out.
5 They have designed a microwave *which* can defrost a frozen chicken in just ten seconds. *that*
6 We went back to look at the house *where* we used to live.
7 Jeremy Irons, *whose* latest film is shot in Venice has said he'd like to work in the theatre again.
8 It was returned to the person *whose* name was inside.
  that; ∅;
9 The number *which* you are dialling is out of order.
10 I prefer to go to Spain in winter *when* there are fewer tourists about.

6 Relative clauses and prepositions

A Look at the following pairs of sentences.
  1 a That's the man to whom I spoke.
     b That's the man I spoke to.
  2 a The speaker, about whom I'd heard so much, gave an extremely interesting talk.
     b The speaker, who I'd heard so much about, gave an extremely interesting talk.
What are the differences between the two sentences in each pair? What rules can you work out?

B Check your answers with section 5 of the Grammar reference on page 207.

7 Use of English

Read the text and fill the gaps with an appropriate word. An example is given.

Jana Schneider, (0) *who* is in her early forties, has an unusual job (1) *for* a woman: she is a war photographer. Jana, (2) *whose* pictures of the devastation of war have earned her worldwide recognition, has travelled (3) *all* over the world in her job. Some call her brave, others crazy, but Jana's secret is knowledge of herself and the enemy. 'You have (4) *to* concentrate on what you want to do and forget about (5) *what* might happen to you,' she says. Jana has faced death several times but says that it does (6) *not* frighten her as she is a religious person.

Her husband, rock musician and composer Tom Wilson, to (7) *whom* she has been married for over 10 years, wants (8) *her* to give up her career. Jana admits that he worries (9) *about* her and is getting tired (10) *of* goodbyes at the airport but says she cannot imagine doing anything else.

8 Expanding a text

A Rewrite this paragraph about Stephen Hendry including the extra information given in *italics*. Add the extra information in the order it is given (you will need to include two pieces of information in the last sentence). Add commas where needed and make any other necessary changes. An example is given.

Stephen Hendry, *who is a professional snooker player,* is a millionaire though he is still only in his twenties. However, Stephen's manager puts most of his earnings straight into the bank. Stephen started playing snooker when he was 12. World champion at the early age of 21, Stephen says his success lies in his killer instinct.
He is a professional snooker player.
His manager controls his finances.
His earnings were over £500,000 last year.
He comes from South Queensferry in Scotland.
Without his killer instinct he believes he would be just another good player.

B Now write a paragraph about someone you admire. Include at least three relative clauses.

Writing

Exam training: Applications 1 Paper 2 Part 2

1 Introduction   A letter of application is a written request for a job, a place at a college or university, or a scholarship or grant. Letters of application are often written in reply to advertisements. They are written in a formal style and contain relevant personal information about the applicant.

2 Model   Look at the advertisement and read the letter of application. Do you think the applicant is likely to be successful? Give reasons for your opinion.

homework – write a letter →

AU PAIRS USA ///

We are looking for au pairs, male or female aged 18–25, drivers/non-smokers, who would like to spend 12 months working and studying in the USA.

Would you like to live with an American family where you can study and learn about America and its people in return for 25 hours of child care each week?

If the answer to this question is Yes and, along with the initial qualifications mentioned above, you are interested in children, keen on sports and available to go to the United States for a year, please send a letter of application to:
The Director, Au Pair (USA), 61, Cannon Street, Leicester LR1 6BA

★ **$100 per week pocket money**
★ **2 weeks paid vacation**
★ **Free return airfare**
★ **Free medical insurance**
★ **Financial support towards study**

Dear Sir or Madam,

where, what date

I have just seen your advertisement in the Daily Globe for au pairs in the USA and I would like to apply.

introduce yourself

I am eighteen years old and will be leaving school in a few months' time. I intend to continue my studies at university but have decided to take a year off between school and university. I have always wanted to visit the United States and this would be an ideal opportunity for me to learn about the American way of life.

her experience

I am a non-smoker and am taking my driving test next month, so I hope to have my licence soon. Although I have not got any experience of looking after very young children, I have a ten-year-old brother and often baby-sit for my neighbours' children, who are aged 4 and 6. I am very keen on sports. I am a good swimmer and also enjoy horse-riding.

conclusion

I hope that you will consider my application. I look forward to hearing from you.

Yours faithfully,

Maria Moreno

Maria Moreno

3 Analysis

Discuss these questions about Maria's letter with a partner.

1 What is the purpose of each paragraph?

2 Why does Maria begin and end the letter as she does?

3 How many examples of formal language can you find in the letter?

4 Think, plan, write

A You are going to write a letter of application for a job at an American summer camp. First, read the advertisement and think about what the job requires.

B Now jot down some ideas, using these questions to help you. You can invent as much information about yourself as you like.

Age

How old do you think the ideal applicant would be?

Availability

When would you be available?

Sports

What sports are popular with children? What sports are you good at? Do you play in any teams?

Other activities

What other activities could you be asked to organize? Do you have any experience of these activities?

Qualities

How could you indicate that you are physically fit?

How could you show your interest and enthusiasm?

In what ways could you demonstrate that you are responsible? Have you any experience of looking after children?

C Expand your notes into a letter of 120–180 words, following this plan. Remember to write in formal English.

Paragraph 1   Say why you are writing and where and when you saw the advertisement.

Paragraph 2   Give relevant details about yourself and your availability.

Paragraph 3   Say what skills and experience you can offer. Be convincing!

Paragraph 4   End your letter in an appropriate way. Refer back to the model if necessary.

D Finally read through your letter, checking grammar, spelling and punctuation.

Camp USA

We are looking for helpers to organize sports and other activities at our American summer camps for children.

You must be 18 or over and able to work for at least 9 weeks, starting June 15.

You should also be fit, enthusiastic and responsible.

Accommodation, food, pocket money, medical insurance and return travel are all provided.

Apply to:
Camp USA, Box 104, Bath

Applications 1

Beginning and ending If you don't know the name of the person, start with *Dear Sir or Madam* and end *Yours faithfully.* If you are given a name, use it in full, for example *Dear Mr Banks,* and end *Yours sincerely.* Remember to sign your full name in both cases.

Content Refer to the advertisement, if appropriate, and say why you are writing. Give relevant information to support your application. Remember that you will need to convince the target reader that you are the best person for the job.

Paragraphing Each paragraph should have a clear topic and purpose.

Applications 2 covers scholarships and grants. p 182

7

beauty

Only skin deep

| Introduction | 1 There is more to a person than their appearance. What else can we talk about when we describe someone? |
| | 2 What determines the type of description we give? |

Listening

| 1 Think ahead | Describe the women in the photos and predict what they are like, what jobs they do, and their interests. |

1   2   *bob*   3

| 2 Listening | You are going to hear a description of one of these women. As you listen, decide which one is being described and circle the number next to the photograph. |

3 Comprehension

A Listen to the conversation again and work out:
- who is describing Diana Jacobs
- who the 'describer' is talking to
- what the context of the description is

Choose a person from list 1, a person from list 2 and a context from list 3. What evidence is there in the description that your choices are right?

1 Describer's connection with Diana
potential employer   acquaintance   friend   someone who fancies her

2 Describer's connection with the listener
friend   acquaintance   colleague   member of family

3 Possible contexts
discussion at work   private conversation   formal speech   casual chat

B You are going to hear two more descriptions of the same person. For each description do the same as for A above.

4 Missing person

Listen to the description of a missing person and complete this report form.

MISSING PERSON	
Name of missing person	Jammie Durie
Reported missing by	mother
Address	64 PRIORY Drive RD.
Phone number	_41709

Age	16	Height	5 feet 8 inch	Build	s/m	Hair	Brown short

Distinguishing features	NO
Clothes	blue jeans & black, T-shirt (plain)

Last seen by	his friend	Date last seen	14th June
Time last seen	9:30 pm	Place last seen	bus station

Signature of officer on duty	Sgt. Paul Banham

5 Appearances

You are going to hear part of a radio talk called 'Judging by appearances'. You will hear the recording twice. Read the sentences below which summarize what the speaker says and complete them with a word or short phrase.

1 The reporter did not realize at first that _which_ was the pilot. _the brown women_

2 When we see someone we don't know, it only takes a few seconds for us to decide if we _find_ _them attractive_.

3 If a stranger looks like someone we know we will probably _like them_ _or dislike them_

4 Some people give a false impression of what they are like by their choice of _clothes_

5 Women have more possibilities than men of changing _opions_

Exam techniques

Use of English: Error correction Paper 3 Part 4

1 Guidelines

Do	Don't
• Read the whole text through quickly to get an idea of what it's about.	➡ Don't worry about mistakes for the moment.
• Read the text again sentence by sentence. Concentrate on the grammar and the meaning. Look out for any unnecessary words.	➡ Don't read the text line by line yet. You often need to read the whole sentence to see if it is correct.
• Now read the text line by line. Tick (✓) any lines you think are correct and mark the extra words.	➡ Don't transfer your answers to the answer sheet yet. You may want to change your mind later.
• Make sure you haven't marked more than one word in each line.	➡ Don't give more than one answer. You will not get a mark if you do.
• Read the text again to see if it makes sense. Write your final choices on your answer sheet.	

Error checklist
- **Verbs** Is an auxiliary verb needed? e.g. *He has arrived last week.* Check what follows the main or modal verb, e.g. *I must to go.*
- **Quantifiers** Check the use of 'of', e.g. *He's done more of than me.*
- **Articles** Is there an unnecessary article? e.g. *He climbed the Mount Fuji.*
- **Prepositions** Is a preposition necessary? e.g. *Are you going to home?*
- **Pronouns** Is a pronoun needed? e.g. *The restaurant which you're looking for it has closed down.*

2 Practice

Follow the guidelines and use the error checklist to help you find the errors in the following text. There are four correct lines.

Someone I know

```
 0   I have known Jonathan, or Jon as I call him, all my life.        ✓
00   The first thing everyone notices about is his height. He is      about
 1   very tall, almost the two metres, but he is only seventeen       _____
 2   years old. The second thing is how skinny that he is.            _____
 3   People tell me that I am thin but I look like very fat           _____
 4   compared to him. But, despite of looking as if he hasn't         of
 5   eaten for several months, he never stops. He doesn't care        ✓
 6   much about his appearance. The last time he has had his          _____
 7   hair cut was at least since six months ago. It's a shame         _____
 8   because he has got a nice, thick, dark-brown hair. He            a
 9   would be quite a good-looking boy if only he smartened           ✓
10   himself up a bit. I imagine he will when he starts to            _____
11   get interested in the girls. At the moment, though, his          _____
12   only interest is his old car, which he spends all his time       ✓
13   and money on it. As a person he is extremely patient and         _____
14   kind. If I can't do my homework, he will always help to          _____
15   me. I know I'm really lucky to have got a brother like him.      _____
```

Vocabulary

1 Describing people
Vocabulary reference p 217

7

8

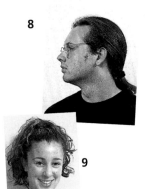

9

10

11

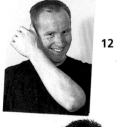

12

13

A How many words do you know for describing what people look like? Make a list using the following headings.

age   height   build   hair   complexion   distinguishing features
slim
fat.   膚色

B Find someone who . . .
Look at the photos. Find people who have the following physical characteristics. Use a dictionary to check words you don't know.

Find someone who is:

going grey 10   *plump* 6   *slim* 3   *tanned* 11
petite 4   *skinny* 2   *stocky* 5   *well-built* 5

Find someone who has:
刀X疤
a beard 10   *dyed hair* 11   *a parting* 10   *a scar* 8   *shoulder-length hair* 9
curly hair 9   *freckles* 12   *a pony-tail* 9   *spiky hair* 11   *a spotty complexion* 7
                庭玫王   (釘状)

C Modifying adjectives and adverbs
1 Some adverbs, like *very*, intensify the meaning of other adverbs and adjectives. Underline the modifiers in the following sentences from the listening and grade them from the most to the least intense.

She's very efficient.   *He's fairly tall for his age.*
It's really straight.   *She usually dresses quite casually.*
She's extremely reliable. informal   *I think she'd fit in pretty well.* quite
They're often a bit late.   *He's rather inexperienced.*
It was incredibly crowded. informal   amazing
                              ↑
Which words occur mainly in informal English? Can you think of any other words like *incredibly*?

2 Some adverbs like *fairly* can intensify or reduce the meaning of adjectives and adverbs. Different meanings are conveyed by different stress.
*He's fairly **tall** for his age* means he's taller than you would expect him to be.
*He's **fairly** tall for his age* means he's tall but not especially so.
Which other modifiers are like *fairly*?

3 Now read the Grammar reference on page 207.

2 Use of English

Read the text and decide which word A, B, C or D best fits each space.

Even though he is always eating crisps and chocolate, Mark has a (1)_____ complexion and never seems to get spots. His hair is brown and already (2)_____ , which isn't surprising as his father lost all his hair when he was only 26. Because there's a touch of red in his hair, he usually comes out in (3)_____ when he's been in the sun. He has a (4)_____ on his left cheek as the result of a cycling accident four years ago but no other (5)_____ features.

perfect

1 A clean   B spotless   C clear   D natural
2 A receding   B retiring   C decreasing   D losing
3 A blemishes 傷疤點 B marks   C moles 黑誌   D freckles
4 A cut   B scar   C wound   D tattoo
5 A diverse   B different   C distinct   D distinguishing

禿前額 ←

3 Word building

unpunctual

A The negative prefixes *un-, dis-, in-, im-, ir-* and *il-* can be added to some adjectives to make opposites. The following general rules may help you decide which prefix to use, but remember there are exceptions.

im- before a word beginning with *m* and *p*   *immature, impossible*
ir- before a word beginning with *r*   *irrational*
il- before a word beginning with *l*   *illiterate*

There are no rules of use for *un-, in-* and *dis-* but it is useful to know that *un-* is the most common negative prefix.

B Look at these adjectives, some of which were in the Introduction on page 91. Add the correct prefix to make the opposite.

un-caring   in convenient   un enthusiastic   un fair
un-fit   in-logical   im patient   im polite
dis-organized   ir-responsible   in secure   un sociable

4 Phrasal verbs

In one of the listening passages, the police officer says, 'There's a good chance he'll *turn up.*' There are several phrasal verbs formed from *turn*. Complete the following sentences with the verb *turn* in the correct tense and one of the words below. Make any other necessary changes to the sentence.

down   into   out   over   up

1 'Turn down that radio! I can't hear myself think!' Alan shouted.
2 John turned up *arrived* after the party had ended.
3 In Agatha Christie's novels the murderer always turn out to be the least likely person. *'something come out in the end.*
4 We had to turn down their invitation as we had already arranged to go out that day.
5 When the omelette is cooked on one side, turn over *it*
6 The room was so cold that they had to turn up the heater to maximum.
7 In six months the tiny puppy turn into a huge dog.

Writing

Describing people

1 Bringing descriptions to life

> 1 My next-door-neighbour is in his late seventies. He's lived next door for as long as I can remember. He's short and a little overweight. He walks with a stick as he has a bad leg. He has a lot of wrinkles because he used to be a farm labourer. He's the most miserable man I know.

> 2 My next-door-neighbour is the most miserable man I know. He complains about everything – the weather is always too hot or too cold and things were so much better when he was young. His face is wrinkled, just like a prune, the 皱纹 result of many years working in the fields when he was a young man.

A Read these two descriptions of the same person. In what ways are they different? Which description do you find more interesting? Give reasons for your answer.

B To what extent do the texts meet the following requirements?
A good description should:
- catch the reader's attention. You should begin with the most interesting facts, not with the most ordinary.
- give details. However, you should be selective; choose the most interesting details. Make some comparisons.
- give examples. Don't just describe a person with a single adjective; expand on this.

C Choose words from the list below to complete the sentences. Then make similar sentences of your own with the remaining words.

affectionate   ambitious   bad-tempered   big-headed   clever   mean *= not generous*
nervous   reliable   reserved *don't show out*   sentimental *多愁善感*   shy

1 My brother always comes top of the class at school. He's very _clever_.
2 Kirsty is extremely _ambitious_. She won't stop till she gets to the top.
3 Anna's very _reserved_. She never asks anyone round to her house and generally keeps herself very much to herself.
4 My father is always giving me hugs. He's very _affectionate_.
5 He's the most _nervous_ person I've ever met. He's a terrible driver because everything makes him panic.
6 Josie has kept all her love letters from all her old boyfriends. She's terribly _sentimental_.
7 Liz is very _shy_. She never looks you in the eye when she speaks to you.

2 Think, plan, write

Describe someone you like or dislike in one or two paragraphs. Use these ideas and examples to help you.
- Begin with their most interesting or distinctive feature.
  a *The first thing you notice about Daniel is (his eyes)*
  b *What I most admire about Tony is (his generosity)*
- Give examples, more detail or both.
  a *They're the bluest blue you'll ever see./ They're as blue as a summer sky and yet everyone else in his family has brown eyes.*
  b *He'll lend you money even when he hasn't got much himself.*
- Expand on your examples and details or choose another interesting feature.

Exam techniques

Listening: Multiple matching Paper 4 Part 3

1 Guidelines

Do	Don't
• Read the instructions and the six options carefully. Try to predict what you might hear.	➡ Don't waste time before the recording starts.
• Try to understand the general meaning the first time you hear the five extracts. Note down key words and make a first choice of answers.	➡ Don't worry about understanding everything. It isn't necessary.
• When the extracts are repeated, listen out for words associated with the options. Remember that one option will not be needed.	➡ Don't make your final choice of answer until you have heard all the extracts twice.
• Make your final choice of answer. Use any notes you have made to help you decide.	➡ Don't leave any spaces. If you aren't sure, make a sensible guess.

2 Practice

A What kind of holiday jobs do students do? Spend a few minutes discussing this.

B Now try out the guidelines. Before you listen to the recording, read the instructions below. Then answer the clue questions in *italics*.

You are going to hear five people talking about temporary jobs they did when they were students. Decide what happened to each of them. Match the options A–F with the speakers 1–5. There is one extra option which you do not need to use.

A The speaker tried out an idea.
  Why do people try out ideas?
B The speaker told a lie.
  Why do people tell lies?
C The speaker was hurt.
  What do you feel when you are hurt?
D The speaker was sacked.
  What sort of things are people sacked for?
E The speaker did a variety of activities.
  What kind of holiday job involves doing many different things?
F The speaker was given a warning.
  When are people given a warning?

Speaker

1 F
2 B
3 E
4 C
5 A

8 Points of view

A burning issue

Introduction

A In Britain you are not supposed to smoke in any of the places in the photos. In which places is smoking allowed in your country? In which places is it prohibited? Do you think people should be allowed to smoke wherever they want to?

二手煙

B What is passive smoking? Do you think it's a health hazard?

C What are the disadvantages of smoking?

health, smell,

Listening

1 Think ahead

1 Which sporting events in your country are sponsored by tobacco companies? Why do tobacco companies use sport for advertising?
2 Should they be forbidden to do this? Why?
3 Are there any restrictions on the advertising of cigarettes in your country? What are they?

2 Listening

You are going to hear part of a radio broadcast on cigarette advertising. As you listen for the first time, see how many of your ideas are mentioned.

3 Comprehension

A Sentence completion
Listen to the recording again and complete the sentences with a word or short phrase.

Every week on 'Burning Issues' people can give their opinions on **1** ~~items in the news~~.

Since 1965 **2** ~~adverlize Tobaca~~ hasn't been allowed on British television.

Tobacco companies are only allowed to advertise in women's magazines if more than 75% of readers are **3** ~~over 24~~.

Posters advertising tobacco can't usually be put up near schools or **4** ~~play grand~~.

The tobacco companies do not sponsor sports which are played mainly by **5** ~~TV. under 18~~.

The tobacco industry started **6** ~~move into sport sponsor~~ in 1965.

The British government doesn't think that banning advertising is the best way to **7** ~~cut down the smokers~~

In Britain in the last 20 years **8** ~~Men~~ have stopped smoking than **9** ~~Women~~.

The tobacco industry **10** ~~Tabaca industry sale less~~ in Britain than ten years ago.

B Matching speakers to topics

1 You are going to hear five different people giving their opinions on whether the government should support a ban on cigarette advertising. Before you listen, make a list of arguments for and against the banning of cigarette advertising.

2 As you listen to the recording for the first time, tick any of the ideas on your list which are mentioned.

3 Listen again and match the speakers 1–5 with the topics A–F. There is one extra topic which you will not need.

A the cost of health care
B personal freedom of choice
C the responsibility of shopkeepers
D the influence of friends and family
E health education in schools
F smoking in public places

Speakers

1 *C*
2 *F*
3 *A*
4 *D*
5 *B*

4 Vocabulary

These sentences all come from the broadcast. Explain the meaning of the words and phrases in *italics*.

1 The number of smokers *has been dropping steadily* for 20 years. *decresing*
2 It's really easy for *kids* to *get hold of* cigarettes if they want to. *buy*
3 The floor's covered in cigarette *butts.* *– yellow parts of cigarette*
4 Your clothes all *stink* of smoke. *= smell*
5 One or two of my younger brother's friends smoke because they think smoking makes them look *big.* *mature*
6 Adverts just influence which *brand* of cigarettes people smoke. *label*
7 The main reason why people start smoking is *peer pressure.* *influence of people*
8 You feel like *an outcast.* You aren't one of the group.
9 It should be *up to me* to decide whether I want to smoke or not. *= make the decision*
10 This ban on advertising cigarettes is just another example of people *poking their noses into* things that *have nothing whatsoever to do with them.* *= ask question about not your business*

汽车用同新牌用
Car–"make"
烟,酒食–brand

5 Over to you

Do you agree or disagree with the following statements from the broadcast? Discuss your ideas in groups.

1 Shopkeepers shouldn't sell cigarettes to children under 16.
2 Children whose parents smoke are more likely to smoke themselves.
3 It's my body and I should be able to do what I like with it.

Grammar and practice

1 Reexported speech

A Look at this statement from the broadcast and how it has been reported by someone else.

1 'I don't think the government is doing enough. I started smoking when I was 8.'

2 Chris Mitchell said that he didn't think the government was doing enough and that he had started smoking when he was 8.

What usually happens to verb tenses in reported speech? What other changes might we need to make when we report what someone has said?

B Read section 3 in the Grammar reference on page 207 before you do the practice exercise.

C Practice

Report these statements made by some other people on the programme.

1 'I have to travel to school by train and when we get on the train it's packed.' (Katie Braithwaite)

2 'One or two of my younger brother's friends smoke because they think it makes them look big.' (Katie Braithwaite)

3 'I support a ban on tobacco advertising though I'm not convinced it will change people's attitudes towards smoking.' (Wendy Johnson)

4 'It's my body and I should be allowed to do what I like with it.' (Gordon Jackson)

2 Reported questions

A Look at these sentences.

1 a 'Do you think the government should support a ban on tobacco advertising?'

   b The presenter asked the listeners if they thought the government should support a ban on tobacco advertising.

2 a 'Why doesn't the government just put a stop to the sale of tobacco altogether?'

   b Dave Snow asked why the government didn't put a stop to the sale of tobacco altogether.

What other changes (apart from changes in verb tenses) need to be made when we report questions? When do we use *if* in reported questions? What other word could be used instead of *if* in the first sentence?

B Check your answers in section 4 in the Grammar reference on page 208.

C Practice

Report the following questions.

1 'Have you got a light?' the girl asked him.

2 'Do you smoke?' Val asked Rob.

3 'How long has Chris been smoking?' Nick asked me.

4 'Why did you start smoking, Sharon?' Rachel asked.

5 'Would you like to give up?' Julie asked Tim.

3 Changing references

A Time references

Look at this sentence.

'I'll see you *tomorrow*,' Lizzie told Graham.

We usually report it like this:

Lizzie told Graham she would see him *the next day*.

However, we can sometimes report it like this:

Lizzie told Graham she would see him *tomorrow*.

When do we need to change the time reference and when can we keep the same time reference? How would we usually report the following time references?

last week   next month   next week

three days ago   today   tomorrow   yesterday

B Other references

Read these pairs of sentences and answer the question.

1 a 'Do you think this meat is all right?' Terry asked his wife.

   b Terry asked his wife if she thought the meat was all right.

2 a 'Shall we eat here?' Carol asked Denise.

   b Carol asked Denise if they should eat there.

What other references may have to change when we report speech?

C Read sections 3C and 3D in the Grammar reference on page 208 before you do the practice exercise.

D Practice

Put the following sentences into reported speech, making all the necessary changes.

1 'Does this work have to be finished today, Mr. Hunt?' Marsha asked.

2 'Were there any phone calls for me yesterday?' asked Mr Gilbert.

3 'This car was used in a robbery two weeks ago,' the police officer informed Ian.

4 'I wrote to her last week and I phoned this morning,' Dorothy said.

5 'I've arranged to meet them after lunch tomorrow,' Matthew said.

E No change in tense

Look at these sentences.

1 'I'm still fit and healthy.' (Gordon Jackson)

2 Gordon Jackson says that he is still fit and healthy.

3 Gordon Jackson said that he is still fit and healthy.

Sentences 2 and 3 both report Gordon Jackson's comment. Why is *be* in the present tense and not the past tense in each case? Check your answer in section 3B in the Grammar reference on page 207.

4 Reported functions

A Look at the following sentences.

1 She suggested { talking it over. *why don't we talk about it.*
{ (that) they (should) talk it over. *should we talk it*

2 She told Bob she was leaving the next day. *I'm leaving tomorrow*

3 She told Bob to leave her alone. *order - leave me alone*

4 She asked Bob why he had done it. *why have you done it.*

5 She asked Bob to leave his keys. *request - could you leave your keys*

6 She warned Bob not to try and get in touch. *Don't try and get in touch with me*

7 Alan advised Bob to try and forget her. *Please try and forget me*

Why is the structure after *tell* different in sentences 2 and 3? Why is the structure after *ask* different in sentences 4 and 5? What structure is used after the verbs *advise*, *warn* and *suggest*?

B Write all the above sentences in direct speech.

C Use of English

Complete the second sentence so that it has a similar meaning to the first sentence. Use up to five words including the word you are given. Do not change this word.

1 'You'd better not swim there. It's dangerous!' the man told us. **warned**
The man _warned us not to swim_ there because it was dangerous.

2 'I wouldn't buy Dave a book if I were you, Pete,' said Laura. **advised**
Laura _advised peter not to buy_ Dave a book.

3 'Take that chewing gum out of your mouth, Claire!' the teacher ordered. **told**
The teacher _told Claire to take_ the chewing gum out of her mouth.

4 'Can you speak Spanish, John?' asked Marie. **asked**
Marie _asked John if he could_ speak Spanish.

5 'I'll pick you up from work if you like, Tracy,' said Jason. **offered**
Jason _offered to pick Tracy up_ from work.

6 'See you after class, Angie!' said Mike. **said**
Mike _said that he would see_ Angie after class.

5 Fluency

Work with a partner. Act out the situations below, taking turns to be the police officer and the member of the public. The member of the public should explain what happened, while the police officer should ask questions and make notes. After you have both had a turn as the police officer, write up a report of the questions you asked and the explanations you received.

1 You have lost the keys to your car and are trying to get into it. A police officer sees you. You have no identification on you.

2 A very pleasant man you met at the airport asked you to post a parcel for him when you got to Miami. You agreed. On arrival at Miami Airport, you are searched by customs officers. The parcel is found to contain two kilos of cocaine. The police are called.

Exam techniques

Reading: Multiple matching Paper 1 Part 4

1 Guidelines

Do	Don't
• Have a quick look at the instructions, as well as the title and opening sentences of the text, to see what it is about.	➧ Don't spend more than 30 seconds on this stage.
• Read the questions carefully. You need to know exactly what information you are looking for.	➧ Don't start reading the text yet.
• Underline key words in the questions and predict words and ideas you may find in the text.	➧ Don't omit this stage. It will make the reading task easier.
• Scan the text for the information you need. Look for key words.	➧ Don't read everything. It isn't necessary and there isn't enough time.
• Go on to the next question if you can't find the information quickly.	➧ Don't spend too long on any one question. You can go back to it later.
• Make a sensible guess if you don't know the answer.	➧ Don't leave any questions unanswered.

2 Practice

As you complete this task, follow the guidelines and use the clues alongside the questions to help you. Underline the words in the text which helped you decide on your answers.

You are going to read some short texts in which people talk about their smoking habits. Answer questions 1–15 by choosing from the people A–H. Where more than one answer is required, these may be given in any order.

Who:

has never tried to stop smoking?	`0 B` `1` `2`	*What other words could be used instead of* **stop**?
doesn't believe in the harmful effects of passive smoking?	`3`	*What are the harmful effects of passive smoking?*
is in a minority in his/her profession?	`4`	*In which professions might you expect people not to smoke?*
was shocked when someone he/she knew died of cancer?	`5`	*What other words have a similar meaning to* **shocked?** *upset*
found smoking helped him/her to get over a personal tragedy?	`6`	*Think of some examples of* **personal tragedies.**
was punished after he/she had stopped smoking?	`7`	*Who might punish someone for smoking?*
admits to having smoking-related health problems?	`8` `9` `10`	*Name some smoking-related health problems.*
started smoking as a student?	`11` `12`	*Which word is often associated with* **student?**
found the effects of giving up smoking unacceptable?	`13` `14`	*Think of immediate negative effects of stopping smoking.*
had special treatment to stop him or her smoking?	`15`	*What treatment can people have to help them stop smoking?*

The evil weed

A Ambrose Huxley
Editor

I refuse to employ non-smokers. They always gang up and try to stop everyone else from smoking. Anti-smokers are so bossy. There's nothing to prove that passive smoking causes cancer. Actually, I gave up recently because I was wheezy and very short of breath, but it won't last. I tried to stop once before. I had electric shock treatment, which was extremely expensive, and I stopped for three months, but then I went back to it.

B Ann Gore
Journalist

I started when I was at university. Everyone else seemed to be doing it. I only realized I was hooked when I discovered I'd run out late one night and walked for miles through the pouring rain to find a shop that was still open. I tell people that I smoke about 30 cigarettes a day but it can be much more. When I'm on a story, and existing on two hours' sleep a day, I smoke non-stop. I don't even enjoy it.

C Rowena Taylor
Novelist

There's no point giving up. Smoking will soon be considered good for us and people with dirty, wasted lungs will have more resistance than people with fresh, tender lungs. That's my excuse anyway. I did stop once for 48 hours after visiting a local shop. The owner, who always had a cigarette in her mouth, had died of lung cancer. That upset me a lot because it was someone I knew. Actually, I'm a bit suspicious of people who don't smoke. I suppose I think they're rather cowardly.

D Graeme Ashbury
Actor

In 26 years I probably haven't gone without a cigarette for more than six hours, except when I'm asleep. I smoke the second I wake up, and would be uncertain how to approach the day without one. No, I've never tried to give up. In New York anti-smokers are very aggressive; people gesticulate at you in the street. But in England, I've only been subjected to exaggerated waves of the hand in restaurants, or to whispered comments. I certainly hope that our six-year-old daughter won't smoke.

E Adrian Daniels
Dancer and choreographer

I retain an old-fashioned image of smoking. I see it as attractive and rebellious, and was a pre-10-year-old smoker. A lot of dancers smoke. It's the hanging around and tension that get to you. I'm sure I'd notice a difference in my dancing if I stopped, but I've never tried. I don't doubt the health risks. Most of my friends smoke and my partner does too. I suppose I might be more self-conscious about it, if they didn't.

F Joanne Archer
Freedom Organisation for the Right to Enjoy Smoking Tobacco

It's not the best thing you can do for your health, but if you have an introverted personality and suffer from stress, cigarettes can become your best friend. When my husband died last year, I would have been utterly lost without cigarettes. The mood against smokers is openly hostile. There should be restricted areas for smokers in all public places. I've tried to give up twice, due to chest problems, but I'm not happy with my personality as a non-smoker.

G Julian Carter
Doctor

Most doctors don't smoke. There are only about 8% of us who still do, but two years ago I replaced my cigarette habit with cigars. My wife forced me to give up. I was on around 15 a day. It all started when I was at university. There was a lot of hanging around and talking, and smoking was very much a part of that. Now I limit myself to two cigars a day. My views are changing. Now I believe that smoking is anti-social.

H Kate Clements
Model

I started to smoke at boarding school when I was 14, but gave it up pretty quickly. Two weeks after I'd quit, the headteacher found an empty packet in my drawer and I was suspended from school for two weeks. I thought, 'If I'm going to be suspended anyway, I might as well smoke.' Now I get through 10–15 a day. At the end of each photographic shoot, I'll light up. I've tried to give up, but gained weight and became so bad-tempered that I started again. Even at 21 I'm short of breath, have chest pains and feel lousy until I've had my first cigarette.

An eye for an eye

NEVER AGAIN.

It's unequal, unjust, and irrevocab

noose *can't change*

Introduction   What message is this poster trying to get across?

Reading

1 Think ahead   What is capital punishment? Can you name any countries which have it? How many arguments can you think of for and against its use?

2 Reading   As you read the article and the missing paragraphs, check to see if your answers and ideas are mentioned.

3 Points of view   Which of the arguments do you agree with?

4 Comprehension   **A** Read the article and the missing paragraphs again. Choose from the paragraphs A–G the one which fits each gap 1–6. There is one extra paragraph which you do not need to use.

Capital punishment has been used throughout history, although its methods and the crimes for which it is used have changed over the centuries.

In the USA, 85% of the population over the age of 21 approve of the death penalty. In the many states which still have the death penalty, some use the electric chair, which can take up to 20 minutes to kill, while others use gas or lethal injections.

The first of these was the case of Ruth Ellis, who was hanged for shooting her lover in what was generally regarded as a crime of passion. The second was the posthumous pardon of Timothy Evans, hanged for murders which, it was later proved, had been committed by someone else.

3

The pro-hanging lobby uses four main arguments to support its call for the reintroduction of capital punishment. First there is the deterrence theory, which argues that potential murderers would think twice before committing the act if they knew that they might die if they were caught. The armed bank robber might, likewise, go back to being unarmed.

The other two arguments are more suspect. The idea of retribution demands that criminals should get what they deserve: if a murderer intentionally sets out to commit a crime, he should accept the consequences. Retribution, which is just another word for revenge, is supported by the religious doctrine of an eye for an eye and a tooth for a tooth.

The arguments against the death penalty are largely humanitarian. But there are also statistical reasons for opposing it: the deterrence figures do not add up. In Britain, 1903 was the record year for executions and yet in 1904 the number of homicides actually rose. There was a similar occurrence in 1946 and 1947. If the deterrence theory were correct, the rate should have fallen.

The other reasons to oppose the death penalty are largely a matter of individual conscience and belief. One is that murder is murder and that the state has no more right to take a life than the individual. The other is that Christianity preaches forgiveness, not revenge.

A By contrast, in Britain, public opinion started to turn against the use of capital punishment after the Second World War. A number of well-publicised cases in the fifties, two in particular, helped to bring about this swing.

B The next argument in favour of bringing back capital punishment concerns public security. If the death penalty were reinstated, it would mean that a convicted murderer could not be set free after serving 20 years or less of a life sentence and be able to go on to murder again. Consequently, the general public would be safer.

C As a consequence, juries were unwilling to convict. This brought about a gradual reduction in the use of the death penalty until finally it was decided that it should only be available for murder and serious violent crimes.

D Nowadays not only are the methods different but more importantly not everyone agrees that capital punishment should be used. People are divided into two distinct groups; those for and those against. This is because this issue is black and white; there is no grey area.

E The fourth and last main pro-hanging argument is the most cold-blooded. It is that it makes economic sense to hang convicted murderers rather than keep them in prison wasting taxpayers' money.

F However, despite this change of opinion, the death penalty was not actually abolished in Britain until 1965. And even now there are many people both inside and outside Parliament who would like it to be reintroduced. There have been 14 attempts to bring back hanging since its abolition.

G The second main argument against reintroducing capital punishment is that innocent people are sometimes wrongly convicted, and while people can be released from prison, they cannot be brought back from the dead if they have been hanged.

B Reading between the lines

1 Which form of capital punishment does the author appear to find the most barbaric? Justify your answer.
2 'There have been 14 attempts to bring back hanging since its abolition.' What does this tell us about British politicians' views on hanging?

C Vocabulary

Choose the best meaning for the words in *italics* from the article.

1 a *convicted* murderer
   A determined
   B declared guilty by a jury
   C one who has committed murder before
2 The other two arguments are more *suspect*.
   A questionable   B understandable   C justifiable
3 The fourth pro-hanging argument is the most *cold-blooded*.
   A convincing   B controversial   C unfeeling
4 The arguments against the death penalty are *largely* humanitarian.
   A mainly   B especially   C also

5 Over to you

1 Do you think the role of prison should be to punish or to reform criminals?
2 What changes would you make to the system of dealing with criminals in your country?

Vocabulary

1 Crime

Vocabulary reference p 217

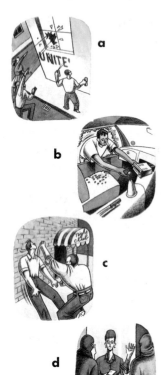

A Breaking the law

Match these crimes with the pictures and write a sentence about each, describing what is happening.

*b*1 theft   *d*2 robbery   *e*3 burglary   *a*4 vandalism   *c*5 assault

B Name the criminal

1 A person who steals from a shop as they walk round it. SH *op Lifter*
2 A person who attacks someone in order to steal their money. M *u g ger*
3 A person who kills someone on purpose. *MURDERER*
4 A person who behaves in a noisy and violent way in a public place.
   H *ooLigan* 棍少年暴郎

C Rob and steal

1 The verbs *rob* and *steal* are similar in meaning and are frequently confused. Say which words each verb can go with.

	a person	a bank	money	a car	a shop	a wallet
rob	✓	✓			✓	
steal			✓	✓		✓

2 Fill in the gaps in these sentences with *rob* or *steal* in an appropriate tense.

1 That bank _has been robbed_ twice this year. Each time over £100,000 _was stolen_
2 More and more people are fitting their cars with anti-theft alarms in an attempt to stop them _being stolen_
3 'Oh, no! I _am being robbed_ ! They've taken everything. My credit cards, cash, the lot!'
4 The thieves were accused of _stealing_ paintings worth over £2 million.
5 Take travellers' cheques when you go abroad in case you _are robbed_.
6 The shoplifter _stole_ £500 worth of goods from the shop.
7 The Aden Gallery _was robbed_ of several of its best paintings last night.

2 Word building

A Unit 3 looked at four of the most common noun suffixes in English: *-tion, -ence, -ness, -ity*. Another common noun suffix is *-ment*. Find examples of nouns with these endings in the text on pages 112–3 and give related verbs where possible.

B Give the nouns related to these verbs and use them to fill the gaps in the following sentences.

accommodate   act   disagree   move   occur   prefer

1 Her resignation was an unfortunate _____ . *occurrence*
2 A package holiday includes the flight and the _accommodation_
3 There was a lot of _disagreement_ over what to do next.
4 Patrick's swift _action_ saved the man's life.
5 'I really don't mind where we go,' said Jane. 'I have no _preference_ at all.'
6 There was a slight _____ behind the bushes.
   movement

Writing

Presenting an argument

1 Discourse markers **A** Read the model answer and fill each gap with an appropriate word or phrase from the ones below. There are two extra words and phrases which you do not need to use.

What are the advantages and disadvantages of a jury system?

Many countries operate a jury system when people are on trial for serious offences like murder. This system, naturally enough, has both advantages and disadvantages. *On the one hand,* 1 _____ there is less chance of a wrong verdict being given. Because twelve people are involved in deciding the verdict as opposed to a single judge, the system is less open to corruption in the form of political interference, threats or bribes. 2 *Another advantage is that* _____ no one person can be blamed or made to feel guilty for a wrong verdict.

3 *On the other* _____, the system is very costly in terms of time and money. It slows down the legal process, which increases the legal costs. 4 *In addition* _____, people may have to take time off work to serve on a jury, which can be inconvenient as some trials last for weeks. 5 *Another disadvantage is that* _____, as members of a jury are just ordinary people, it is relatively easy for skilled lawyers to influence their opinions.

6 *On balance* _____, although there are disadvantages, most people feel that a jury system is fairer than the alternatives.

Another advantage is that

In addition

Instead

On balance

On the one hand

On the other hand

Another disadvantage is that

In contrast

B The words and phrases below are all used for one of the following purposes:
1 to introduce additional information.
2 to introduce information which contrasts with what has come before.
3 to summarize or conclude an argument.
Group them according to their purpose.

apart from that /
however ∨ 2 無論如何
in short ∨
on the contrary 3
to summarize 3

as well as (that) /
in conclusion 3
2 nevertheless ∨ 雖然
on the whole 3
to sum up 3

besides (this) /
in contrast 2
on balance 結果 3
to conclude 3
/ what is more

2 Arguing your point **A** How many main points are made in the model? Underline them. The first one has been done for you.

B What is the function of the parts of the text you have not underlined?

C Practice
Support the following statements and opinions with additional information. Write one or two sentences for each one.

Example   Most crime today is drug-related. *Addicts commit crimes in order to finance their habit.*

1 Schools should have programmes which educate young people about the dangers of taking drugs. *Young people have been educated the dangers of taking drugs,*
2 Most crime is against property not people, and most crimes are not carefully planned. *The crimal should be have another reform.*
3 Drinking too much can lead to crime. *most crimes*
4 Fitting a car alarm is a waste of money.

Writing

Exam training: Compositions 1 Paper 2 Part 2

1 Introduction

A discursive composition is a piece of formal writing which includes information and opinion. It can take the form of a balanced argument which discusses the pros and cons of the question under discussion (the *advantages and disadvantages* composition) or it can be a statement of the writer's personal opinion with supporting arguments (the *opinion* composition).

2 Model answers

You are going to read two models. The first is an *advantages and disadvantages* composition and the second is an *opinion* composition.

A Read the first question. How many advantages and disadvantages can you think of? Read Model 1. How many of your ideas are mentioned?

> Community service is being used more and more as a punishment for young offenders, as an alternative to imprisonment. What are the main advantages and disadvantages of this system?

B Read the second question. Think of arguments you could use to disagree with the statement. Then read Model 2 and see how many of your ideas are mentioned.

> Many people think that community service is a better punishment for young offenders than locking them up in prisons or special institutions. Do you agree?

1

Nowadays young people who are convicted of a crime are as likely to be given community service as they are to be locked up. Naturally, this system has both advantages and disadvantages.

In the first place, young offenders are often first offenders. If they are sent to prison, they may be pushed towards a life of crime. In contrast, community service may help integrate them into society. Another advantage is that it is a cheaper alternative to prison as the offender continues to live at home. Besides, the offender is giving something back to the community instead of taking from it.

The main disadvantage is that while the idea of going to prison might act as a deterrent for some people, community service would not. Also, not all young offenders are first offenders. Some have been committing crimes from an early age and are already hardened criminals. They would regard community service as a 'soft option'.

To sum up, it seems that there are as many advantages as disadvantages, and that while community service may work for some offenders, it fails for others.

2

I do not agree that it is preferable to give young offenders community service instead of imprisonment, unless the crime they have committed is minor, such as petty theft.

First of all, I believe that if someone commits a crime, they should be punished for it. But, while prison punishes offenders by taking away their freedom, community service does not punish them at all. In my opinion, young people need to be taught from an early age that crime does not pay.

Another reason why I am against community service is that it does not make people think twice before committing a crime. The only real deterrent is the thought of possibly facing a prison sentence if they are caught.

To conclude, community service should, in my view, only be used as an alternative to locking young offenders up when the crime committed is minor and is a first offence. I believe that this view is shared by most victims of crime, who wish to see the people pay the price for the suffering they have caused.

3 Analysis

1 What is the function of the opening and closing paragraphs in each composition? How do they differ?

2 How many main points are made in each composition? What are they?

3 What additional arguments are used to support the main points?

4 Language study

1 Underline all the discourse markers used by the writers, e.g. *In the first place...* Group them according to their purpose:

a to introduce an argument.

b to introduce additional information or supporting points.

c to introduce information which contrasts with what has come before.

d to summarize or conclude the arguments.

2 Make a list of all the words and phrases in the second composition which emphasize that the writer's opinion is being given. Can you add any other words and phrases to this list?

Home work.

5 Think, plan, write

A You are going to write a composition in answer to this question.

戒律 思想 (訓練)

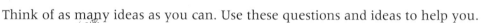

Write 120–180 words on the advantages and disadvantages of a form of discipline that is used in schools in your country.

Think of as many ideas as you can. Use these questions and ideas to help you.

1 What offences are pupils punished for? e.g *Fighting* 犯罪

2 How are pupils punished? e.g. *They are suspended.* 休學

3 Do some forms of punishment work better as a deterrent than others?

4 What effect can badly-behaved pupils have on the rest of the class?

B Remember that you can only write a maximum of 180 words, so choose two advantages and two disadvantages to include. Plan your composition and make notes under these headings.

Introduction What general information could you start your composition with? How will you finish the paragraph?

Advantages/Disadvantages Note down the main points. Add details if there's room.

Conclusion Summarize your ideas. Include your own opinion here if you like.

C Expand your notes into a composition, using appropriate phrases like the ones you listed in 4. When you have finished, read the composition through to make sure your arguments are clear. Finally, check grammar, spelling and punctuation.

Compositions 1 Advantages and disadvantages

Introduction   Make a general statement about the topic.

Paragraphing   Write your advantages and disadvantages in two separate paragraphs.

Content   Choose one or two main points for each

paragraph and back these up with supporting statements.

Conclusion   Summarize your arguments. You may include your opinion but do not add personal words or expressions.

Compositions 2 covers the opinion composition.   **p 156**

Vocabulary

1 Use of English

Read the text below and decide which word A,B,C or D best fits each gap.

Crime prevention

You can make life more difficult for thieves by (1)_____ your wallet in an inside pocket instead of a back pocket. But make sure that you still have it if somone bumps into you in a (2)_____ . Most pickpockets are very skilful. Never let your handbag out of your (3)_____ . On public transport, (4)_____ hold of it. You are also (5)_____ to take travellers' cheques rather than cash when you go abroad, and to use cash dispensers which are on (6)_____ streets, or are well lit at night.

A quarter of all crimes are car thefts or thefts of things from cars, like radios and cassette players. If your car is (7)_____ , you may not get it back. One in four are never found, and even if it is, it may be badly (8)_____ . Always lock all doors and windows, and think about fitting a car alarm too. If you are buying a new radio/cassette player, it is (9)_____ choosing one that is security-coded or removable by the driver. These precautions will help to (10)_____ thieves.

1 A taking	B holding	C carrying	D bringing
2 A mass	B band	C crowd	D group
3 A view	B sight	C visibility	D vision
4 A keep	B catch	C take	D have
5 A suggested+Ving	B told	C informed	D advised
6 A main	B important	C principal	D major
7 A robbed	B burgled	C stolen	D hijacked
8 A hurt	B damaged	C spoilt	D injured
9 A beneficial+toV	B practical	C worthwhile+Ving	D sensible
10 A put off "deter	B put down	C put out "fire	D put back

2 Phrasal verbs

Look at the following sentence from the reading text on page 112. 'The armed robber might *go back* to being an ordinary robber.' Here *go back* means to return. *Go* can be used with other particles to express different meanings. Fill the gaps in the sentences below with the correct form of *go* and the appropriate particle.

off out over through with

1 The room was freezing because the fire _____ .
2 Food _____ very quickly in the summer if it isn't kept in a fridge.
3 The gun accidently _____ as Phil was cleaning it.
4 Mike's spotted tie _____ his striped shirt. They look awful together.
5 The teacher _____ the exam, pointing out all the students' mistakes.
6 In British prisons the lights _____ at 10 p.m.

9 Interaction

Hooked = addicted

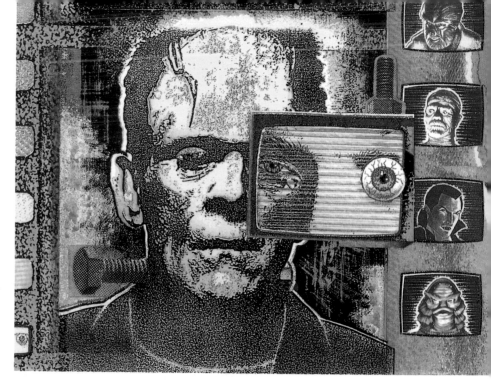

Universal monsters

Dracula has risen from the grave … and he's not alone. Frankenstein, the Mummy, and even the Creature from the Black Lagoon are among the foul fiends also set to appear on your screen when you buy **Universal Monsters**. This game will breathe new life into the undead stars of Universal's horror film classics and bring them into your home. Not to be played late at night.

A lost childhood

We live in a seaside town. On sunny days you would expect 13-year-old boys to be down at the sea, brown and healthy, having the time of their lives. Instead, they and their friends retire into darkened rooms with the curtains drawn, playing computer games hour after hour, killing or being killed by weird creatures which pop up on the screen. The boys and their friends have pale, unhealthy faces, and they have become aggressive and irritable. It breaks my heart to see my boys wasting their young lives on this rubbish.

Toys for the grown-up boys

Barbie Goes Shopping will soon be in computer game shops alongside *Pitfighter*, *Streetfighter* and *Bad Dudes vs Dragon Ninjas*. Nintendo have at last brought out a computer game for girls.

Since their *Gameboy* arrived in Britain in 1988, it has been just that – a toy for the boys.

Despite this, there are no plans to bring out a *Gamegirl*. If the company started to market the game at females, boys might stop buying it. A spokeswoman explained: 'Girls don't mind joining in male activities, but it never works the other way round.'

Introduction

A Read the three short texts above. What do they have in common? Where do you think they are from? Which text does the illustration go with?

B Why are the games like the one described in the first text so popular?

C Do you think the parent in the second text is right to be worried?

D Is it true that girls like playing boys' games, but that boys don't like playing girls' games? Can you think of examples from your own experience which prove or disprove this idea?

tngle 刺々群々的痛.
anti-social

Listening

1 Think ahead

addicts

advisers

aerials

average

compensation

equipment

eyes

fingers

intended

screens

sold

A Read this information about computer games. Fill the gaps with words from the list on the left.

1 There are at least 50 million Nintendo _addicts_ around the world.

2 Fifty per cent of Japanese homes have Nintendo games connected to their TV _screens_.

3 The hand-held Gameboy was _intended_ for 18 to 25-year-olds, but is being played by six-year-old children.

4 An American girl who played with her Gameboy for two hours a day for a year has developed numbness and tingling in her _fingers_. She is suing the Nintendo company for $10,000 _compensation_

5 Five hundred Nintendo _advisers_ answer 500,000 queries a week from players with problems.

B Make a list of as many ways as possible that computer games could be harmful.

2 Listening

mental

A Listen to the first part of a radio phone-in programme and complete these sentences with a suitable word or phrase.

1 The radio programme is about the link between computer games and . _children physical mental health._

2 Helena Brook is a . . _children psychologist_

3 Jim Edwards is a . . . _secondary school Head teacher_

4 The first person who telephones the programme is from . . . _London_

B Listen to the rest of the programme. Are any of the harmful effects you listed in Think ahead B mentioned by the speakers?

3 Points of view

Do you think Marion Jeffries is over-reacting? Whose view do you most agree with?

4 Comprehension

11

t-6hrs

passing face
= 18→轉時期

A Read the statements below, then listen to the second part of the programme again. Decide whether the statements are true or false.

T 1 Marion Jeffries thinks her son spends too much time playing computer games.

F 2 She is worried because her son doesn't mix with other children.

F 3 The child psychologist thinks Marion has good reason to be worried about her son's behaviour.

T 4 The psychologist expects Adam to lose interest in computer games soon.

F 5 According to the head teacher, children who play computer games do badly at school. 成績表好不好

F 6 The head teacher advises Marion to take the game away from the boy.

F 7 According to Oliver's research, computer games affect everyone in the same way.

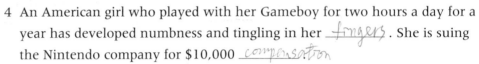

B Listening between the lines

1 What do you think Adam's personality was like before he became addicted to his computer games?

2 Why do you think the child psychologist suggests that Marion should try ignoring her son? 我沒內容48

3 What does Oliver Newton mean by 'outlet for their aggression'? What other outlets for aggression can you think of?

C Read these extracts from the radio programme. Match the words or phrases in *italics* with the definitions.

became very angry

c 1 If I shout to get his attention, he *loses his temper*.

h 2 When he's finished playing, he's completely *uncommunicative*.

b 3 What should I do about Adam's *obsession*?

g 4 He's like a two-year-old having a temper *tantrum*.

e 5 Obsessions like this are *a passing phase*.

d 6 It might just *do the trick*.

a 7 . . . if he continues to play *for hours on end*.

f 8 You'd be *asking for trouble*.

i 9 He's got a *flair* for computers.

a for a long time without stopping, continuously

b something you can't stop thinking about

c become very angry

d succeed in producing the right result

e a habit or stage in a person's life that does not last

f increase the chance of problems occurring

g a sudden noisy or violent outburst of anger

h unwilling to talk or listen to other people

i a special talent

5 Use of English

Read this text and fill the gap in each line with a word formed from the word in capital letters.

Many parents are becoming (1) *increasingly* worried about   INCREASE
their children's (2) *addiction* to video games. They believe   ADDICT
that playing for too long can be (3) *harmful* to their health.   HARM
Parents are afraid that their children's (4) *personality* will   PERSON
be affected, and many have frequent (5) *argument* with   ARGUE
them about their playing habits.
Actually, there is no (6) *scientific* proof that video games   SCIENCE
are (7) *dangerous* even if played for many hours a day.   DANGER
Another (8) *difficulty* for parents is that, although most   DIFFICULT
basic computer (9) *equipment* is quite cheap, the games   EQUIP
themselves are often very (10) *expensive*   EXPENSE

6 Over to you

Marion Jeffries thinks her son is addicted to computer games. What other kinds of addiction do you know of? Make a list.

Grammar and practice

1 Suggestions, advice and warnings

A Rank these three statements in order of strength.

advice 1 You really ought to stop worrying.

Warn 2 Don't stop your son from playing altogether, or you might make the situation worse.

suggestion 3 You could try ignoring Adam altogether.

Which statement is:

a a suggestion – an idea or plan put forward by someone?

b a piece of advice – someone's opinion or recommendation?

c a warning – strong advice with a mention of what may happen if this advice is not followed?

B Here are some more statements. Are they suggestions, advice or warnings?

advice 1 If I were you, Marion, I'd point out to Adam that he could do damage to his eyes.

advice 2 I wouldn't do that.

warn 3 Encourage him to keep up his other hobbies, otherwise he'll lose all his friends.

sug 4 Why don't you tell him he's got a flair for computers? *a fib*

C Advice and suggestion phrases *in your shoes*

ad 1 Sentence 1 above starts with *If I were you*. Do you know any similar ways of giving advice which start with *If I were . . .?*

Su 2 Rephrase sentence B4 above, starting with these phrases.
What about . . .? You could . . . How about . . .?

regret **D** What does Marion Jeffries mean when she says, 'I shouldn't have bought it for him. I realize that now.'?

E Check your understanding of suggestions, advice and warnings in the Grammar reference on page 208.

2 Practice

A Respond to these statements with suggestions or advice. *What about you go to part time work*

1 'I need to find a way of earning money so that I can afford a holiday next summer.' *You should —*

2 'I'm finding it really difficult to revise for my school exams.' *How about working harder.*

3 'My parents are always arguing. I don't know what to do.' *If I were you, I should shout back.*

B What would you say to your friends in these situations? Give them warnings. *Don't drive*

1 Your friend has got a new car and drives too fast.

2 Your friend drinks too much alcohol at parties.

3 Your friend, who has plenty of money, has got into the habit of stealing small things from shops for fun.

C Read this brief news report. What should or shouldn't the airport worker have done?

An airport baggage handler was in a plane's luggage compartment waiting for the last bag. He was tired after working an 80-hour week, so he lay down to rest and unfortunately fell asleep. When he woke up the plane had taken off. He cried for help and was freed by one of the plane's stewards. When he got back home, he was sent a bill for £298 – the cost of the return flight.

3 Conversation

Fill the gaps in this conversation with an appropriate word. Many of the missing words are to do with advice and suggestion.

John You look terrible. Are you all right?

Alan Yes thanks, I'm just very tired.

John What time did you go to bed last night?

Alan Quite early actually. The problem was I (1) *couldn't* get to sleep. It was the neighbours again. Every night they're up late, talking and playing loud music.

John Why (2) *don't* you ask them to make less noise?

Alan I have asked them. They promised they (3) *would* try to be a bit quieter, but it hasn't really made any difference.

John What (4) *about* going to see a solicitor?

Alan That's not a bad idea. I (5) *could* do with some expert legal advice.

John I (6) *can* give you the name of a good one.

Alan Thanks, that (7) *will* be very useful. I've never been to a solicitor before.

John I'm afraid, the law's slow and solicitors aren't cheap.

Alan I know, and all the time I'm getting (8) *more* and more exhausted.

John You know, if I (9) *were* you, I'd report them to the police. *serious*

Alan That's a bit drastic, (10) *isn't* it?

John I know, but (11) *what* else can you do?

Alan I don't know. Perhaps I'll just call the local council. Maybe they (12) *could* help.
can

4 Regrets and criticisms

A When Marion Jeffries says *I shouldn't have bought it for him . . .*, she means that she regrets buying her son the computer game.
In this sentence the speaker uses *You shouldn't have* to criticize:

> *You shouldn't have borrowed the car without asking me first.*

Write sentences – criticisms or regrets – which could follow these six statements, using *should have* or *shouldn't have* . The first one has been done for you.

1 I've got no money left.
   You shouldn't have spent so much on new clothes.
   I shouldn't have bought four CDs.
2 I've got an enormous phone bill to pay.
3 I didn't get high enough exam grades to get into university.
4 I got soaking wet in that heavy rain.
5 I've been waiting for him for nearly two hours.
6 I couldn't sleep after the party. I felt terrible.

B Write about things you have done but now regret.

5 Fluency

A Work in groups of three or four. Each choose a different problem from the list below. Think about how the people with the problems are behaving and how they have changed recently. Decide exactly why you are worried.

1 Your sister is addicted to gambling. You know she rarely wins, and loses much more money than she earns each week.
2 You think your best friend may be taking drugs. He / she is unsociable and never has any money.
3 Your friend has just got a credit card and is spending far more money than he can afford.

B Now present your problems to the group. The rest of the group should give advice. Make sure the advice you give is clear and helpful.

6 Linking ideas

A These extracts from the reading and listening texts each include two main ideas. Find these ideas and underline the words which link them. The first one has been done for you.

1 The boys and their friends have pasty faces <u>and</u> they have become aggressive and irritable.

2 Since Nintendo's Gameboy hit the British market in 1988, it has been a toy for the boys. <u>Despite this,</u> there are no plans to bring out a Gamegirl.
3 Girls don't mind joining in male pursuits, <u>but it</u> never works the other way round.
4 Don't let him give up his other hobbies, <u>otherwise</u> he'll lose all his friends.   *= In spite of*   *"even though"*
5 <u>Although</u> the children who play these games behave more aggressively, they also develop improved powers of observation.

B Discuss these questions about the sentences in A above.
1 How are the two ideas in the extracts related? Match each extract with one of these definitions.
   a one idea is an addition to the other
   b the two ideas are in contrast to each other
   c one idea is conditional on the other
2 Which words are used to link contrasting ideas?
3 Can you think of any more words or phrases which link contrasting ideas?

C Before doing the next exercise, read the Grammar reference on page 209.

7 Practice

Link these pairs of contrasting sentences in as many ways as possible.   *Although*
1 John's very fat. He does a lot of exercise.   *but*
2 We've got three television sets at home. I never watch TV.   *Although = Despite*
3 I drink several cups of coffee every night. Coffee keeps me awake.   *Even though*
4 I went to work as usual yesterday. I had a terrible cold.   *Although = even though*
5 My brother can't find a job. He is very well qualified.   *even though*
6 My sister always gets good marks in exams. She never does any revision.

9 Interaction

On the right track

1 Calling all students
Thanks to their extended summer vacations, students are in the enviable position of being able to travel round Europe by rail and see the sights on the cheap. This article points out some of the pros and cons of travelling by train.

2
The sense of freedom offered by rail travel is unrivalled by any other, except perhaps the less safe option of hitch-hiking. Trains are also a great way to meet local people and, compared with other long-distance modes of transport, the Greenest you can get. Rail travel allows you to explore the hidden corners of the continent, especially areas where rural lines are still open and trains are still the most common form of public transport. It's also a relaxing way to travel, whether you're using it as a cheap bed for the night, or as a ring-side seat for a series of stunning views.

3
The first step before you go is to choose one of the Eurorail schemes available. After that, there are a few tips to bear in mind before you leave. Budgeting always causes headaches and it's worth finding out which are the 'expensive' and the 'cheap' countries. It's sensible to take some cash, but you should take most of your money in traveller's cheques. Choose a well-known brand and buy small denominations.

4
Your most important piece of equipment is your backpack, and it's worth choosing one that's comfortable and light, sits just above your hips, and is 'high' rather than 'wide' when full. A day-pack is useful for sightseeing, and a pair of comfortable walking shoes is vital, along with dark, hard-wearing

---

Introduction

If you had as much money and time as you wanted, what kind of holiday would you choose to have? Which methods of transport would you use?

Reading

1 Think ahead

Imagine you're going on a month's holiday travelling around Europe by train. What problems might you encounter? Make a list. What precautions would you take?

2 Reading

The leaflet above gives advice to students on travelling round Europe by train. As you read it, underline any of the ideas you thought of in the Think ahead section.

3 Comprehension

A Choose suitable headings for the eight sections of the leaflet from this list. There is one heading you do not need to use. Write the section numbers in the spaces.

Beware of criminals __7__
Fill your time __X__
Planning a sensible schedule __6__
Take care but enjoy yourself __8__
Calling all students __1__

Money matters __3__
Packing the essentials __4__
Minor irritations __5__
Trains! They're the best __2__

B Read questions 1–6. Then read the leaflet again and choose the correct answers.
1 The main purpose of this text is to
   A highlight the problems associated with rail travel.
   B emphasize the many advantages of rail travel.
   C give advice to students about rail travel.
   D promote and advertise rail travel.

Eurorailing

clothes. As a general rule, put out everything you want to take – then halve it. Some things, however, should not be left behind. An alarm clock (so you don't miss those early trains); a scarf to cover your shoulders or legs for visits to churches or mosques; photocopies of all your important documents – best packed separately or given to a travelling companion; toilet paper, soap and a universal plug; a Swiss army penknife; numerous plastic bags; a water bottle and a small first aid kit.

5

The fun really starts once you're out there, of course – hunting for a hostel at 10 p.m., being ripped off by a taxi driver who claims there are no buses to your campsite or being turned away from a famous tourist attraction for wearing shorts. There are compensations for these frustrations

(which make the best stories afterwards, anyway!), but many problems can be avoided if you're aware of the potential pitfalls before you leave.

6

The golden rule is not to try to cram too much into the time available. Trying to see the whole of Europe in a month, by spending every night on a train and an afternoon in each capital city will result in an unsatisfactory blur of shallow impressions. It is also a recipe for disaster, as you will be tired, grumpy and unreceptive for most of your trip. Instead, try to vary your route, mixing visits to cities with relaxing spells on the beach or in the countryside.

7

Each year a few unlucky travellers have their valuables stolen. The best way to

prevent this is to carry them with you at all times, preferably in a money belt or a neck pouch. This is especially important on night trains, where most thefts occur. Another sensible precaution is not to sleep rough – you're just asking for trouble. Watch out for conmen at stations: they'll try to persuade you to accept a room, tempting you with glamorous pictures of a hotel which turns out to be awful and whose price will have doubled by the time you reach it. Far better to go and see accommodation yourself before accepting it. And, if you're on a tight budget, it's always worth asking if they've got anything cheaper.

8

These ideas are really just common sense, but it's amazing how often they're overlooked. But the most important tip of all is – have fun!

2 The writer advises students to take
   A no cash.
   B money in more than one form.
   C only traveller's cheques.
   D a credit card.

3 When they are packing for a rail holiday, the writer advises students to
   A include only small objects.
   B take more than they think they'll really need.
   C take less than they really want to.
   D leave behind nothing they think they may need.

4 According to the writer, the best thing about bad experiences on holiday is that you
   A forget about them later.
   B may receive compensation afterwards.
   C can learn something useful for the future.
   D can tell people about them later.

5 When planning a route, the writer advises students to
   A see as much as possible in the time they have.
   B visit places but also rest from time to time.
   C go sightseeing in the afternoons and travel by night.
   D see everything in a month.

6 What should travellers do to prevent their valuables from being stolen?
   A They should keep them with them all the time.
   B They should not travel on trains at night.
   C They should not fall asleep on trains.
   D They should be especially careful at stations.

4 Over to you   What is the most interesting journey you have ever had? Tell your group about it.

Vocabulary

1 Travel and holidays
Vocabulary reference p 217

A Modes of transport
Complete these sets of travel words.

1 car   to _drive a car_   to go by road
2 _train_   to travel on a train   to go by _train_
3 ship   to _sail on a ship_   _to go by ship_
4 _airplane_   to fly _____   to go by _air_

B Noun–verb collocations
If the vehicle and the verb can be used together, tick the correct space in the table. For example, you can say *catch* or *miss a bus*, but not *catch* or *miss a bicycle*.

Types of vehicle	car	bicycle	boat / ship	bus	motorbike	plane	taxi	train
Verbs catch / miss			✓	✓		✓		✓
get into / get out of	✓			✓			✓	✓
get on / get off		✓	✓	✓	✓	✓		✓
ride		✓			✓			
take	✓			✓		✓	✓	✓
drive	✓			✓			✓	✓

C Fill the gaps in the following sentences with one of the following words.
trip journey tour excursion 游览、团体旅游

1 Do you know, my _journey_ to work took over four hours this morning.
2 For our holidays next year, we're going on a ten-day _tour_ of the Australian outback.
3 We always go on a day _trip_ to France in December to buy Christmas presents.
4 The price of this holiday includes a full-day _excursion_ to a place of cultural interest.
5 He's hoping to go on a(n) _trip_ to the Himalayas next year.

2 Colloquial language
The words and phrases in *italics* in these extracts from the Eurorailing leaflet are all informal or colloquial English. Match them with their meanings.

1/2 d e   There are a few *tips* to *bear in mind* before you leave.
3 g   Budgeting always causes *headaches* . . .
4 f   . . . being *ripped off* by a taxi driver . . .
5 b   . . . many problems can be avoided if you're aware of the potential *pitfalls* before you leave.
6 a   . . . you will be tired, *grumpy* and unreceptive for most of your trip.
7 h   . . . mixing visits to cities with relaxing *spells* on the beach . . .
8 c   . . . if *you're on a tight budget*, it's always worth asking if they've got anything cheaper.

a bad-tempered
b unexpected difficulties
c you haven't any money to spare
d pieces of advice
e think about / remember
f cheated / misled
g worrying problems
h periods of time

Writing

Exam training: Transactional letters 2
Paper 2 Part 1

1 Sample question

Read all the information carefully, so that you know exactly what to do.

> A group of foreign students is visiting your town next month. You have been asked to write a letter inviting them to a 'Welcome evening' at your school. Read the Director's memo and the notes you have made. Then write a letter to Tom Wilde, the leader of the group, covering all the director's points and including the information in your notes.

Memo

Central High School

To   Student representative
Date   12 May
From   Director

Subject   **Invitation to Welcome Evening for foreign students**

Thank you for agreeing to write a letter on the school's behalf. You should write to the leader, Tom Wilde. Please make sure you include these points.

1   Some brief information about the school.
    No. of students & local reputation

2   Date, time and venue of the Welcome Evening (as we agreed). *6th June 8.30 - 11.00
    Main Hall (school)*

3   Programme for the evening – don't forget my speech at 9.00 pm. *Welcome drinks
    Entertainment - disco*

4   Directions from the town centre to the school.
    send map

2 Think, plan, write

A Think

1 Try to visualize what a 'Welcome Evening' might be like in the school you attend now, or in one you have attended in the past.
2 Here are some specific points to think about.
  a What would your visitors like to know about the school?
  b What kind of entertainment could your school put on?
  c How long should the formal entertainment programme last?
  d When should the disco start?

B Plan

1 Plan your letter, using all the information provided and incorporating any ideas you have just come up with.
  Follow this paragraph plan:
  Paragraph 1   Say who you are and why you are writing.
  Paragraph 2   Information about the school.
  Paragraph 3   Details of the Welcome Evening.
  Paragraph 4   Directions to the school and a concluding sentence.
2 Decide on an appropriate style. Remember that although you are writing on behalf of the school, you want to sound friendly and welcoming.

C Write

Now write your letter of invitation, following your plan and making sure you don't leave out any of the points mentioned in the question. Finally check grammar, spelling, punctuation and style.

Transactional letters (2)	p 54 Transactional letters 1
Viewpoint Try to think yourself into the position of the writer and write from this point of view.	For a less formal letter, start with *Dear + name* and end with *Yours sincerely.*
Style Choose an appropriate style, remembering what the purpose of the letter is.	**Paragraphing** Work out a paragraph plan before you start writing. Each paragraph should have a specific purpose.

Exam techniques

Use of English: Vocabulary cloze Paper 3 Part 1

1 Guidelines

Do	Don't
• Read the whole text through to get a general understanding of what it is about.	➡ Don't look at the four choices or try to fill the gaps until you understand the overall meaning of the text.
• Read the text again, trying to fill each gap as you come to it. Study the four choices A–D and the words on both sides of the gap.	➡ Don't simply choose the first word which seems to fit. Some of the choices are intended to mislead you.
• If you are not sure of the answer, read the sentence to yourself, filling the gap with each of the four words in turn. One may seem more natural than the others.	➡ Don't leave any gaps blank.
• Try to eliminate three of the four alternatives.	
• If you still can't decide, make a sensible guess.	

2 Practice

A Follow the guidelines as you work through this text. There is an example at the beginning and clues in *italics* for 1–7, to help you.

When you have chosen your answers, try to think of reasons why the other three alternatives in each question are not possible.

Example
(0)   A at   B on   C for   D in

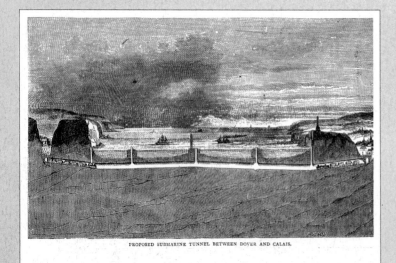

PROPOSED SUBMARINE TUNNEL BETWEEN DOVER AND CALAIS.

The history of the Chunnel

The Channel tunnel, which joins Britain to mainland Europe (0) *for* the first time, was officially opened in 1994, but the history of the 'Chunnel' (1) _____ back nearly 200 hundred years.

At the beginning of the nineteenth century, a British politician went to France to discuss closer trade links (2) _____ the two countries. The (3) _____ of a tunnel was mentioned in talks with Napoleon. A French engineer prepared plans for a tunnel in two sections, meeting at an (4) _____ island built in the middle of the English Channel. Another plan involved the laying of air-filled wooden tubes

D 1 A turns   B looks   C starts   D goes
*Which of these verbs combined with **back** refers to the past?*

A 2 A between   B among   C within   D inside
*Two of these prepositions indicate a relationship. Which of these two can refer to **two** things or people?*

C 3 A belief   B opinion   C idea   D thought
*Which of these words can mean **a plan about something new**? Which are commonly followed by **of**?*

A 4 A artificial   B false   C imitation   D imaginary
*The island was going to be 'real', but not natural. Which of these words can mean the opposite of **natural**?*

B 5 A end   B bottom   C bed   D base
*Which one of these nouns cannot follow the preposition **at**? Which of the other three refers to water, e.g. rivers, seas?*

A 6 A two   B both   C twin   D all
Two of these words cannot be used in this position in a sentence. Which of the other two is appropriate here?

C 7 A came   B went   C broke   D brought
*Which of these verbs combined with **out** means **start suddenly**?*

B Now try questions 8–15 on your own. Ask yourself the sort of questions that were in the clues for 1–7.

B 8 A written   B signed   C agreed   D decided
C 9 A soil   B earth   C land   D ground
A 10 A completed   B ended   C done   D terminated
B 11 A view   B opinion   C belief   D idea
C 12 A thought   B put up   C considered   D taken on
D 13 A thrown   B left   C refused   D rejected
A 14 A financial   B market   C trading   D economical
B 15 A by   B until   C in   D prior

at the (5)_____ of the sea. These (6)_____ schemes were abandoned when war (7)_____ out between Britain and France.

In 1875 a Tunnel Committee was formed, and a Convention was (8)_____. The British Channel Company bought (9)_____ near Dover and started digging. There were still arguments about whether there should be a tunnel. The British were against the idea, saying that once the tunnel was (10)_____, Britain would no longer be an island. Public (11)_____ was increasingly hostile and in 1884 all work stopped.

In the early twentieth century the idea was (12)_____ again but was soon forgotten when the First World War began. Throughout the twenties and thirties the idea was always (13)_____ because of security and (14)_____ worries. After that, it was not (15)_____ the 1960s that the two governments started talking seriously again about the tunnel.

Vocabulary

1 Use of English
Vocabulary reference p 218

Read this text and decide which of the alternatives best fits each gap.

Holidays

We've just come back exhausted after a two-week holiday in France. We were really stupid, on the last day we drove non-stop from Marseille to Calais – we should have (1)_____ our journey in Lyon or Paris. As if that wasn't enough, the sea was so rough in the English Channel that the (2)_____ took three hours instead of one and a half. Next year we've decided we're going on a cheap (3)_____ holiday to Italy. It sounds marvellous – the cost of the flight, the hotel and all our meals are (4)_____ in the price. While we're in Rome we'll be going on a guided (5)_____ of the Colosseum. The last time I was in Italy, I was on a business (6)_____ – I can't say I saw many of the famous tourist (7)_____ on that occasion.

1 A stopped   B paused   C broken   D interrupted
2 A expedition   B crossing   C cruise   D passage
3 A party   B package   C overall   D inclusive
4 A included   B involved   C contained   D combined
5 A view   B tour   C sightseeing   D trip
6 A trip   B journey   C excursion   D travel
7 A views   B sights   C scenes   D visits

2 Word building

Roots

The words in 1-3 are from the reading texts in this unit.

1 What are the roots of these nouns? What parts of speech are they?
goodness   observation   reaction   amusement   valuables
(observe, react, amuse, value)
Example   The root of the noun *goodness* is the adjective *good*.

2 What are the roots of these adjectives? What parts of speech are they?
darkened   addictive   resentful   unrivalled   unlucky   glamorous
(addict, resent, unrival, glamour)
Example   The root of the adjective *darkened* is the adjective or noun *dark*.

3 What are the roots of these adverbs? What parts of speech are they?
honestly   enviably   especially
(a. / envy v. / a.)

3 Phrasal verbs

This sentence is from an article at the beginning of the unit. 'Nintendo have at last *brought out* a computer game aimed at girls.' Here *bring out* means introduce to the market. *Bring* can be used with other particles to express different meanings. Fill the gaps in these sentences with the correct form of *bring* and one of these particles: *back in round on up.*

1 Last year the government __brought in__ a new law making it compulsory for people to wear seat belts in the back of cars.

2 I __was brought up__ by my parents to know the difference between right and wrong.

3 Don't feel sorry for him. He __brought__ all his problems __on__ himself.

4 Visiting Spain again __will bring back__ so many childhood memories.

5 It took doctors an hour to __bring__ him __round__ after the accident.

Restrictions

Within limits

3 Professional ballet dancers

4 Doctors

2 Top fashion models

5 Monks

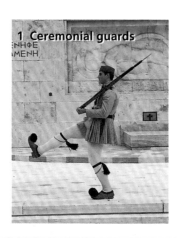

1 Ceremonial guards

8 Sumo wrestlers

6 Heads of state

7 Schoolboys

Introduction

A Look at the people in the photographs and discuss your answers to these questions.

1 Who has the hardest life?

2 Who has the easiest life?

3 What makes these people's lives harder or easier than the others?

People's lives are governed by a variety of restrictions, from national laws to rules and regulations associated with their jobs. Think about the special restrictions which govern the lives of some of the people in the photographs and compare ideas.

Examples   *Ceremonial guards have to wear special uniforms and take part in official ceremonies.*
Heads of state can't go anywhere without bodyguards.

B Can you think of people whose lives are restricted in other ways?

Listening

1 Think ahead

Many people have several different images – a private image and one or more public images. How many images do you have? How would you describe them?

2 Listening

A You are going to hear five people talking about something to do with clothing or fashion. They are:
1 Suzie 2 Jenny 3 Becky 4 Sheila 5 Mary.

As you listen for the first time, decide who is talking. Match the names with the list of people A–F. There is one more person than you need.

A a model   B an unknown actress   C an artist   D a fashion designer
E a schoolgirl   F a parent

B Listen again and decide the subject of each extract. Match the names with the list of subjects A–F. There is one more subject than you need.

Which speaker is talking about

A her general appearance   _____? B pros and cons of her lifestyle _____?
C where her ideas come from _____? D the clothes she has to wear   _____?
E clothes for small children   _____? F buying fashionable shoes   _____?

3 Points of view

Have you ever had to wear a uniform? What was it like? Did you enjoy wearing it? Why? Why not? Compare ideas with a partner.

4 Comprehension

Listen to the five speakers again and answer these questions by choosing the best of the three alternatives A, B or C.
1 At the first speaker's school, a boy was sent home because
   A he was wearing earrings.
   B his hair was too long.
   C he wasn't wearing a tie.
2 Adriano wants expensive trainers mainly because
   A they are more comfortable than the others.
   B his schoolfriends are all wearing them.
   C they are better designed than the others.
3 The third speaker designs clothes for people who
   A have to be careful with their money.
   B normally buy second-hand clothes.
   C have plenty of money to spend.
4 Most of the time the fourth speaker wears clothes that are
   A attractive.
   B smart.
   C comfortable.
5 The last speaker says that people like her need to
   A take some time off.
   B avoid putting on weight.
   C get media attention.

5 Vocabulary

In English there are a number of adverbs which have two forms. In some cases the forms have different meanings. For example *rough* and *roughly*.

*. . . teenagers who sleep **rough***.	in the open air, outside
*Their parents treat them **roughly***.	violently, cruelly

Here are some more pairs of adverbs. Decide which form should go in which sentence.

1 a He _____ refused to help his mother with the housework.
  b He tripped and fell _____ on his face.   *flat, flatly*

2 a In some countries old people travel _____ on the buses.
  b There's no one listening, so we can talk quite _____ .   *free, freely*

3 a Some people work _____ and get very little money.
  b Other people _____ do any work and are paid a fortune.   *hard, hardly*

4 a Where's Gloria? I haven't seen her _____ .
  b Don't worry, she's coming. She always arrives _____ .   *late, lately*

5 a It is _____ known that the President is about to resign.
  b At the dentist, you have to open your mouth _____ .   *wide, widely*

6 a Be careful not to drive _____ the edge of the cliff.
  b Someone I know _____ had a terrible accident last week.   *near, nearly*

6 Over to you

Look at these two photographs of the supermodel Claudia Schiffer. Which image do you prefer and why? Discuss ideas in pairs or groups and then write 60–80 words expressing your ideas.

Grammar and practice

1 Modal verbs

A Obligation and necessity

Read these sentences from the listening extracts and underline the verbs which express obligation and/or necessity, or absence of necessity.

1 You don't have to worry about what to put on in the mornings.
2 Pupils must wear ties at all times.
3 Boys must not wear earrings while at school.
4 You must come and see my new collection.
5 I have to lose a couple of kilos for the next job.
6 You mustn't let the press attention go to your head.
7 I need to get right away from the business.

Which sentence or sentences express:
a a necessity?
b a strong suggestion, a piece of advice or an invitation?
c a rule, law or prohibition?
d a personal obligation outside the speaker's control?
e a lack of necessity or obligation?

B

Rewrite these sentences, without changing their meaning, and without the verbs in *italics*. The first one has been done for you.

1 You *mustn't* drive if you've drunk too much alcohol. *It's against the law to drive if you've drunk too much alcohol.*
2 You *shouldn't* sunbathe for too long. It can damage your health.
3 British people *needn't* vote in general elections if they don't want to.
4 Soldiers *don't have to* wear uniforms when they're off duty.
5 You *mustn't* worry about me. I've travelled on my own before.

C didn't need / needn't have

What is the difference in meaning between these sentences?

1 I didn't need to hurry. There was plenty of time.
2 I needn't have hurried. There was plenty of time.

In which sentence did the speaker hurry?

D

Fill the gaps in these sentences with *didn't need to* or *needn't have* and the correct part of the verb in *italics*.

1 I went to the airport to meet him. Unfortunately he was ill and had to cancel his trip, so I _____ *drive* all that way.
2 I was about to go shopping, when Dad arrived home with everything we needed, so I _____ *go* after all.
3 The car was really dirty, but then it rained for a couple of hours, so I _____ *wash* it.
4 I carried my umbrella round all day but it didn't rain once. I _____ *take* my umbrella.
5 Last year my father won £1 million. He _____ *work* any more, so he gave up his job.
6 That was a lovely meal, but you _____ *go* to so much trouble.

E

Check your understanding of these verbs in the Grammar reference on page 209.

2 Practice

A

Read this extract from a speech made by a college director talking to a new group of students. From the list below choose the best verb to fill the gaps. Sometimes more than one answer is possible. In these cases, give the alternative verbs and explain any differences in meaning.

must mustn't should don't have to will need to

First of all, and most importantly, you (1)_____ enrol and pay your fees today, otherwise you will not be allowed to start your course. According to the college regulations, you (2)_____ attend a minimum of 80% of your classes, but actually, if you want to do well in your exams, you (3)_____ try to attend all your classes. If you have no classes on a particular day, you (4)_____ stay at the college. You can stay at home if you like. If you are planning to come by car or motorbike, you (5)_____ get a permit from the college office. And lastly, please remember that this is a no-smoking college, which means that you (6)_____ smoke inside the building at any time.

B This leaflet gives tourists information about driving on British motorways. *Must* is used for all legal obligations, *should* for anything which isn't law, and *need* for things that are physically necessary. Read the leaflet, and fill the gaps with the affirmative or negative form of one of the three verbs.

Drive carefully . . . ⚠

Although motorways are safer than other roads, nevertheless accidents do sometimes happen – and they can nearly always be avoided.

Before you leave

◆ If you are feeling tired, you ¹_____ drive.

◆ Learner drivers ²_____ not use motorways.

◆ Petrol stations may be up to 80 miles apart on some motorways. You ³_____ make sure you have enough petrol before joining the motorway.

As you go

◆ Drive at a safe speed. You ⁴_____ under any circumstances drive faster than 70 m.p.h.

◆ If you have a mechanical problem and you ⁵_____ stop, pull on to the hard shoulder and switch on your hazard warning lights. You ⁶_____ use the hard shoulder for casual stops.

◆ If driving long distances makes you feel sleepy, you ⁷_____ stop regularly at service stations and walk about.

hard shoulder – area at the side of a motorway where drivers are allowed to stop in an emergency

. . . arrive safely

3 Permission

A This chart gives information about the ages at which young people in Britain are allowed to do certain things. Study the information and make sentences using *can* and *be allowed to*.

Examples   *When you're 12 you're allowed to buy pets.*
You can't buy pets until you're 12.

Age	buy pets	get a part-time job	go into a pub or bar	drink alcohol in a pub or bar	leave school	buy cigarettes	vote in elections	become a member of parliament	become a soldier	get a driving licence
12	✓									
13		✓								
14			✓							
15										
16					✓	✓			✓	
17										✓
18				✓			✓			
19										
20										
21								✓		

B Check your understanding of ways of talking about permission in the Grammar reference on page 210.

C Make a similar chart like this for your country. Compare charts with other students.

4 Fluency

Working in pairs, act out this situation. Instructions for Student B are on page 198.

Student A
You are a famous sumo wrestler training for the world championships. You are tired of weighing 180 kilos, and want to be slim. Tell your trainer you have decided to go on a diet, and explain why.

Writing

Exam training: Articles 2 Paper 2 Part 2

1 Model

A Look at this exam question.

> You see the following announcement in an English-language magazine for young people and decide to write an article.

B As you read the model answer think about these questions.

First paragraph — How does the writer attract your attention and persuade you to read the rest of the article?

Last paragraph — What effect does this paragraph have on you?

> **YOU WRITE – WE PRINT**
>
> Can you explain why some teenagers choose to wear clothes their parents dislike? Can you explain parents' reactions to their children's clothes? Write an article giving us your views. The three most interesting articles will win cash prizes and be published in our next issue.

You're not going out like that!

Have your parents ever said: 'You're only wearing those clothes to embarrass me, aren't you?' This is what my mother said to me the other day, when she saw my torn jeans.

In my case, I just wanted to look like everyone else, but many people believe that clothes reflect children's attitudes to their parents. I have got friends who deliberately buy things they know their parents will dislike. In my opinion, children want to prove their independence and parents don't want to admit their children are growing up.

In addition to this, I think that people's clothes indicate their social situation. For example, people of my grandparents' age, who remember being poor, prefer to mend clothes than to buy new ones. By contrast, those who were teenagers in the 1960s are used to having money to spend on themselves. However, their children definitely prefer the second-hand look.

Let's face it, when it comes to fashion, we all laugh at the generation before us and are shocked by the generation that follows.

2 Analysis

A Here are some common techniques used in the first paragraphs of articles. Which of them are used in the model?

1 Giving an interesting example to illustrate the topic of the article.

2 Describing an unusual scene or situation.

3 Addressing the reader in a direct way about something relevant to them. This may include asking personal questions.

4 Surprising the reader with strong opinions.

5 Describing a puzzle or a problem which needs an answer.

B What is the main purpose of the last paragraph?

1 To summarize the main points of the article.

2 To leave the reader with something to think about.

3 To express a final personal opinion on the theme of the article.

4 To round off the article.

3 Practice

Here are some more first and last paragraphs of articles.
A Match a beginning with an appropriate ending.
B Which techniques are used in the first paragraphs?
C What is the main purpose of the last paragraphs?

Beginnings

1   Are you still wearing your Reeboks or your Nike Airs? I replaced mine with a pair of black boots six months ago, when I heard that trainers were out of fashion.

2   I have changed my mind on many subjects in the last few years, but school uniform is not one of them. When I had to wear it, I thought it was ridiculous and I still do.

3   I'm in a restaurant and this is the scene. A young Englishman with clothes full of holes is ordering a meal. At a table, a Japanese couple are talking to their baby. A German professor is leaving hurriedly. What have these people got in common? They're all wearing blue jeans – Levis to be precise.

Endings

A   So, clothes that started in the 1850s as tough trousers for American workers have become an important part of a world uniform. Whatever happens in the world of high fashion, it is likely that blue denims will last for another 150 years.

B   The test of any fashion is, will people wear it even if it is extremely uncomfortable, like mini skirts in winter? Recently I've seen young people walking about with their boots undone. It reminded me of how I wore my trainers. Now, where did I put them?

C   If wearing uniform is really about preparing kids for adult life, they should all be wearing oily overalls, or dark suits. Perhaps T-shirts and jeans would be more suitable, like those worn by the thousands who can't find work?

4 Think, plan, write

YOU WRITE – WE PRINT

What can you tell about a person from their hairstyle and their clothes? Write an article giving us your views. The six most original articles will be published in our spring issue.

A Think

In pairs or groups discuss this topic. Here are some points to think about.
1   What do you first notice about a person?
2   Do you look closely at people's clothes?
3   Do people's hairstyles reflect their personality?

B Plan

1   Will the readers belong to one age group? Choose an appropriate style.
2   Work out a suitable title for your article.
3   Plan your article paragraph by paragraph.
4   Think particularly carefully about your first paragraph.
5   Start a new paragraph for each main idea. How will you link the paragraphs?
6   Think about your last paragraph. What effect would you like it to have?

C Write

1   Write a first draft of your opening paragraph and exchange it with a partner. Tell your partner whether their beginning makes you want to continue reading.
2   Rewrite your first paragraph if necessary. Then complete the article and check grammar, spelling and punctuation.

Articles 2   ◀ p.46 ◀ **Articles 1**

First paragraph Together with the title, this should attract readers and make them want to continue the article.

Last paragraph This should round off the article, by summarizing, reaching a conclusion or expressing

a personal opinion; it may also leave the reader with something to think about.

Paragraphing Make sure new ideas are given new paragraphs and that all paragraphs are connected by linking devices.

10

Space

Introduction

A Imagine yourself in the position of the astronauts shown in the photographs. How safe would you feel? What could go wrong?

B How do you think your daily routine would differ from the normal routine on earth?

C How would you occupy any free time you had?

Reading

1 Think ahead

If you saw an advertisement for the job of an astronaut on a future space flight, would you apply? Why? Why not? What mental and physical qualities do you think an astronaut needs to have? How many of these qualities do you have?

2 Reading

Read the article quickly to find out whether you do have any of the qualities needed to be an astronaut. Don't worry about the missing sentences yet.

What it takes to be an astronaut

One afternoon in the summer of 1989, a 27-year-old food technologist called Helen Sharman was listening to the radio. She heard an unusual position being advertised: 'Astronaut wanted – no previous experience necessary.' Quickly she wrote down the phone number and the next day sent off her application.

Sharman was one of 13,000 hopefuls who applied to become Britain's first astronaut when the British government agreed to co-operate with the Russians in the Juno space mission. Applicants for the Juno Project had to take tough psychological and physical tests. They needed to be scientifically trained, had to speak a foreign language and had to be able to deal with difficult situations without panicking. [1] Sharman was a highly trained scientist, could speak several languages and was well-known for her ability to remain calm. Obviously, physical fitness was also important and although Sharman often played squash and regularly went cycling and swimming, she now admits that she was no great athlete when she applied. [2] In space there's almost no gravity, so the movement of food through the stomach is entirely dependent on muscle power.

To Sharman's surprise, her application was successful and six months later she was in Russia beginning 18 months of training at the Yuri Gagarin Cosmonaut Centre. [3] 'Actually, it's extremely difficult to do this on earth,' explains Sharman, 'because to weigh absolutely nothing you have to be positioned between two planets so that the force of their gravity is pulling you in opposite directions.' The nearest it is possible to get to these conditions on Earth is in a plane that is flying in enormous loops. 'We used huge freighter aircraft. [4] Each experiment only lasted about 23 seconds – not very long, otherwise it would hit the ground.' Once she was aboard the space shuttle, Sharman found it easy to get used to weightlessness, despite a little initial discomfort.

Another important part of Sharman's preparation included learning about the technical aspects of space travel. There were only three people in the spacecraft, and they are all needed to be able to operate it. [5].

On 18 May 1991, Sharman boarded the Soyuz spacecraft in the Kazakhstan Desert with two Russian cosmonauts. Once it was in space, the craft was going at a speed of 29,000 km/h. [6]. She says living up there was not as frightening as it sounds. 'Eating wasn't too difficult. We sucked coffee and tea out of tubes and ate a lot of tinned food.' The on-board lavatory was an interesting piece of environmentally correct technology – amazingly a proportion of the waste matter produced was recycled.

In space Sharman carried out experiments on various materials to be used for new drugs and electronics. [7].

Although she would like to go back into space, these days Sharman is happy enough working as a part-time consultant to a company making satellites. The rest of her time she spends trying to persuade schoolchildren to take up a career in science and technology.

3 Comprehension

A Choose from sentences A–H the one which fits each gap in the article. Remember, one of them does not fit anywhere.

A But the Russians wanted to make sure Helen could operate all the systems she would need to survive on her own in an emergency.

B One of the most interesting parts of her preparation was a set of tests which simulated weightlessness.

C The results were brought back to earth for analysis by the Russians.

D The experiments that she would be doing in space were tested in towers where the conditions also simulated weightlessness.

E It docked with the Mir Space Station two days later.

F When the plane gets to the top and starts to fall, you fall with it, so you feel as if you're weightless.

G A strong digestive system was also vital.

H Helen Sharman turned out to be ideal.

B Reading between the lines

1 Why do you think so many people wanted to become astronauts?
2 Why do you think it is so important for astronauts to be able to stay calm?
3 What arguments do you think Helen Sharman uses to try to persuade children to take up careers in science and technology?

Grammar and practice

1 Adverb and prepositional phrases

Here are some adverbs and prepositional phrases from the article about Helen Sharman. Group them under these six headings:

- manner (*how*)
- place (*where*)
- time (*when*)
- frequency (*how often*)
- degree (*how much*)
- viewpoint (what the writer thinks)

six months later   obviously   quickly   very
one afternoon   amazingly   in space   often
almost   the next day   on earth   regularly
now   extremely   entirely   absolutely   to the
top   actually   these days

2 Position of adverbs

A The position of adverbs in sentences is tricky in English.
The adverbs or adverb phrases in bold in most of the lines in this text are in the wrong place. For all the wrong lines mark the place where the adverb should be. An example is given.

> Sharman feels **strongly** that Britain needs more qualified scientists and technologists, so she is hard working to do everything she can **possibly** to persuade people that science
> 5 is fun. She spends a lot of time talking **now** to schoolchildren. 'We need to get them **genuinely** interested in science from an early age,' she **enthusiastically** says , 'Primary school teachers have **often** no scientific
> 10 background and cannot make science interesting. **Definitely** I think children should learn about space when they're **very** young - it's a good way of teaching them basic science.'
> Sharman knows **quite well** that scientists
> 15 themselves **always** aren't the best people to talk about their subject. 'Many of them are **extremely** shy people who are not great communicators.'

B Now look at the rules for the position of adverbs in the Grammar reference on page 210.

3 Too, enough, very

A Fill the gaps in these sentences from the space text with *too, enough* or *very*.
1 Each experiment only lasted about 23 seconds – not _____ long . . .
2 Eating wasn't _____ difficult.
3 . . . at the moment Sharman is happy _____ working as a part-time consultant...

B Which of the three words, *too, enough* and *very*
1 intensifies an adjective or adverb?
2 means *more than is needed or wanted*?
3 means *sufficient*?
Which of the three words can come
4 before an adjective or adverb?
5 after an adjective or adverb?
6 before an uncountable noun or a plural countable noun?

C Use the information given to complete the unfinished sentences. If possible, complete the sentences in two different ways, with *too* and *enough*.
1 When I was sixteen, I fell in love with a boy of 18. We wanted to get married, but my parents said no. They wanted me to wait for two or three years.
My parents thought we _____ .
2 We've been looking for a new flat for ages. There's a fantastic one right in the town centre but we can't afford the rent. Unfortunately, this flat _____ .
3 I was thinking of going to India for my holiday next year, but I don't think I could stand the high temperatures.
I think India _____ .
4 My brother started training to be a teacher, but he gave up after a year because he found he didn't have the patience necessary for the job.
My brother gave up the idea of teaching because _____ .

Vocabulary

1 Clothes

Vocabulary reference p 218

A Clothes can be categorized in many ways. List as many items as you can under the following headings.

Winter clothes   Summer clothes   Sportswear
Indoor clothes   Nightwear

B Think about your clothes and decide what you would wear on the occasions below. Describe the clothes you have in mind, mentioning material, colour, pattern and style. The Vocabulary reference on page 218 will help you.

a a formal interview tomorrow
b a friend's birthday party this evening
c a day on the beach at the weekend

Example   *For a formal interview tomorrow, I'd wear my lightweight cotton suit. It's pale green, and looks very smart.*

Compare ideas in pairs, and give reasons for your choices.

2 Prohibition

Choose the correct word to fill the gaps in these sentences.

1 He was found guilty of dangerous driving and _____ from driving for three years.
   A forbidden   B banned   C prevented   D stopped
2 Smoking is strictly _____ on underground trains in London.
   A prohibited   B banned   C disallowed   D prevented
3 It is now _____ for all passengers in cars to wear seat belts.
   A enforced   B obliged   C allowed   D compulsory
4 Because he got home two hours late, he was _____ to go out for a week.
   A forbidden   B prohibited   C prevented   D banned
5 Relatives were only _____ to visit patients on weekday afternoons between four o'clock and half-past five.
   A let   B prevented   C permitted   D prohibited

3 Phrasal verbs

Choose the appropriate phrasal verb to fill the gaps in these sentences. You may need to change the form of the verbs.

1 Last year scientists _____ experiments to find out the effect of weightlessness on the human body.
   carry out / carry on
2 These days, more girls are _____ jobs in scientific research.
   take over / take up
3 It doesn't matter what you say, I'm not going to _____ to your demands.
   give in / give up
4 The interviewer _____ everything the president said in his speech.
   write off / write down
5 As soon as I heard about the match, I _____ for tickets.
   send off / send out

Exam techniques

Use of English: Key word transformations Paper 3 Part 3

1 Guidelines

Do	Don't
• Read through the first sentences and the second gapped sentences you have to complete.	➡ Don't start writing immediately.
• Focus on each key word you are given and think about how it can be used grammatically in its gapped sentence.	➡ Don't forget that you must not change the key word in any way.
• Starting with the ones you are sure about, complete each gapped sentence, using between 2 and 5 words. Remember that the second sentence must have a similar meaning to the original sentence.	➡ Don't waste time worrying about the sentences you cannot complete. Try them again later.
• If you aren't sure, make a sensible guess.	➡ Don't leave any spaces.
• Finally, read the sentences to check that they make sense and are grammatically accurate.	

2 Recognizing structures

A Key word transformations can test a wide range of structures, involving grammar, vocabulary and conversational language. They could include conditionals; verbs and adjectives followed by gerunds or infinitives; time phrases; passives; reported speech; prepositions after verbs; phrases for invitations, suggestions, etc; phrasal verbs; words which are often confused, for example *so* and *such* ; *although* and *despite*.

B Look at the key word transformations below, which practise some of the grammar in Units 1–10. Some are incorrect. Tick the correct ones and correct any mistakes in the others.

Example Motorbikes are faster than mopeds. **so**
Mopeds·are *not so fast than* motorbikes
Mopeds are *not so fast as* motorbikes ✓

1 You can't drive without a licence.　**if**
   You can't drive *if you haven't got a licence.*

2 He prefers staying in to going out.　**rather**
   He'd *rather to stay in than* go out.

3 Is there an earlier flight than this?　**the**
   Is this *the earlier flight* there is?

4 He has been playing golf for six months.　**ago**
   Six months *ago he has started playing* golf.

5 I've never eaten snails before.　**first**
   This is the *first time I am eating* snails.

6 We haven't got enough money to buy a new car.　**if**
   We could buy a new car *if we had enough* money.

7 'Why don't you apply for the hospital job Linda?' said Larry.　**suggested**
   Larry *suggested Linda should apply* for the hospital job.

8 My parents taught me to be independent.
   brought
   I was *brought me up* to be independent by my parents.

9 I got home very late last night – that's why I didn't phone you. **would**
   If I hadn't got home so late last night, *I would have phoned* you.

10 The film was so boring that I fell asleep half way through. **such**
   It was *a such boring film that* I fell asleep half way through.

3 Guided practice

Use the guidelines as you work through the following exercise. There are also clues in *italics* to help you.

1 A holiday in Miami is cheaper than one in Bermuda. **expensive**
   A holiday in Bermuda is _____ in Miami.
   How is the comparative form of **expensive** *different from the comparative form of* **cheap**?

2 The last time I saw Jimmy was at Stephen's party. **since**
   I _____ Stephen's party.
   Which verb tense is often used with **since**?

3 Many people are sorry that they ever started to smoke. **regret**
   Many people _____ smoke.
   What structure follows **regret**?

4 My brother was always on time until he got friendly with Mick. **used**
   My brother never _____ until he got friendly with Mick.
   What construction follows **used** *? What is the opposite of* **on time**?

5 If you aren't a member, you can't come in. **unless**
   You can't come in _____ a member.
   What is the difference in meaning between **if** *and* **unless**?

6 I'd rather drive than be driven. **prefer**
   I _____ be driven.
   Which two structures can follow the verb **prefer**? *Which one is correct here?.*

7 I'll finish this book before Monday. **finished**
   By Monday _____ this book.
   Which future tense uses a part of the verb like **finished**?

8 If he didn't eat so much chocolate, he wouldn't be overweight. **because**
   He is overweight _____ so much chocolate.
   When does/did he eat the chocolate? Now or in the past?

9 My parents said 'Well done' when I passed my driving test. **congratulated**
   My parents _____ my driving test.
   What structure follows the verb **congratulate**? *Is a preposition needed?*

10 He was not allowed to drive for a year after the accident. **banned**
   He _____ for a year after the accident.
   What construction follows **banned**? *Is a preposition needed?*

Writing
Bringing descriptions to life

1 Introduction and models

When we describe something, it is the details we give that bring it to life. These details can be factual or descriptive. Read these two descriptions and list examples of interesting details under these headings.

Factual details – Example *300 days a year*
Descriptive details – Example *sparkling blue sea*

At Antalya, the pine-covered Toros mountains sweep down to the sparkling blue sea to form an irregular coastline of rocky headlands and secluded bays. The region, which enjoys brilliant sunshine for 300 days a year, is perfect for swimming, sailing, mountain-climbing, hunting and caving.

Four brave individuals have set out to discover whether humans can live under the same conditions as battery chickens. If they survive for a week, they will each receive £2500 from the vegetarian author Rebecca Hall. The human chickens will have to live on boiled brown rice and beans, which will be fed to them down a pipe on to a metal tray outside the cage. The cage has no toilet and is one metre square by two metres high.

2 Practice

A Read this description of a public demonstration against a new motorway. The spots (•) indicate points where details could be added. Some suggestions of the type of details you can include are given underneath. Add an example to each list. Then rewrite the text including information from the lists.

Yesterday morning, • **1** • **2** protesters marched • **3** through the • **4** town. When they arrived at the town hall, they stopped and formed a • **5** crowd. Some were carrying • **6** placards with • **7** slogans written on them. Others were shouting and shaking their fists • **8** at the • **9** officials working inside the • **10** building.

1	How many?	large crowds of / hundreds of
2	What mood are they in?	angry / good-tempered
3	How?	slowly / briskly
4	Which part?	outskirts of the / centre of the
5	What is it like?	noisy / silent
6	What size or shape?	large / square
7	What kind?	political / anti-motorway
8	How?	furiously / violently
9	What sort of people?	invisible / nameless
10	What is it like?	modern / enormous

B If you use more than one adjective to describe something, what order should these be in? Rewrite these phrases if the adjectives are in the wrong order.
1 a Spanish old large city
2 a tall modern beautiful building
3 huge square red placards
4 green cotton wonderful baseball caps
5 narrow impressive ancient streets
6 wooden, small, sixteenth-century houses
Check your answers in the Grammar reference on page 211.

3 Think, plan, write

Describe a public event which you have seen in real life or on TV.
A Choose an event and note down ideas using these questions.
Paragraph 1. What kind of event was it? Where and when did it take place?
Paragraph 2. Who was involved? What did they do?
Paragraph 3. How did the event end?
B Write a description of 80-100 words using your notes. Finally, check your grammar, spelling and punctuation.

Speculation

Follow that

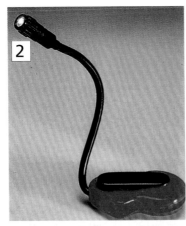

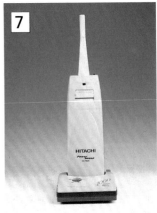

Introduction

A Read the dictionary definitions of *gadget* and *appliance*.

1 Look at the photos and decide which objects could be described as appliances, which as gadgets, and which as either appliances or gadgets.

2 What do you think the gadgets and appliances are used for?

B Read these three descriptions and try to match them with three of the objects above. Would you buy any of them? Why? Why not?

gadget small mechanical device or tool: *a new gadget for opening tin cans.*

appliance piece of equipment for a particular purpose in the house, esp. one that works by electricity or gas.

▶ Make fuel from waste paper – reuse your old newspapers and paper waste to produce fuel briquettes. They are easy to make, non-toxic, cost nothing and burn steadily for up to two hours. ▨

▶ Forecast the weather electronically with this sleek and accurate digital barometer, which gives the temperature, humidity, an illustrated weather forecast, barometric pressure chart, plus alarm clock. Requires 4 x AAA batteries. ▨

▶ This long-reach flexible torch is invaluable for seeing clearly behind large household appliances, heavy furniture and in small awkward areas for maintenance and DIY. Pocket clip gives hands-free advantage. Requires 2 x 1.5v batteries. ▨

C Points for discussion

1 What gadgets or appliances do you have, at home or at work, which you couldn't do without? What are they for?

2 Have you ever bought a gadget that didn't live up to your expectations, or one that was particularly useless? What was it, and why was it disappointing?

Listening

1 Think ahead

What special equipment do you need to pick up satellite television where you live? What difficulties might you have if you tried to install the system yourself?

2 Comprehension

A You are going to hear part of a panel game called 'Follow that'. Before you listen, read the sentences below carefully and decide what kind of information is missing. As you listen, complete the sentences by writing a word or short phrase in the space provided. You will hear the recording twice.

There are [1   ] people in each team.

Every time Anita stops talking, the teams try to work out
[2   ].

A correct answer from the whole team will get [3   ]
points.

The principal character in the story is Anita's [4   ].

Peter thinks that dishwashers were invented [5   ].

Eric always does things quickly so that he can [6   ].

The problem with the television the first time was that
[7   ].

To solve the problem, Eric [8   ].

It was [9   ] that caused the fire.

The first things to catch fire were [10   ].

B Vocabulary

Match these words and phrases from the recording with their meanings.

1	I'd *go for* the phone.	a	in the middle of the game
2	I'm *pretty sure* they were around before colour television.	b	getting the right idea
		c	correctly, in the right way
3	Eric doesn't always do things *properly*.	d	easily set on fire
4	A fire-engine *drew up* outside.	e	choose
5	Am I *on the right track*?	f	almost certain
6	If you're going for *full marks*.	g	stopped
7	It must have been something *flammable*.	h	maximum points
8	*At the halfway stage*, Nigel's team has 0 points.		

3 Over to you

A You are going to discuss the following question.

Which of these technological inventions has had the greatest effect on people's lives – the telephone, the computer or the television?

 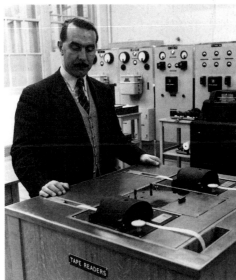 

1 If you already have an opinion, jot down two or three ideas of how the invention has affected people's lives. Mention positive and negative effects. If you haven't got an opinion, use the following questions to help you decide.
   - How many people have one?
   - Where is it used?
   - What did people do before it was invented?
   - What has it enabled people to do that they couldn't do before?
   - How else has it changed people's lives?

2 Get into groups with others who share your point of view. Together note down as many arguments supporting your opinion as you can.

3 Split up into small discussion groups with someone in each group arguing for each invention. Try to convince the others of your point of view.

B Anita's story is an 'urban myth', that is, no one knows if the story is really true or where it came from. Do you know any urban myths?

Grammar and practice

1 Certainties and possibilities

A Read these sentences from 'Follow that'.

1 The dish might have reflected the sun onto something in the other house.
2 Well, it can't have been anything solid, like a table, because the dish had only been up for a few hours.
3 It must have been something flammable and near the window.
4 It was net curtains at the window.

How certain is the speaker of each extract about what caused the fire? What structures or words helped you answer?

B Look at the sentences below which are also from 'Follow That'. In all of them the speakers show their attitude to what they are saying. Which speaker:

a is fairly certain the idea is right?
b isn't sure about the idea?
c is fairly certain the idea is not right?

1 Could be anything, couldn't it? It could be a dishwasher.
2 There again, it might be a portable phone.
3 Well, if it wasn't a phone, it must be satellite television.
4 No, it can't be a dishwasher. I'm pretty sure they were around before colour television.

C Read the extracts again and underline the words or structures which the speakers use to indicate their attitudes. Think of other words or structures you know which have similar meanings, for example, *maybe*.

2 Past, present or future?

A Read the following dialogues and decide whether speaker B is talking about a past, present or future event or situation. Which structure follows the modal verb in each case?

1 A I saw Joe in a new car the other day.
  B He must have sold his old one, then.
2 A I haven't seen Jenny for ages!
  B She might be studying. She's got exams soon.
3 A Isn't Mick coming?
  B He might come later.

4 A I'm starving!
  B So am I. It must be almost lunchtime.

B Now read the Grammar reference on page 211.

3 Practice

Use an appropriate modal verb to rephrase the parts of the sentences in *italics*. The first one has been done for you.

Fiona   I've seen Rachel out with another boy so *I'm pretty sure she isn't going out with Robert any more.* (1)
        ... she can't be going out with Robert any more.

Pat   I can't find John anywhere. Have you seen him?
Liz   *Maybe he's in the canteen.*(2)
Pat   No. I've looked there.
Liz   Well, *perhaps he's gone home early.*(3) He sometimes does on Thursdays.

Linda   It was an excellent meal. Steve's a good cook, isn't he? We had pork casserole for the main course and a lemony pudding for afters.
Bev   *I'm sure it wasn't pork that you had.*(4) Steve's a vegetarian.

Douglas Maggie still isn't speaking to me. I sent her some flowers like you suggested.
Michael *Perhaps they haven't arrived yet.*(5)
Douglas No. *I'm sure she's got them.*(6) The shop promised they'd be delivered first thing.
Michael Well, if that's the case, *I guess she's still very angry.*(7)

Jack   What's the time?
Bill   Three o'clock.
Jack   *That's impossible.*(8) I left the house at one!
Bill   *Maybe your watch is slow.*(9)
Jack   So it is. I forgot to take it off when I had a bath last night. *Water's probably got into it.*(10)

4 Picture discussion

Do the following activities with a partner.

Activity 1

You are both FCE candidates. Discuss what you think is happening In photograph A. Try to include some of the structures you have studied in this unit, for example *might be, can't have (done)*.

Photograph A

Activity 2

Student A: You are an FCE candidate. Answer the questions which your partner asks you as fully as possible.

Student B: You are an FCE examiner. Ask your partner some more general questions about the subject of photograph A. There are brief notes on the photograph and some ideas for general questions on page 197.

Photograph B

Activity 3

Repeat the same procedure as in Activity 1 for photograph B.

Activity 4

Repeat the same procedure as in Activity 2 for photograph B but exchange roles. Student A will find brief notes on photograph B and some ideas for general questions on page 198.

Vocabulary

1 Gadgets and appliances

Vocabulary reference p 218

Match these descriptions to the gadgets and appliances below. Write similar descriptions for the ones you haven't matched.

1 It can be made entirely of metal or have a plastic handle. It has a sharp tip for cutting through metal.
2 It is an electrical appliance and is made mainly of plastic. You can do many things with it like chopping, slicing, mixing. It's a big time-saver.
3 It's quite a large appliance and is fairly expensive to run. It's particularly useful if you have a large family and live somewhere cold and wet.
4 It's made of glass, and wood or plastic. It's easy to use. You just turn it upside down!

egg timer	electric whisk	food processor	microwave oven
remote control	tin opener	tumble dryer	wine cooler

2 Word building

Adjectival suffixes

One of the most common adjective endings in English is *-able*, as in this example from the listening section: *It must have been something **flammable** and near the window.* Fill the gaps in the following sentences with appropriate adjectives. Some letters are given to help you.

1 I'll have to buy a new bed. This one is so _ _ c _ _ _ _ _ _ able.
2 The hotel wasn't expensive. In fact it was very r _ _ s _ _ able.
3 The reading lamp is a _ _ _ lable in three different colours: red, black and white.
4 If a film has an X-certificate it means that it isn't s _ _ table for children.
5 Old cars are not very r _ _ _ able. They're always breaking down.
6 The view from the top of the mountain was _ _ f _ _ g _ _ _ able. I'll remember it as long as I live.
7 The weather in Britain is very c _ _ _ g _ able. One minute the sun is out and the next it's raining.
8 It is always a _ v _ _ able to phone the airline in advance in case the flight has been rescheduled.

3 Phrasal verbs

In 'Follow that', Anita said about her neighbour 'He was the first to get colour TV when that *came out*.' Here, *come out* means to become available to the public. *Come* can be used with other particles to express other meanings. Try to work out the meanings of the following phrasal verbs from their contexts and explain them.

1 I *came across* some old family photographs while I was looking through some boxes in the spare room.
2 'Why don't you *come round* for a drink on Thursday?' Angela suggested.
3 When Jane heard the news, she fainted. When she *came round*, she didn't know where she was at first.
4 'I'm sorry but I won't be able to see you this evening after all,' Ian apologized. 'Something's *come up*.'
5 'I've *come up with* a brilliant plan. It can't fail.'

Writing

Connecting ideas

You can improve your writing if you join your ideas logically with a suitable word or phrase.

1 In sentences

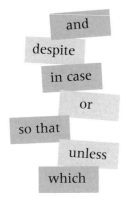

and
despite
in case
or
so that
unless
which

Join these clauses by choosing an appropriate word or phrase to fill each gap.

1 Richard immediately patented his invention _____ no one could steal his idea.
2 Take some extra batteries with you _____ these run out.
3 Thomas Edison invented the record player _____ the electric light bulb.
4 Millions will die of AIDS in the next decade _____ a cure is found.
5 The system of drug testing, _____ is carried out on all winning athletes, is not 100% reliable.
6 There is still no cure for the common cold _____ the advances that have been made in medical science.
7 Most people take their temperature by placing the thermometer under their tongue _____ in their armpit.

2 Between sentences

As a result
However
In contrast
On the contrary
On the whole
What is more

Think about the relationship between these pairs of sentences. Then fill each gap with one of these linking words or phrases. Use each one once only.

1 A conventional fridge needs to be defrosted about once every six weeks. _____, the new frost-free fridges never need defrosting.
2 Smoking does not help people relax, as is commonly thought. _____, it speeds up the heart rate and makes the smoker more tense.
3 Communication satellites were first put into space in 1957. _____, people can now watch events around the world as they happen.
4 A microwave oven can cook even frozen food extremely quickly. _____, it saves on electricity.
5 Scientific and technological advances have brought many changes to our society. _____, these changes have been positive.
6 Many parents disapprove of the time their children spend playing games on their computers. _____, a computer can be a valuable teaching aid as well as a toy.

3 Referring words

Referring words also help to link the text together. There are many kinds, of which the most common are personal pronouns, e.g. *he,* and demonstratives, e.g. *these.* Identify the referring words in 1-5 and say what they refer to.

1 Since they first appeared in the shops in the Eighties, the sale of camcorders has risen dramatically.
2 Jane decided to get an answering machine. It was a sensible idea, as she was rarely at home.
3 Researchers argue that testing drugs on animals is necessary. However, many people would disagree with them.
4 If the appliance is under guarantee, the makers should repair it free of charge.
5 Less money is being spent on space exploration. It looks as if this will continue.

Living on the edge

Playing with fire

A Volcanic eruptions have been a fact of life since the earth first formed as a solid planet, and they have taken a huge toll of human life over the centuries. One of the earliest recorded
5 disasters was the Vesuvius eruption in AD 79, which buried the Italian city of Pompeii under ash, killing an estimated 16,000 people. The most violent eruption of modern times was in Krakatoa, Indonesia, in 1883, when more than
10 36,000 people were killed and debris was scattered across the Indian Ocean as far away as Madagascar, off the east coast of Africa.

B There are about 500 active volcanoes in the world today, though it is always unsafe to
15 assume that any volcano is on the retired list. The types of eruption vary greatly. The simplest kind, found in Hawaii and Iceland, is a more or less continuous fountain of fire, sometimes reaching incredible heights. Next in order of
20 complexity are eruptions that follow the Stromboli* pattern, where the lava is less fluid and the rate of eruption is not so high – from one every few seconds to one every couple of hours.
25 **C** But even well-behaved volcanoes can turn nasty if water gets into them. It boils to produce steam and this increases explosive power. When a section of rain-sodden ground fell into Mount Etna in 1979, blocking the flow
30 of lava, pressure built up so much that when it was released the huge explosion killed nine tourists who were peering inside.

D Even more dangerous is the *nuée ardente* (a burning cloud), which occurs in volcanoes
35 where the lava is viscous and rich in gas. Pressure builds up gradually and imperceptibly, though towards the end a distinct swelling of the mountain may be detected, as if it is getting ready to give birth. When the eruption
40 finally happens, the gas is released like the fizz in a well-shaken bottle of champagne throwing out a mass of dust, ash and solid chunks of lava at speeds of up to 100kmh and at temperatures between 100 and 900 °C. The
45 hot gases destroy the delicate tissues of the lungs, which can no longer absorb oxygen from the air. Death is by suffocation.

E Studies by volcanologists show that there is no real evidence of an accelerating pace in the
50 number and frequency of eruptions, but that increasing world populations mean that when a volcano does erupt, it may well affect more

Introduction

1 What natural phenomena are shown in the pictures on these two pages?
2 What effect can these phenomena have on the landscape?

Reading

1 Think ahead

How many countries can you name where there are volcanoes? List them.

2 Reading

As you read the article for the first time, tick off any of the places which are on your list.

3 Points of view

1 Have you ever seen a volcano or a volcanic eruption? What was it like? How did you feel?
2 If you haven't seen one, would you like to? Why? Why not?

4 Comprehension

A Look at questions 1–15 below and then read the article again. For 1–15, choose the correct paragraph from A–I. When more than one answer is required, they may be given in any order.

Which section or sections refer to:
research into volcanoes?
specific volcanic eruptions?
how volcanoes can benefit a community?

1	2	
3	4	5
6	7	

people. In fact, this is already happening. The eruption of Pinatubo, in the Philippines, in 1991 has affected the entire world population. More than a year after the eruption, a belt of ash and chemicals still circles the Equator at an altitude of about 30 kilometres, disrupting the ozone layer and the planet's climate.

F We have yet to see the full capacity for devastation of a volcanic eruption in the modern world. If a major eruption were to occur in Japan, New Zealand or California, as is possible in the near future, we might be counting the dead in millions rather than tens of thousands, and looking at the destruction of a nation's economy and a serious destabilisation of world power rather than the loss of a few billion pounds.

G There are 15 capital cities in the world in a position to be wiped out or seriously damaged by volcanic eruptions. So why do people continue to live alongside them? Many are poor and have little choice, while others disregard the risk–which is, after all, rather less than smoking or driving a car. But it is the land around volcanoes which attracts people; the soils from volcanic ashes are light, easily worked, drain well and are full of plant nutrients. A light fall of ash, though it may destroy one year's crop, pays back in future years by the fertility it adds to the soil. Coffee in Colombia, vines in Italy, and rice in Japan are just a few of the crops that flourish on volcanic soils.

H In Italy, New Zealand, the United States and Iceland the subterranean heat is used to generate electricity. And in many places, the ability of the lava flows to concentrate minerals makes them attractive to mining companies.

I People will clearly not abandon the mountains that have played so large a part in the history of the Earth and its civilisation, though some of them may one day wish they had. Although growing scientific understanding is helping to predict when a volcano may be about to erupt, we will never be certain.

* **Stromboli**: a continuously active volcano off the north-east coast of Sicily

possible future eruptions? | 8 | | 9 |

positive effects on the environment? | 10 |

the differences between volcanoes? | 11 |

loss of human life? | 12 | | 13 | | 14 |

negative effects on the environment? | 15 |

B Reading between the lines

1 Why do you think it is always unsafe to assume that any volcano is 'on the retired list'? (line 15)
2 What do you think a 'well–behaved volcano' is? (line 25)

C Vocabulary

Rewrite the formal words and phrases in *italics* in informal English.

1 they have *taken a huge toll of human life* (line 3)
2 *an estimated 16,000 people* (line 7)
3 *the rate of eruption is not so high* (line 22)
4 *the entire world population* (line 55)
5 *in a position to be wiped out* (line 71)

5 Over to you

Environmental disasters are not all natural. What man-made environmental disasters are there? Choose one and discuss its causes and its effect on the environment. What can and should be done to prevent it happening?

Grammar and practice

1 Wishes

A Form and use

Look at this sentence from the article.

Some of them may one day *wish they had*.

> People will clearly not abandon the mountains,
> though some of them may one day *wish they had*.

The sentence could have been written as follows:

> Some of them may one day *wish they had left the mountains*.

Under what circumstances would people wish this and why?

B We use *wish* to talk about situations we would like to change but can't, either because they are in the past, or because they are outside our control. Match sentence beginnings 1, 2, and 3 with their endings, 4, 5, and 6, and their uses, a, b, and c.

1 *I wish he would write more often,*
2 *I wish he had written more often,*
3 *I wish he wrote more often,*

4 *but he didn't.*
5 *but he doesn't.*
6 *but he won't.*

a talking about a present situation
b talking about a past situation
c complaining about a present situation

C Check your answers with the Grammar reference on page 212.

2 Practice

A Use of English

Complete each of these sentences so that it has a similar meaning to the first sentence. Use up to five words including the word you are given. Do not change this word.

1 Unfortunately, I haven't got enough money to go on holiday this year. **afford**
I wish _____ on holiday this year.
2 You never clean the bath when you've finished! **wish**
I _____ the bath when you've finished!
3 Pete regrets forgetting to send Sally a Valentine card. **remembered**
Pete wishes _____ Sally a Valentine card.
4 'It wasn't a good idea to go to bed so late,' said Justin, yawning. **earlier**
'I wish I _____ ,' said Justin, yawning.
5 'I'd love to be the same height as my sister,' said Jodie enviously. **tall**
Jodie wishes _____ her sister.
6 I regret telling John. **only**
If _____ John.

B What do you think the people in the following situations are thinking or saying? Think of as many sentences as you can for each one.

Example   1 *I wish I had been honest.*

Exam techniques

Listening: Selecting from two or three answers Paper 4 Part 4

1 Guidelines

Do	Don't
● Look at the whole task before listening to the recording for the first time. You will have to choose between two or three possible answers. The question types may include true/false; yes/no; multiple choice; identifying which speaker said what.	➡ Don't neglect this stage. It is important to be sure you know exactly what you have to do.
● Try to build up a picture of the topic from the instructions and the questions. Then predict what you might hear.	➡ Don't waste your time. Predicting the topic and content of a recording will help you to understand it.
● As you listen for the first time, try to understand the general meaning. Note down any answers you are confident about.	➡ Don't stop listening as you write down any answers.
● In the pause before the recording is repeated, look at the questions you haven't answered so that you can pay particular attention to these when you listen again.	➡ Don't misuse your time. You can always check your answers.
● As you listen for the second time, write your remaining answers and check any you have already given.	➡ Don't leave any questions unanswered. Make a sensible guess if necessary.

2 Practice

Now try out the guidelines on this practice exercise.

You will hear a conversation which takes place in a village shop, between the owner of the shop, Vera Wallace and a customer, Graham Mann.

Answer questions 1–7 by writing
W for Vera Wallace
M for Graham Mann
or **B** for both
in the boxes provided.

Who discovers some new information? `1`

Who is pleased at the news? `2`

Who will be affected by the change? `3`

Who may leave the village? `4`

Who was born in the village? `5`

Who disagrees with the work schedule? `6`

Who has an unselfish attitude? `7`

Writing

Exam training: Compositions 2 Paper 2 Part 2

Think, plan, write

A You are going to write an opinion composition in answer to this question.

Which environmental issue is of greatest concern to you?

B Work with someone who is interested in the same topic as you. Use the pictures and the questions below to give you some ideas. Make notes as you discuss these questions.

1 **Pollution**
Which kind of pollution do you feel most strongly about? e.g. *air pollution*
Why? *Because it causes acid rain.*
What solutions are there? *Increase the price of petrol to make people use their cars less.*

2 **The hole in the ozone layer**
What has caused it? e.g. *use of aerosol sprays*
What are the effects? e.g. *damage to eyesight*
What measures can be taken? e.g. *use of pump sprays rather than aerosols*

3 **Animal welfare**
How are animals threatened? e.g. *the fur trade*
In what ways are animals treated cruelly? e.g. *They are often kept in cramped conditions.*
Which issue do you feel most strongly about? e.g. *experiments carried out on animals to try out new beauty products*
Why? *The animals suffer a lot.*
What solutions are there? *Human volunteers could be used instead.*

C Read through your notes and choose two or three of your best ideas for the main part of your composition. Make sure that you have included examples and reasons to support your opinion. Group your notes into paragraphs.

D Write your composition in 120–180 words. Remember to:
1 state your opinion clearly in the first paragraph.
2 introduce each argument with appropriate expressions.
3 include examples and reasons to support your opinion.
4 write a conclusion. It is a good idea to repeat the opinion you expressed in your first paragraph but you should use different words here.

When you have finished check grammar, spelling and punctuation.

Compositions 2 Opinion	◀ **p 116** ◀ **Compositions 1**
Introduction State your opinion clearly but do not use too many personal opinion words.	referring words to connect your ideas within and across paragraphs.
Paragraphing Begin a new paragraph for each main idea. Use linking words and phrases and	**Conclusion** Re-state your opinion, using different words.

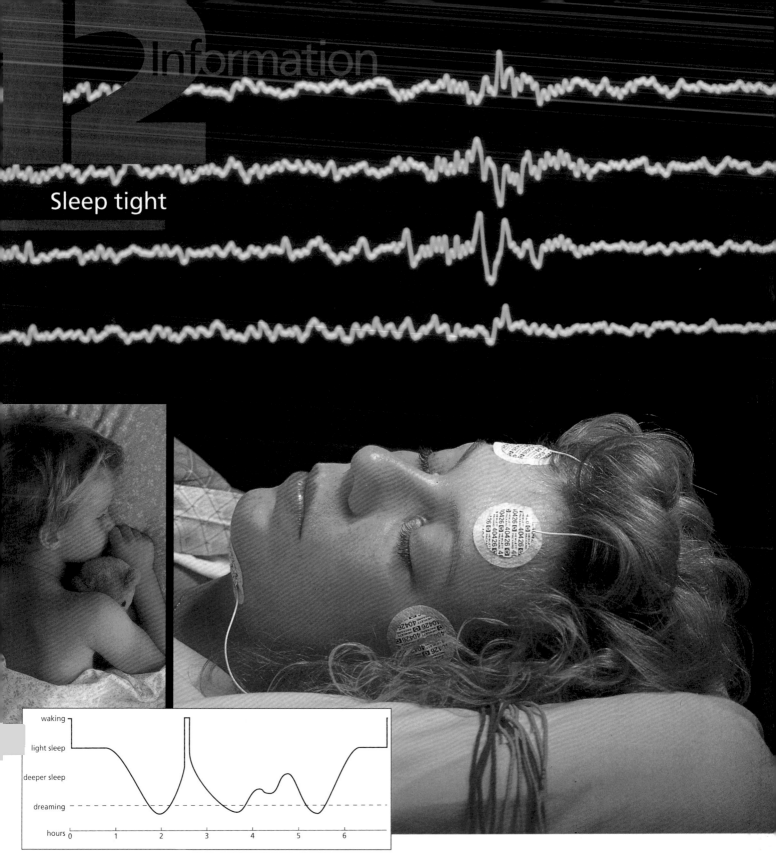

12 Information

Sleep tight

Introduction

A What do you think is happening to the woman in the photograph? According to the information given in the graph, do we dream when we are in *light sleep* or when we are in *deeper sleep?*

B What time do children under seven go to bed in your country?

C How much sleep do you usually have? How much sleep do you need? What effect does lack of sleep have on you?

Reading

1 Think ahead
How many different words do you know for *sleep* in English?

2 Reading
Read the text through quickly. Don't worry about the missing sentences. Do you think the text comes from an encyclopaedia, a scientific journal, a magazine, or a school textbook? Give a reason for your choice.

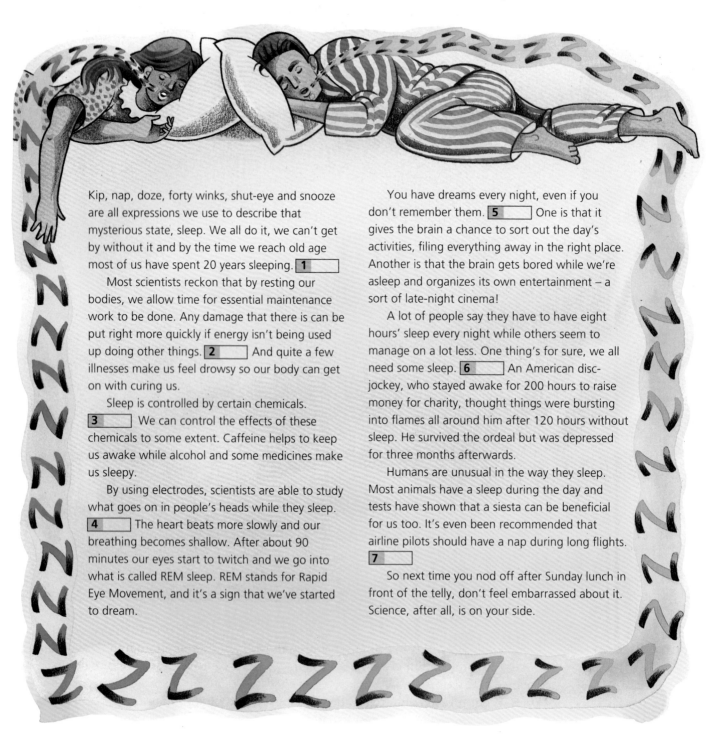

Kip, nap, doze, forty winks, shut-eye and snooze are all expressions we use to describe that mysterious state, sleep. We all do it, we can't get by without it and by the time we reach old age most of us have spent 20 years sleeping. **1**

Most scientists reckon that by resting our bodies, we allow time for essential maintenance work to be done. Any damage that there is can be put right more quickly if energy isn't being used up doing other things. **2** And quite a few illnesses make us feel drowsy so our body can get on with curing us.

Sleep is controlled by certain chemicals. **3** We can control the effects of these chemicals to some extent. Caffeine helps to keep us awake while alcohol and some medicines make us sleepy.

By using electrodes, scientists are able to study what goes on in people's heads while they sleep. **4** The heart beats more slowly and our breathing becomes shallow. After about 90 minutes our eyes start to twitch and we go into what is called REM sleep. REM stands for Rapid Eye Movement, and it's a sign that we've started to dream.

You have dreams every night, even if you don't remember them. **5** One is that it gives the brain a chance to sort out the day's activities, filing everything away in the right place. Another is that the brain gets bored while we're asleep and organizes its own entertainment – a sort of late-night cinema!

A lot of people say they have to have eight hours' sleep every night while others seem to manage on a lot less. One thing's for sure, we all need some sleep. **6** An American disc-jockey, who stayed awake for 200 hours to raise money for charity, thought things were bursting into flames all around him after 120 hours without sleep. He survived the ordeal but was depressed for three months afterwards.

Humans are unusual in the way they sleep. Most animals have a sleep during the day and tests have shown that a siesta can be beneficial for us too. It's even been recommended that airline pilots should have a nap during long flights. **7**

So next time you nod off after Sunday lunch in front of the telly, don't feel embarrassed about it. Science, after all, is on your side.

3 Comprehension

A Choose from the missing sentences A–H the one which best fits each gap 1–7. There is one extra sentence which you do not need to use.

A These build up during the day, eventually reaching levels that make us tired.
B There are all sorts of theories about why we dream.
C Going without it can have some very strange effects.
D Dreams can have very frightening results indeed.
E Injured animals certainly spend more time asleep than usual while their wounds are healing.
F That way they are more alert for the tricky business of landing.
G They have discovered that when we first drop off everything slows down.
H Yet nobody knows why we do it.

B Paragraphs
Read the paragraphs containing sentences 2–7 again, to check your answers. What question could each paragraph answer?
Example   Paragraph 2 *Why do scientists think we sleep?*

4 Points of view

What's the longest you have gone without sleep? What was the reason? How did you feel?

5 Vocabulary

Choose the best meaning for each of the words or phrases in *italics* from the text.
1 *Yet* nobody knows why we do it.
   A and   B but   C so
2 We can control the effects *to some extent*.
   A occasionally   B partially   C totally
3 He *survived the ordeal*.
   A He got through a difficult experience.
   B He made a lot of money for charity.
   C He didn't suffer any after-effects.
4 That way they are more *alert* . . .
   A calm and relaxed   B cool and prepared   C awake and ready
5 . . . the *tricky business* of landing
   A boring job   B exciting prospect   C difficult task

6 Reading between the lines

1 What bed-time drinks would you not recommend for someone who had problems getting to sleep?
2 What age group might be embarrassed about 'nodding off in front of the telly'? Why?

7 Over to you

Do you remember a particular dream? What makes it memorable? Is it a recurring dream or a nightmare? Working in groups, see if you can find any explanations for your dreams.

Grammar and practice

1 Passives

A Form and use

1 Read these sentences from the text. Underline the verbs. Which are passive and which are active? Name the tenses.
   a Any damage that there is can be repaired if energy isn't being used up doing other things . . .
   b Sleep is controlled by certain chemicals.
   c We can control the effects of these chemicals to some extent.
2 How is the passive formed?
3 Rewrite sentences b and c putting the passive verb into the active form and the active verb into the passive form. How do the changes you have made affect the meaning?

Only sentence b has an agent, i.e. the person or thing responsible for the action. Why has an agent not been included in sentence a?

B Read the Grammar reference on page 212 before doing the following practice exercises.

2 The agent

Why is there no agent in the following sentences? Match the sentence with the most appropriate reason, a–d. There may be more than one reason.
Example   The secretary was given a pay rise.
          c The agent is obvious. It must be her boss.
1 Gauguin's most important paintings were produced during his time in Tahiti.
2 Silence must be observed at all times.
3 The house had been re-decorated since my last visit.
4 I was told to be here by five at the latest.
5 I've been robbed.
6 Smith was given a five-year sentence for his part in the robbery.

   a The agent is probably not known.
   b The agent is not considered important.
   c The agent is obvious.
   d The agent has already been mentioned.

3 Practice

A Advertising

1 Match the products and services in the photos with sentences a–e from their advertisements and brochures. There is one extra product. Which words helped you make your choice?
2 Fill the gaps in the sentences with one of the verbs below. Use the correct form and tense of the passive. There is one extra verb that you do not need.

a This product should reach you in perfect condition. If it does not, please return the product and its wrapper, stating when and where it _____ .
b We insist our shoes _____ by a trained assistant.
c Every effort _____ to ensure that a warm welcome awaits all our guests.
d Once opened, this pack should _____ in an airtight container.
e Any electrical work that _____ to install this appliance should _____ by a qualified electrician or a competent person.

   buy   carry out   fit   make   offer   require   store

B Put the following passages into the passive. Do not include the agent unless it is important.

1 The police arrested Smith at Newtown Hospital last night. Doctors were taking him to the operating theatre when the police arrived. One of his accomplices had accidentally shot him in the knee during the get-away. The police are interrogating Smith at Sunhill Police Station. They will charge him with armed robbery. They have charged him twice for similar offences in the last five years.

2 The government will close three more coal mines over the next two years. They have already closed a total of six since they came into office. They are asking miners to consider voluntary redundancy.

C Services

1 Fill the gaps in the hotel brochure below with the passive form of one of the verbs below. All verbs should be in the present simple tense.

The George Hotel

A friendly atmosphere (1)_____ at the George Hotel, which (2)_____ in a quiet residential area in the historic heart of the city, just a few minutes' walk from the centre. All 30 bedrooms (3)_____ to a high standard and most have en suite facilities. All rooms (4)_____ with colour TV, tea and coffee-making facilities and direct-dial telephones. Some rooms (5)_____ for non-smokers. A full English breakfast (6)_____ in the price and (7)_____ between 7 a.m. and 10 a.m. in the Breakfast Bar. Dinner is available between 7 p.m. and 10 p.m. and can (8)_____ at Reception. A supplement of £3 (9)_____ for a single room.

book   charge   equip   furnish   guarantee   include
reserve   serve   situate

2 Now write a similar text about the hotel in the photograph. Use the information in the key and your imagination to write about the hotel.

4 Use of English

Read the text and fill the gaps with an appropriate word. An example is given.

Friday the 13th

Fear of Friday 13th, and of the number 13 generally, is (0) *more* common than you might expect. A recent survey carried out (1)_____ Britain revealed that 41% of British people feel uncomfortable about Friday 13th while 4% live in dread of it.

The unwillingness of superstitious sailors to sail on Friday 13th was once considered to (2)_____ reached such a level that in 1791 (3)_____ government attempted to prove that the superstition was both ridiculous and false. Construction (4)_____ started on a new ship on Friday 13th; she was named HMS Friday; she was launched on a Friday (5)_____ she began her first voyage from London on a Friday. Neither the ship (6)_____ the crew was ever heard of again.

Richard Hall, from Sheffield, has (7)_____ involved in four crashes on Friday 13th. He has also broken several bones, fallen (8)_____ a river, been knocked down (9)_____ a motorbike and walked through a glass door. Now he never gets out (10)_____ bed on that day.

Friday 13th interferes with hospital schedules (11)_____ many patients refuse to have operations on that date (12)_____ it does not seem to be the case that (13)_____ accidents happen on Friday 13th than on any other Friday.

However, experts claim that the number 13 is not really as unlucky as people say. What (14)_____ really brings is surprises, which can (15)_____ good as well as bad.

Exam techniques

Speaking Paper 5 Part 3 and Part 4

1 Guidelines for Part 3 – Carrying out a task

Do	Don't
• Carefully study the photograph or drawing that the interviewer gives you.	➡ Don't just glance at this. It contains important information which you need to know.
• Listen carefully to what the interviewer tells you to do.	➡ Don't panic if you don't understand. Ask the interviewer to explain again.
• Discuss with your partner not the interviewer.	➡ Don't look at the interviewer or the assessor during the discussion.
• Let your partner talk too. If your partner isn't contributing much, ask him or her some questions.	➡ Don't talk all the time. You must carry out the task together.
• Keep to the task the interviewer has given you.	➡ Don't start discussing something else.

2 Model

A You are going to hear a recording of a model Part 3. Before you listen, look at the house plan below and the information about the family who are going to move in. Talk with your partner and decide which would be the best bedroom for each member of the family.

B As you listen, note down both candidates' ideas. Were yours the same?

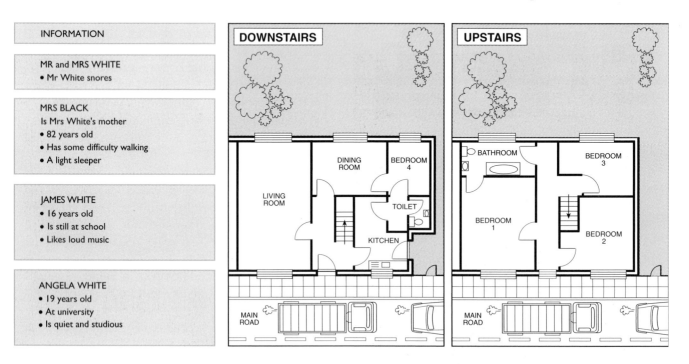

INFORMATION

MR and MRS WHITE
• Mr White snores

MRS BLACK
Is Mrs White's mother
• 82 years old
• Has some difficulty walking
• A light sleeper

JAMES WHITE
• 16 years old
• Is still at school
• Likes loud music

ANGELA WHITE
• 19 years old
• At university
• Is quiet and studious

3 Practice

Work with a partner. Choose two members of the family and talk about how they might decorate and furnish their bedrooms.

4 Guidelines for Part 4 – Topic-related discussion

Do	Don't
• Answer the interviewer's questions as fully as you can.	➡ Don't give one-word answers. The interviewer and assessor need to hear you talk.
• Talk to your partner not the interviewer. Listen to what your partner says and relate what you say to this.	➡ Don't concentrate solely on what you are going to say.
• Start speaking when your partner has finished.	➡ Don't wait for the interviewer to ask you personally.
• Try to speak with confidence.	➡ Don't worry about making mistakes. Speaking fluently is important too.

5 Model

A You are going to hear a recording of a model Part 4.

Before you listen, think about how you would answer the interviewer's first question: *How important do you think it is for young people to have their own bedroom?*

Exchange ideas with a partner.

B As you listen, note down both candidates' opinions. Were yours different?

6 Practice

Discuss these questions with a partner. Say as much as you can about each one.
1 Do you think the location of a bedroom is more important than its size?
2 How important is the decoration of a room?
3 Do you have any problems sleeping or know anyone who does? What advice would you give them?

12

Remember, remember

Introduction

What is happening in the photos? Are fireworks and fires associated with any special festivals in your country? Describe one festival.

Listening

1 Think ahead

You are going to hear some people talking about a festival called Bonfire Night, which is celebrated in Britain. What do you know about this festival?

2 Comprehension

A Listen to part of a radio broadcast giving information about Bonfire Night celebrations in the local area. Fill in the spaces in the information sheet below. You will hear the recording twice.

	Venue	Date	Time of firework display	Entrance fee Adult	Child
1	The Green Man	4 Nov	_____	_____	free
2	_____	5 Nov	_____	and includes a baked potato and _____	_____
3	_____		6 p.m. and 9.30 p.m.	_____	£1.25 and includes _____

B You are now going to hear five people talking in different situations. For each question, choose the best answer A, B or C.

1 Listen to this radio interview. What has the man being interviewed just written a book about?
 A traditional British festivals
 B Britain in the 17th century
 C a historical event

2 Listen to this woman talking to her children. What is she telling them?
 A what to do if they feel hungry
 B what to do if they get lost
 C what to do if they have an accident

3 You hear someone talking on the phone. Where is the person he is talking to?
 A in a newspaper office   B at the police station   C at the fire station

4 You overhear a woman talking to a friend. What is the woman complaining about?
 A the smoke   B the noise   C the rubbish

5 You hear a man talking on the phone. What does he want the other person to do?
 A organize the food   B buy the fireworks   C find a new site

3 Over to you

1 What other special days are celebrated in your country, e.g. Mother's Day? When and how are they celebrated?
2 If you could choose to celebrate something which is not celebrated at the moment, what would it be and how would it be celebrated?

Grammar and practice

More passives

A Look at the two pairs of sentences below. In which sentence does the speaker present the information as being factual? How do the passive forms *is considered* and *is believed* alter the meaning of sentence b in each pair? What other verbs could replace them?

1 a Professor Ellett is one of the leading authorities on 17th century British history.
 b Professor Ellett is considered to be one of the leading authorities on 17th century British history.

2 a Guy Fawkes was the brains behind the plot.
 b Guy Fawkes is believed to have been the brains behind the plot.

B Now read the Grammar reference on page 213.

C Practice
You are preparing a news report for a radio station. You are not sure whether all the information you have received is correct and you have underlined any unconfirmed information in your notes. Write up your news report using the present passive form of the verbs below, followed by the infinitive or perfect infinitive to show which information is unconfirmed.

say   believe   report   think

Example   Elizabeth Taylor was not accompanied by her husband. <u>He is in Paris.</u>
   He is believed / thought, etc. to be in Paris.

1 A Boeing 747 has crashed in Peru. The plane was carrying 250 passengers. <u>Several of the passengers were British</u>. The plane was on a routine flight between Madrid and the capital, Lima. <u>It ran into problems as it was coming in to land</u>.

2 An Essex man has dug up some coins in his garden. <u>The coins are Roman. They date from the first century BC</u>.

3 The police are looking for two men in connection with a robbery which took place at Goodbuy Supermarket at 5 p.m. yesterday. <u>One of the men has a scar on his left cheek. The other speaks with a northern accent</u>.

Writing

Reporting an opinion

1 Extracts

Where would you expect to read these extracts? What are they about?

1 The majority of the people interviewed said that they were satisfied with the measures taken by *Burger Express* to reduce the amount of litter dropped by their customers.

2 It has a light crisp aroma and is excellent value for money at £3.99 a bottle.

3 Surprisingly, only 10% felt that their diet was unhealthy although 30% thought that they ate too many chips.

4 The decor is simple but pleasing. The service, however, could be better, and, at £20.00 per person for a three-course meal, excluding wine, it is rather over-priced.

5 Many people consider that the advantages far outweigh any disadvantages it might have. They would argue that rather than being responsible for encouraging bad eating habits, it has freed women from being tied to the kitchen stove.

6 It is interesting that nowadays almost as many men as women believe that they are overweight. More men than ever are going on a diet. The number and type of slimming products on the market is beginning to reflect this trend.

2 Analysis

A In which extracts does the writer give his or her own opinion? In which extracts does the writer report other people's opinions?

B List the verbs that are used to introduce other people's opinions. What other similar verbs can you add to this list?

C In two extracts, the writers' attitudes to the opinions they are reporting are indicated by a particular word and phrase. Find these. Do you know any similar words or phrases to express attitude in this way?

D Underline the opinion words and phrases in extracts 2 and 4. There are no phrases like *I think* or *In my view* to introduce the opinions in these extracts. Why not?

3 Practice

A You are going to conduct a survey on the eating and drinking habits of the other students in your class. Think of a topic area to ask questions about, e.g. eating out; the school canteen or cafeteria; breakfast; dieting. What questions should you ask? At least one of your questions must require an opinion. Here are some ideas:

Do you think it's important to have breakfast? Why? Why not?
Where do you have breakfast?
What do you usually have for breakfast?

B Before you conduct your survey, decide what answers and opinions you think most people will give and make a note of these. If they are different from what you expected, indicate this in your report by using appropriate expressions, e.g. *Surprisingly . . . .*

C When you have interviewed everyone, write up the results in the form of a short report. Use the extracts on this page to help you to write in an appropriate style.

Vocabulary

1 Celebrations

Vocabulary reference p 218

A Read the text through quickly and decide which of these three titles best describes what the text is about.
1 Australian festivals
2 The origins of Australia Day
3 Celebrating Sydney style

B Use of English

Decide which word A, B, C or D best fits each space. An example (0) is given at the beginning.

0	A domestic	B public	C government	D state

Australia Day, which is a national (0) _public_ holiday, is (1)_____ on January 26th, in the middle of the Australian summer. It commemorates the (2)_____ of Sydney in 1788.

 Australia Day is a (3)_____ day, and many families go out for a picnic. Some people go to the beach, where they go surfing or sunbathe, but the (4)_____ of Sydney (5)_____ for The Rocks, the oldest (6)_____ of Sydney and the site of the first colonial settlement. The Rocks, which (7)_____ Sydney Harbour, is packed on this day. Parades with brass (8)_____ march through the narrow (9)_____ and hundreds of small boats (10)_____ part in races in the harbour.

 Wherever people go, it is (11)_____ to have a barbecue and drink beer. The traditional (12)_____ is 'Pavlova', a sweet cake made of meringue with fruit on the top, and 'damper', a bread made with flour, water and sugar and cooked in the fire.

 The festivities in Sydney (13)_____ with a huge firework (14)_____ . The yellows, blues and greens light up the night sky and fall like shooting stars into the water (15)_____ . It's a memorable sight.

	A	B	C	D
1	performed	enjoyed	held	celebrated
2	achievement	foundation	beginning	creation
3	family	household	domestic	familiar
4	tenants	neighbours	visitors	residents
5	go	start	head	aim
6	part	place	region	section
7	glimpses	views	overlooks	observes
8	groups	bands	orchestras	musicians
9	avenues	ways	roads	streets
10	take	make	play	have
11	ordinary	regular	general	usual
12	course	food	meal	plate
13	stop	complete	end	halt
14	exhibition	demonstration	show	display
15	below	under	down	underneath

2 Confusing verbs

The verbs *raise* and *rise* are often confused. So are *lay* and *lie*. Before you do the following exercise, check that you know how to form the past tense, present participle and past participle of these verbs. Also make sure that you understand the different meanings (*lie* has two different forms and meanings).

Fill the gaps with the appropriate form and tense of *lay, lie, raise* or *rise*.
1 Please _____ your hand if you want to ask a question.
2 _____ in bed on a Sunday morning is one of life's pleasures.
3 When you've finished _____ the table, could you give me a hand?
4 Prices _____ 10% since this time last year.
5 People often start _____ about their age when they reach 40.
6 The subject of inflation _____ by a delegate at the conference.

3 Phrasal verbs with *up*

Look at this sentence from the text on sleep. 'Any damage that there is can be put right more quickly if energy isn't being *used up* doing other things.'

Use up means to use totally. The word *up* adds a sense of completion to the meaning of the verb. There are some more common verbs of this type in list A. Match them with one of the nouns in list B and make sentences which illustrate their meaning. An example is given.

A	B	
1 tidy up	letter	*I was so angry that I tore the letter up into small pieces.*
2 tear up	desk	
3 drink up	present	
4 eat up	milk	
5 fill up	mess	
6 clean up	dinner	
7 wrap up	car	

4 Phrasal verbs with *get*

A Some of the most common phrasal verbs in English are *get* + particles. Work out the meanings of these phrasal verbs from their context.
1 Quite a few illnesses make us feel drowsy so our body can *get on* with curing us.
2 We can't *get by* without sleep.

B Fill the gaps in the following sentences with *get* + one of the particles below, making any other necessary changes. Use a dictionary to check your answers.

away   by   down   on   out   over

1 She decided to leave home _____ from her parents.
2 Mary Lou asked me how Neville _____ at school.
3 Eric _____ with his brother when they were young but they're quite good friends now.
4 Even if you haven't time for a proper holiday, try _____ for a few days.
5 I hate winter; the cold weather and short days really _____ me _____.
6 When we were in Greece, we _____ with sign-language and the half dozen words of Greek that we knew.
7 Keith still can't _____ the shock of winning so much money.
8 The prisoner _____ by climbing over the high wall that surrounds the gaol.

Writing

Exam training: Reports 2 Paper 2 Part 2

1 Model

Read the following question and Reports 1 and 2. Which answer would get a better mark in the exam and why?

Your school / college is planning a fête for staff, students and their families. The fête will include a bonfire and a firework display. The head teacher has asked you to investigate two possible sites and to present your findings and recommendations to him in a short report.

Report 2

To: Mr Davidson
From: Heidi Weiss
Subject: Possible sites for school fete

Introduction
The aim of this report is to describe and assess the suitability of the following sites for the school fete.
Site A: The field next to the Community Hall.
Site B: The field behind St. David's School.
It is assumed that about 500 people will attend the event.

Location
Both sites are well-situated and easily accessible to those using public transport. Both also provide parking facilities. The Community Hall car park provides space for 150 cars while the school car park provides space for 50. Neither site is near trees or buildings, which minimizes the risk of fire.

Facilities
The Community Hall will allow the use of their toilets and the hall itself for a small charge. Food and drink stalls could be set up here. The school will allow free use of their toilets but will not allow vans to sell food in the car park.

Conclusion
It is recommended that the event is held at site A as it offers better facilities.

Report 1

I think the best site for the school fete is the field next to Green's pub. In my opinion, it has lots of advantages.

Firstly, the site is big enough and people will be able to park their cars on the field, so there won't be any parking problems. The only problem would be if it rained, when the cars might get stuck in the mud. Also, if people want to come by train or bus, the railway station and the bus station are quite near.

Another reason is that you could have a bonfire there as long as you built it at the end of the field, far away from the pub.

Finally, the landlord of Green's has said that we can use their toilets and we could put a big tent up in the middle of the field and serve the food and drink there.

2 Analysis

A The language of reports should be formal and should sound objective. How are the following ideas expressed formally and objectively in Report 2?

Example   I'm writing this report to . . . *The aim of this report is to . . .*

1 say how suitable the sites are
2 I assume that
3 go to the fete
4 easy to get to
5 have car parks
6 means that there isn't much risk of fire
7 We'll be able to use the Community Hall toilets
8 We could set up food and drink stalls here
9 We won't have to pay to use the school toilets
10 I recommend

B Find examples of inappropriate language in Report 1 and suggest something more suitable.

3 Think, plan, write

A Read the following question.

> The head teacher of your school has received several complaints about an outdoor music festival which the school organized recently. You have been asked to investigate the reactions of people living in the area and to make suggestions as to how things can be improved for next year.

B Brainstorm ideas. First, think about the following questions and make notes.
• What do you think people complained about? e.g. *noise*
• What were the causes? e.g. *the loud music*
• What were the effects? e.g. *people couldn't sleep*
• How could the problems be minimized or avoided in the future? e.g. *have the event in a non-residential area*

C Decide how many people you interviewed, what percentage of these complained and what the most common complaints were.

D Think of suitable sub-headings for your report. Plan what you are going to write in each section and make notes. Remember to make some suggestions in the conclusion. If you give opinions make them sound objective.

E Write your report in 120–180 words. Remember to write in a formal and objective style. Then check grammar, spelling and punctuation.

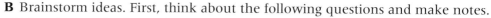

Reports 2	p82 ◄ Reports 1
Introduction State the aim and content of your report.	**Layout** Summarize the information you give under suitable sub-headings.
Conclusion Make clear suggestions or recommendations.	**Style** Write in formal English. Express facts and opinions objectively.

13 Skills and abilities

Memory

Introduction **A** Do this quiz.

 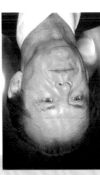 

Have you got a memory for faces?

Do you recognize these famous people? An inverted face is much harder to recognize than, for example, an inverted building, because different sub-processes are involved. It is also difficult to recognize the expression on a face that is turned upside down. It is believed that the right-hand side of the brain remembers images, sounds, odours and fantasies, while the left-hand side of the brain remembers words, ideas and numbers. This would explain why some people recall people's faces perfectly but can never remember their names.

B Answer this questionnaire.

How good is your memory?

Find out with our questionnaire. Write the letter A, B, C or D after each of these questions, according to your answer.
A = often   **B** = occasionally   **C** = rarely   **D** = never

1 Do you ever forget where you put things?
2 Do you find it difficult to remember the storylines of television serials?
3 Do you ever have to check whether you have done something you meant to do, like locking the door or turning off the gas or the lights?
4 Do you ever forget to take things with you when you go out?
5 Have you ever told someone a story or joke that they told you?
6 Have you ever repeated to someone what you have already told them?
7 Do you ever start to read a book or an article you have read before without realizing it?
8 Have you ever had a word 'on the tip of your tongue' but been unable to remember it?
9 Do you ever forget to do things you have promised to do?

10 Have you ever forgotten what you did the day before?
11 When talking to someone, have you ever forgotten what you have just said?
12 Do you ever forget to pass on important messages?

When you finish, work out your score. Give yourself:
1 point for every **A** answer
2 points for every **B** answer
3 points for every **C** answer
4 points for every **D** answer

What does your score mean?
• 46–48   You have an excellent memory.
• 40–45   You have a good memory.
• 28–39   You have an average memory.
• Don't worry too much if you scored less than 28. It may just mean that you lead a very busy life!

C Points for discussion
1 What do you do to help you remember things?
2 Have you ever been embarrassed or annoyed with yourself because you've forgotten to do something?

Reading

1 Think ahead

How much do you know about memory? Read these statements and decide whether they are true or false.

1 There is a limit to how much people can remember.
2 Most people can't remember much from before they were three years old.
3 Some people are born with a better memory than others.
4 People tend to remember pleasant things and forget unpleasant things.
5 Once we learn something we never forget it.

2 Reading

Read the article quickly to see if you were right. Don't worry about the missing headings yet.

Memories are made of this

1

To even imagine a world without memory is impossible. There would be no then, only a now; no way of learning new skills, recognizing faces, remembering words or referring to the past. In fact, without memory we would lose our sense of what we are. It is our capacity to remember that makes us human.

2

Memory is defined as the ability to store and receive information. Humans have remarkable memories: adults can remember between 20,000 and 100,000 words. Added to this we are able to learn complex skills like driving a car, acquire a foreign language, and have specialist knowledge of things related to our work and hobbies. Memory, it seems, is almost limitless.

3

Some theories argue that people have no memory before they can speak, although more recent studies suggest that memory may actually begin before birth. At any rate, it seems that you are unusual if you can remember much from before the age of three. And if you are one of those people who never go on

to develop a good memory, there is no need to feel inadequate. Our capacity for memory is determined by our genes*, so some people have better memories than others just as some people are taller than others.

4

Memory is also affected by factors other then personal ability. We recall an exciting or frightening day more vividly than we do an average day because chemicals like adrenalin boost memory. At the same time, events associated with pain and anxiety are repressed and forgotten more readily than pleasant incidents. This is because forgetting some past events can be as essential to our survival as remembering others.

5

For most of us the problem is not forgetting but remembering. Some theorists say that once something is learnt it is never forgotten, but remains in the brain. The reason we cannot remember something is a problem of access. There are two traditional theories of forgetting. One argues that a memory simply fades rather like ink exposed to the sun. The other claims that subsequent learning interferes with an existing memory. Now it is thought that to some extent both these processes occur.

6

Until quite recently memory was treated as a single thing. Now there are

considered to be three types of memory: sensory, short-term and long-term. Sensory memory, which involves the retention of a piece of information until the next comes along, lasts only a few tenths of a second. Short-term memory lasts for about 30 seconds. It can be compared to a bucket with holes in it through which events pass without being recorded, and it is vital for everything we do. For example, to read a sentence we need to retain the beginning until we reach the end. Long-term memory, however, stores information for considerable periods of time.

7

Research shows that the probability of remembering something depends on how often it has been called to mind and reinforced.

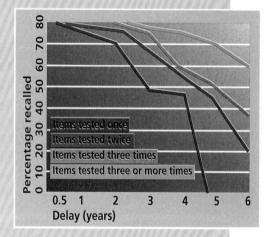

*genes: parts of cells in all living things which determine factors like eye colour, height, etc.

3 Comprehension

Read the article again and the headings A–H. Choose the most suitable heading for each part (1–7) of the article. There is one extra heading which you do not need to use.

6 A What are the different kinds of memory?
4 B Why do we remember some things more easily than others?
  C Why does memory decline with age?
  D If you don't use it, you'll lose it.
2 E What is memory?
  F Why do we forget?
1 G Why is memory so important?
3 H When do we start to remember?

4 Points of view

Would you like to have a better memory? What advantages would it bring you? Can you think of any disadvantages it would bring?

5 Vocabulary

Explain the meaning of these words and phrases from the article. The paragraph number is given in brackets.

a remarkable (2)   f vividly (4)
b limitless (2)   g readily (4)
c at any rate (3)   h access (5)
d inadequate (3)   i fades (5)
e recall (4)   j retention (6)

6 Over to you

What are your earliest memories? Do you have any particularly vivid memories? Describe them.

7 I remember . . .

Now write a description of one of your memories in about 60–80 words. Try to make your description as detailed as possible.

Grammar and practice

1 Can, be able to

A The structures *can* and *be able to* are often interchangeable. Rephrase sentences 1 and 2 from the article using the alternative form.

1 We *are able to* learn complex skills like driving a car.
2 The reason we *cannot* remember something is a problem of access.

In sentences 3 and 4 it is not possible to use the *can* form. Why not?

3 She *hasn't been able to* finish all the letters yet.
4 *To be able to* play a musical instrument well, you need to practise.

B Practice

Look at the following sentences. Rewrite them using the alternative form where possible. If both forms are possible, but one is more usual, underline the more usual form. If it is not possible to use the alternative form, say why not.

1 He's able to run 100 metres in just over 12 seconds.
2 I was able to climb a mountain without getting out of breath when I was younger.
3 They had eaten such a big breakfast that they weren't able to finish their lunch.
4 The climbers won't be able to reach the summit if the blizzard continues.
5 Even if you'd come over, I wouldn't have been able to spend much time with you.

C In sentences 1 and 2 below, the *can / be able to* forms are interchangeable but in 3 they are not. Can you think why?

1 Before Dave started smoking, he *could / was able to* hold his breath for three minutes.
2 Despite their attempts, the doctors *couldn't / weren't able to* save the woman's life.
3 After nine hours the firefighters ~~could~~ */ were able to* put out the fire.

D Check your answers with the Grammar reference on page 213.

2 Other ability structures

In sentences 2 and 3 in C, *can* and *be able to* forms can be replaced by the verbs *manage* and *succeed*.

Examples   After nine hours, the firefighters *managed* to put out the fire.
After nine hours, the firefighters *succeeded* in putting out the fire.

Can you think why it is not possible to rephrase sentence 1 using these verbs?

3 Practice

A Fill in the gaps with the verb in bold along with another appropriate verb, making any other necessary changes. An example is given.

1 He *managed to win* the election, despite strong opposition. **manage**
2 Although they searched for several hours, the rescue party _____ the climbers. **succeed**
3 He did his best but he _____ all his work before the boss got back. **be able to**
4 Jerry was thrilled when he _____ his driving test first time. **succeed**
5 Although there were several people in the house, the burglar _____ and steal the video without being noticed. **manage**
6 Ann _____ three lengths of the pool when she was Bobby's age. **be able to**
7 Richard's interview was this afternoon, wasn't it? I wonder if he _____ the job. **manage**
8 I was so tense that I _____ despite the fact that I was extremely tired. **be able to**
9 The police _____ the man from his fingerprints. **be able to**
10 Despite the fact that he didn't have a corkscrew, he _____ the bottle. **succeed**

Which sentences can be rewritten using *could / couldn't*?

B Fill in the gaps with one of the following structures in the correct tense, along with any other words that are necessary, such as other verbs and prepositions. Use each structure once only.

succeed
learn how
manage
be good

Evelyn Glennie was born in Scotland in 1965. As a young child, she loved music and (1)_____ her reluctant parents to let her have music lessons. She was delighted to find that she (2)_____ it. Then, when she was ten years old, she became profoundly deaf. She was determined to carry on with her music, however, and (3)_____ feel music through her body. She earned a place at the Royal College of Music, where, despite her deafness, she (4)_____ several major prizes. She is now one of the world's best and most popular percussionists.

Now write a similar paragraph using as many of the above structures as you can. It could be about someone famous or simply a friend.

C Quiz

Think of something you can do or used to be able to do. It could be a sport or an activity like tossing a pancake, whistling or walking on your hands. The other students will ask you questions to find out what it is. Answer only *yes* or *no*. Here are some suggested questions.

Can you still do it?
Did you learn how to do it?
Did someone teach you how to do it?
Can anyone do it? Do you need special skills?
Is it easy to do?
Do you need special equipment to do it?

4 Use of English

Fill each gap in the following text with an appropriate word.

A great achievement

Stephen Hawking was born in Cambridge in 1942. Hawking (1)_____ known to millions of people all over the world (2)_____ his best-selling science book 'A Brief History Of Time', (3)_____ has helped to bring about a revival of popular interest (4)_____ science.

Diagnosed as having motor neurone disease (5)_____ he was only twenty-one, Hawking has had to overcome many obstacles. Motor neurone disease causes gradual paralysis and by 1970 Hawking could (6)_____ walk nor write. Fortunately, the disease does (7)_____ affect the parts of the brain which control thought and memory, so he has been (8)_____ to continue with his research into the origins of the universe.

Now in (9)_____ fifties, Hawking weighs less (10)_____ 40 kilos and is almost completely paralysed. But, (11)_____ he can only speak by means of a computer and voice-synthesizer, his attitude to life remains the same – cheerful (12)_____ positive.

Hawking, who is considered (13)_____ many to be the world's greatest living scientist, (14)_____ achieved far (15)_____ than most able-bodied people could ever accomplish. Or, for that matter, would ever dream of accomplishing.

Writing

Exam training: Set book Paper 2 Part 2 (Question 5)

1 Introduction

There is a choice of two tasks, 5a and 5b. You may be asked to write a composition, a letter, a report or an article on the book you have read.

2 Sample questions

Answer these questions in relation to the sample exam questions 1–7 below.
a Which question or questions ask for a mainly factual answer?
b Which question or questions ask for a personal response?
c In which questions are you required to use your imagination?
d In which questions would you write most about the plot?

1 Describe a minor character in the book you have read. What relation does this person have to the main characters?
2 What do you learn from the book you have read about the people, customs and life of the country or region in which the book is set? How important is this information to the story?
3 What is the most important event in the book you have read? Why is it so important?
4 Is there a character in the book you have read who you have strong feelings about? Say why you feel as you do.
5 Which part of the book did you particularly enjoy? Say what you liked about it.
6 Is there an episode in the book that you found disappointing? Say why you didn't like it and make some suggestions as to how you would improve it.
7 Did the story end as you expected? Do you think a different ending would have been better?

3 Model

Read the model answer on page 177. As you read it, decide which of the exam questions above is being answered.

Crime never pays - various authors

A character I feel sympathy for in the book 'Crime never pays' is Loren Amory, one of the main characters in the short story 'Sauce for the goose' by Patricia Highsmith.

The reason I feel sympathy for him is that he is an extremely kind-hearted person and doesn't deserve what happens to him. When his wife Olivia falls in love with the unknown actor Stephen Castle and asks for a divorce, Loren suggests she and Stephen have a three-month separation. He does not suggest this for selfish reasons but because he doesn't think Stephen will make her happy. He wants her to be absolutely sure before she takes a decision.

During the separation, which Olivia agrees to, Loren's kindness is shown in other ways. At one point he even tells Olivia to telephone Stephen when she appears to be unable to cope any longer.

In short, Loren Amory's good nature and trusting character make it easy for Olivia to murder him, and he goes on believing her lies until seconds before his death.

4 Analysis

Read the model answer again and answer these questions.

1 What is the purpose of the first paragraph?
2 What is the purpose of the first sentence in the second paragraph?
3 What function does the rest of this paragraph and the third paragraph have? Why do you think the writer has divided the information contained here into two separate paragraphs?
4 What is the purpose of the last paragraph? Which words indicate the writer's purpose?

5 Think, plan, write

You are going to write an answer to one of the sample questions above. Your target reader is another student in your class who is less familiar with the book than you. Decide which question you are going to answer and then follow this procedure.

A Get into groups with other students who have decided to answer the same question as you. Brainstorm your ideas. First of all, see how many ideas you can think of without looking at the book. Make a note of these. Then check the book to see that your information is correct and look for further examples.

B Select your best ideas. Then follow the normal procedure for writing an opinion composition (see page 156). Write 120–180 words. Finally, check grammar, spelling and punctuation.

Set book question

Title You will have to write the title of the book at the top of the answer page.

Content Be specific. Name the characters you are writing about and support your opinions with well-

argued reasons. Only include relevant information; don't describe the whole plot.

Format Remember which type of writing you have been asked to do and use an appropriate style and layout.

13 Skills and Abilities

The silver screen

Introduction

A Can you name these actors? What films are they famous for? Who are your favourite actors? Why do you like them?

B How often do you go to the cinema? Why do you go?

C To what extent has home video replaced going to the cinema in your country?

Listening

1 Think ahead

How many words do you know connected with the cinema? Make a list.

2 Comprehension

You are going to hear eight short recordings which are all connected in some way with the cinema. Before you listen, read the questions and the possible answers carefully. As you listen, choose the best alternative, A, B or C.

1 You are going to hear part of an interview. Why does the speaker think the actor is so popular?
   A Because he is very attractive.
   B Because he is a very good actor.
   C Because of the parts he plays.

2 Listen to this woman speaking to a friend. What does she want him to do?
   A get her a part in a film
   B arrange a meeting with the director
   C introduce her to an actor

3 You will hear someone talking about a new film. What was his opinion of it?
   A He thought it was too long.
   B He thought it was excellent.
   C He thought parts of it were good.

4 Listen to this man phoning a box-office. What does he want the woman in the box-office to do?
   A change his tickets
   B change his seats
   C refund his money

5 Some people are discussing plans for an old cinema. What does the speaker want to do?
  A knock it down and build a new one
  B make alterations and modernize it
  C turn it into a conference hall

6 You are going to hear part of a telephone conversation. What has the man's son done?
  A forgotten to buy some tickets
  B lost some tickets
  C bought the wrong tickets

7 Listen to this conversation. What are the film director and his producer talking about?
  A changing an actor
  B filming a scene again
  C cutting a scene

8 Listen to the woman on TV talking about someone famous. How does the woman know her?
  A They went to the same secondary school.
  B They went to the same university.
  C They went to the same drama school.

3 Points of view

If you had the option of going to university or going to drama school, would you make the same choice as the last speaker? Give your reasons.

4 Over to you

1 Do you think acting is a natural talent or an acquired skill? Can it be inherited?
2 Why do children of famous people often follow their parents into the same kind of work? Does this just happen with famous people?

Grammar and practice

Question tags 📼

A Listen to these examples of question tags from the listening.

1 That was the one with Jack Lemmon, wasn't it?

2 He's got a really good sense of humour, hasn't he?

In which sentence is the person asking a question? In which sentence does the person simply expect agreement? How do you know?

B Listening

1 Listen to the following sentences and decide if the speaker is asking a real question or expecting agreement. Put Q or A next to the sentences.

a You couldn't lend me a fiver, could you?
b It isn't 3 o'clock already, is it?
c He'll never pass his exams, will he?
d You can come tomorrow, can't you?
e Let's have a break, shall we?
f You know Jane, don't you?

2 Listen again. This time repeat the sentences after the speaker.

C Forming question tags

Look at the above examples. What are the rules for forming question tags?

D You are going to hear some incomplete sentences. The question tags are missing. Repeat the sentences after the speaker and add the missing question tags. Use falling intonation on all the tags.

Vocabulary

1 The mind and the senses

Vocabulary reference p 219

Complete the following sentences with an appropriate word connected with the mind and the senses. All of these words are in the Vocabulary reference on page 219.

1 The man's ____ was so bad that we almost had to shout to make ourselves understood.
2 Angela's ____ wasn't good enough to read the last line of the optician's chart.
3 Don't ____ that plate! It's very hot.
4 When you have a cold, you don't enjoy eating as you can't ____ your food.
5 The woman only caught a ____ of the thief as he ran away.
6 He cooks with garlic so often that his whole house ____ of it.
7 As a child, I was told that ____ at people was rude, and that I should look at them out of the corner of my eye.
8 Rachel's got a terrible ____ for faces, but she's good at remembering names.
9 I didn't hear what you said. I was ____ to John.
10 Actors must spend days ____ their lines.

2 Money

Vocabulary reference p 219

A Quiz

1 Who gets a pension?
2 Who gives pocket-money?
3 Who gets a grant?
4 Who do people give tips to in your country?
5 Why might you have to pay a fine?
6 Why might you ask for a refund?
7 How can you pay for purchases?
8 What's the difference between a gross salary and a net salary?
9 Who pays a mortgage?
10 Who pays rent?

B Phrasal verbs

The phrasal verbs below can all be used when talking about money. Fill the spaces with an appropriate verb, making any necessary changes.

pay back	*pay into*	*pay off*	*put down*
put towards	*run out*	*save up*	*take out*

1 Every month Richard _____ a third of his salary _____ his deposit account and gives another third to his mother to pay for his keep.
2 Jill and Mike _____ to get married since their engagement last April.
3 If you _____ a deposit of £100, you can pay the rest in easy instalments.
4 Graham _____ a bank loan last week to pay for the extension to his house.
5 Don't lend Sharon any money. She never remembers _____ .
6 They hitch-hiked round the world and came back six months later when their money _____ .
7 My parents said they _____ £50 _____ the cost of the repair if I was prepared to pay the remainder myself.
8 The employee had stolen from his firm _____ his gambling debts.

C Use of English

Read the following text and decide which word A, B, C or D best fits each gap.

Many adults spend the largest part of their (1)_____ on accommodation, but while some actually buy a flat or house, others prefer to (2)_____ one. Buying one's home used to be considered a sensible (3)_____ as most people made a good (4)_____ when they sold it. Now, however, many properties are (5)_____ less than their owners originally paid for them.

1	A payment	B winnings	C earnings	D budget
2	A borrow	B rent	C hire	D lend
3	A interest	B income	C salary	D investment
4	A profit	B earnings	C receipt	D income
5	A priced	B valued	C worth	D cost

3 Memory verbs

A The verbs *remind* and *remember* are often confused. Fill the gaps in the following sentences with the correct verb in an appropriate form. You will need to make some sentences negative.

1 Could you _____ me to tell Robert that the meeting has been cancelled?
2 I'm afraid I _____ meeting you. Where did you say it was?
3 Please _____ to water the plants once a week and feed the cat twice a day.
4 He _____ me of his father. He used to get impatient when he couldn't do things too.
5 I _____ John asking me to do it, but I suppose he might have done.
6 'Isn't it your birthday soon?' Jane asked.
 'Oh, _____ me,' said Emma, 'I'll be 30!'
7 Many people write down messages to _____ themselves to do things.

B Which two structures can follow *remind* and which two can follow *remember*? What are the differences in meaning between all four?

Writing

Exam training: Applications 2

1 Grant application

Do you want to improve your English?

Cultural Exchange is offering 25 students the chance to study in Britain for one month this summer absolutely free. Grants will cover fees, accommodation with a family, and travel costs. Applicants must be 16 or over and have a reasonable command of English.

Apply in writing to:
The Director
Cultural Exchange Programme
16, George Street
Glasgow G45 5DJ

A Read the advertisement and the letter of application. The writer has sometimes used inappropriate words and language which is too informal. Suggest improvements to the parts underlined.

B What other kinds of information could the writer include to improve his chances of getting a grant?

Dear _Director_,

I saw your _ad._ in _the paper_ _the other day_ and I _want_ to _ask_ for a grant to study in Britain for one month this summer.

_I'm 16_ and have been studying English _for ages, well 5 years._ _I'm_ taking the _First Cert._ in June and, if I _get it_, I _want_ to study for a higher exam next year. _I've_ never had the _chance_ to go abroad before and _it'd be absolutely fantastic_ to be able to improve my English and learn about the British way of life at the same time.

I hope you will _give me a grant._ _Write back soon._

Yours sincerely,
Federico Accinni

2 Think, plan, write

You are also going to apply for one of the grants.

A First, make some notes. Include relevant personal details; your reasons for applying for the grant; how it would benefit you.

Remember that you have to persuade the Director that you need the grant and convince him or her that you would benefit from it.

B Plan your application like this:

Paragraph 1   Begin the letter in an appropriate way. Say why you are writing and where and when you saw the advert.

Paragraphs 2 and 3
              Give any relevant details about yourself. Say why you are applying for the grant and how you expect to benefit from it.

Paragraph 4   Include a suitable final sentence and end your letter in an appropriate way.

C Expand your notes and plan into a letter of application of 120–180 words.

D Read through your letter and check that you have written it in an appropriate formal style. Check grammar, spelling and punctuation.

Applications 2	p 96 ◀ Applications 1
Content Say why you are writing in your opening paragraph. Support the application with relevant personal information. Give reasons why you would benefit from the grant or scholarship. **Beginning** If you are given a name, include it in full,	e.g. *Dear Mr Thomas*. Otherwise, write *Dear Sir or Madam*. **Ending** If you have included a name at the beginning, finish with *Yours sincerely*. Otherwise, write *Yours faithfully*. In both cases, sign your full name.

14 Cause and effect

That'll teach you

Introduction

A Look at these four photographs, which show different ways of learning.
1 Which of these four situations have you experienced?
2 In which situations did you learn the most and the least?
3 Which situation did you find the most interesting or enjoyable?
4 What made that situation interesting or enjoyable?
5 Have you experienced any other ways of learning? What was good and bad about them?
Discuss your ideas with a partner.

B Education
1 Read these statements about education and decide whether you agree with them. Compare ideas in pairs or small groups.

Students learn best by doing practical tasks.

The main purpose of education is to prepare people for jobs.

Educated people are more intelligent than uneducated people.

Education is about learning and remembering information.

Formal written tests and exams are the best means of finding out how good students are.

2 What do you think the purpose of education is? Has your own education achieved this aim?

Reading

1 Think ahead

Before you read the article discuss these questions.

1 How important is it for you to get high-level educational qualifications?
2 What would the effect be on you and on your friends and family if you failed your next examination?

2 Reading

Read the article quickly and answer these two general questions.

1 Who is the article aimed at?

  A teachers and parents   C students

  B employers   D the general public

2 The article is trying to show that

  A it is of great importance to pass exams.

  B it is possible to succeed without passing exams.

  C students should work hard to pass their exams.

  D students need advice about how to pass exams.

Bernie Grant

The stars who did their own thing

The results of this year's summer exams are due out next week. They will almost certainly result in misery for many and happiness for a few. It seems likely that these results will cause more problems than they solve. On the one hand, if you did well, then you might find there are fewer places available in higher education; on the other hand, if you did poorly, news reports of a general trend towards better results nationwide will hardly make you jump for joy. In times of high unemployment, many people work hard for exams to give themselves a better chance of getting a good job. But there are people who have made it to the top without being born with a silver spoon in their mouth and without getting A grades in their exams. We talked to a number of personalities about their success.

A **Caitlin Moran,** who is 18, is a journalist with a regular column in the Times newspaper. She is also the presenter of the Channel 4 TV programme, *Naked City*. Caitlin was brought up on a council housing estate and claims to have only one certificate – and that is in swimming. 'University? My higher education was pubs and music. I only spent two weeks in the sixth form of my local grammar school and then left because I had already made my mind up to be a writer and broadcaster. I wasn't discouraged by the education system, I just knew what I wanted from the word go.'

B **Bernie Grant** is 49 and is a Member of Parliament. He did very well in his O level* exams at school and went on to get 3 A levels*, but left university after two years. 'It

was growing up in the Caribbean that made me confident. There are contests for everything there, from how loud your stereo sound system would go to your academic ability. I did pretty well in most of these. On balance I don't see any problem with competitive exams. It's good practice for kids who are going out into the wider world.'

C **Barrie K Sharpe,** who is a 33-year-old fashion designer, comes originally from London's East End and now works in Soho. He says he is not sure what his qualifications are. 'Higher Education in my field would be a complete waste of time. If someone asked me in a job interview how many subject exams I'd passed, I'd say ten without any hesitation. I mean no-one's going to check up on you, are they?'

D **Des'ree**, the 24-year-old pop star, took 5 A level subjects. 'My mother wanted me to do a degree in journalism, but after I passed my A levels, I had to sit her down and explain that I knew in my heart what I wanted to do. Although I'm not sure that my A levels prepared me for the world of the music business, I still feel education has to be taken seriously.'

E **John Fashanu**, the 29-year-old footballer, TV presenter and businessman, didn't get any O levels. He describes himself as 'working class'. 'Kids from the middle and upper classes just don't have the same hunger. On the football pitch or in business, the kids with degrees are usually too self-centred. Exams are just exams and at the end of the day the best education you can get is at the university of life. For example, when I am importing coffee, I don't need to be a mathematical genius or have a degree in Business Studies to get it right, do I?'

* In British schools, O (Ordinary) level exams were taken when students were 16 years old. This exam is now called GCSE (General Certificate of Secondary Education). A (Advanced) level exams are taken at the age of 18 and are regarded as university entrance qualifications.

3 Comprehension

A Read the article again and answer the questions below by choosing the appropriate person (A–E). Where more than one answer is required, these may be given in any order.

A Caitlin Moran   **B** Bernie Grant   **C** Barry Sharpe

D Des'ree   **E** John Fashanu

Who:

went to university?   `1`

works in the media?   `2`   `3`

believes that a good education is important?   `4`   `5`

has no formal educational qualifications?   `6`   `7`

claims to have had an unconventional education?   `8`

started but did not finish a course of higher education?   `9`

criticizes people with high level qualifications?   `10`

claims that coming from a poor social background

    makes people more ambitious?   `11`

was brought up in a competitive society?   `12`

B Vocabulary

Guess the meanings of these expressions, which are used in the article.

1 to make it to the top (Introduction)
2 to be born with a silver spoon in your mouth (Introduction)
3 from the word go (A)
4 to go out into the wider world (B)
5 to know in your heart (D)
6 at the end of the day (E)
7 the university of life (E)

C Reading between the lines

1 What kind of 'higher education' do you think Caitlin Moran got from 'pubs and music'?
2 What problems do some people associate with competitive exams?
3 What does John Fashanu mean by 'Exams are just exams'? Do you agree?

4 Over to you

1 Think of successful people you know who were *born with a silver spoon in their mouth.* How do you feel about these people?
2 Do you know anyone who has been a success because of an education at *the university of life*?

5 My last exam

Think back to the last exam you took. Write two paragraphs about how you felt before and after the exam. Each paragraph should be about 50 words long. Compare your feelings with those of other students.

Grammar and practice

1 Cause and effect

A Read these sentences from the article. Underline the verbs or verb phrases which show the effects of actions. The first one has been done for you.

1 They <u>will</u> almost certainly <u>result in</u> misery for many and happiness for just a few.
2 It seems likely that these particular results will cause more problems than they solve.
3 News reports of a general trend towards better results nationwide will hardly make you jump for joy.
4 It was growing up in the Caribbean that made me confident.

B Work out and note down the causes and effects referred to in each of the above sentences. The first one has been done as an example.

cause	effect
1 exam results	misery and happiness

C Make

1 The verb *make* is used in two of the sentences above to refer to cause and effect. What words or grammatical structures follow *make* in each case?
2 Before continuing, check your understanding of *make* in the Grammar reference on page 214.

D Using *make,* think of several answers to each of these questions.

Example   What makes you cry?
Sad films make me cry.
Peeling onions sometimes makes me cry.

1 What makes you laugh?
2 What do you do that makes other people laugh?
3 What makes you feel guilty?
4 What makes you angry?
5 What do you do that makes other people angry or annoyed?

2 Purpose

A Read this sentence from the text and underline the phrase which introduces the purpose for people's hard work.

Of course, in times of high unemployment, many people work hard for exams in order to give themselves a better chance of getting a good job.

B Underline the purpose words or phrases below.

1 People do exercise to keep themselves fit.
2 I'm going to study really hard this week so I can have Friday off.
3 In order to improve his spoken French, he spent the month before his oral exam in Paris.
4 My friend went to the library so that he could study in peace.

C Check your understanding of purpose expressions in the Grammar reference on page 214.

3 Practice

Answer these questions about everyday activities in different ways, using purpose phrases.
Example   Why do people wear clothes?
in order to keep warm
so that they attract attention
to look fashionable

1 Why do young men drive so fast?
2 Why do people go on diets?
3 Why do people go to nightclubs?
4 Why do people take exams?

4 Fluency

What you would do if you were faced with these dilemmas? Compare ideas in groups.

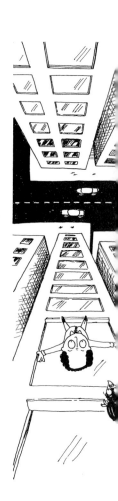

1 You look out of a window on the 10th floor of an office block, and you see someone on the ledge outside. It's a man who says he's going to jump. What do you do to stop him?
2 Having rescued the man on the ledge, you get into the lift to go to the ground floor. The lift starts to move, but suddenly you hear a strange noise. The cable has broken and the lift is out of control. What do you do?
3 Fortunately, you get out of the wrecked lift with only cuts and bruises, but you decide to go to hospital, for a check-up. You get into your car and head for the hospital. Soon you're travelling at 110 kmh. You get to the hospital and try to slow down, but the car brakes don't work. What do you do?

Vocabulary

1 Education

Vocabulary reference p 219

A Quiz

1 What are the jumbled subjects a–g? Match them with the symbols.

  a grayphoge
  b shyriot
  c thasm
  d reofing unalagge   e seccine   f comicnose   g shiplacy tinudeaco

2 What are the three branches of science commonly taught in schools? Here are the first and last letters of the subjects.
1 b_____y   2 c_____y   3 p_____s

3 Many sciences and other subjects of study end in *-ology*. How many *-ologies* do you know? Here are some definitions.
1 The study of the mind and how it functions.
2 The using of scientific knowledge for practical purposes.
3 The study of the earth's surface, including rocks.
4 The scientific study of society and social behaviour.
5 The study of past civilizations by an analysis of the physical remains of those civilizations.

B What is, or was, your favourite school subject? And your least favourite subject? Write 50 words about each of these two subjects, explaining why you liked or disliked them.

2 Word building

A Complete this table of words relating to education.

Noun	Person	Verb	Adjective
1 examination			X
2	educator		a
			b
3			competitive
4 qualification	X		
5	X	X	intelligent
6	X	revise	X
7		fail	

B Fill the gaps in this conversation with the correct form of one of these verbs.

fail pass re-sit revise take

Tony   I'm 1_____ an important music exam tomorrow.
Jane   Good luck, I hope you 2_____ .
Tony   So do I. I've 3_____ every night for six weeks!
Jane   You've always done well in exams – I'm sure you won't 4_____
Tony   I hope you're right. I couldn't face 5_____ the exam in December.

Writing

Checking your work

1 Introduction

When you take Paper 2 of the FCE exam, make sure you allow some time for checking and if necessary correcting what you have written.

First of all, here is some general advice.
- Don't write more than you need to. It's better to write a short piece which is correct than a long piece which is full of mistakes.
- Use all the time available to check what you have written.
- Don't change anything unless you are sure it's wrong. First ideas are often correct.

As soon as you have finished writing, carefully check these points in this order:
1 Grammatical accuracy particularly: verb tenses, articles, word order and punctuation.
2 Vocabulary: appropriate choice of words and spelling
3 Final points – change these only if you can do so quickly: organization – the ordering of ideas in paragraphs, the use of titles and headings; style.

2 Answering the question

Read this composition which was written in answer to the question *Should girls and boys be taught in separate schools?* As you read, decide if it answers the question or not. Give examples to support your view.

> The fact that girls and boys are separated can be good because they have different interest. The communication is easier if there are only girls or boys. For example, boys and girls seldom play together because the first ones prefer fighting or playing cars, whereas the others like puppets. Also that permit to organize the subjects in different ways. So, the boys could have more sport, and the girls could do cooking or drawning.
>
> However, we can notice some disadvantages as having a bad atmosphere. I explain: if girls are all the time together, it can makes problems. Otherwise, because girls are more mature, they can help the boys to grow up. At last, if boys and girls are mixed, that contribute to a rivality between each other and the results can be better.
>
> In my opinion to separate boys and girls is not a good idea because they have to live together and they should learn it the youngest as possible. Apart from that I don't see the reason to separate them. They can bring something each other.

3 Editing

How accurate is this sample composition? Answer YES or NO to these questions and underline all the mistakes, making as many corrections as you can.

1 Grammar
- Are the articles *the, a* and *an* used correctly?
- Is the word order correct?

2 Vocabulary
- Have the right words been used?
- Could any words be added?

3 Spelling and punctuation
- Is everything spelt correctly?
- Has punctuation been used where necessary?
- Have the correct punctuation marks been used?

4 Organization
- Are the main ideas clear?
- Have paragraphs been used appropriately?
- Is the information connected with appropriate linking words and phrases?
- Are the ideas introduced with appropriate markers? e.g. *One advantage is...*

5 Style
- Is the style appropriate?
- Have short verb forms or slang been used? If so, is this suitable?

4 Correct your own writing

A Write an opening paragraph for each of these exam questions. Write about 40 words in each case.

1 An English-language magazine is running a series of articles about schools in various countries. Write an article describing what young people like and dislike about schools in your country.

2 An English examination organization is considering bringing out a new English exam. You have been asked to write a short report about what such a new exam should contain. Base your writing on your own views and those of your friends.

B As you finish each paragraph, check the accuracy of what you have written, correcting any mistakes you find.
Work through the list of questions in 3 above.

C When you have checked your writing thoroughly yourself, exchange paragraphs with a partner and check each other's work.

Cause and effect

Face the music

Introduction

In groups, think of answers to these questions. Spend one minute on each question. In that time note down as many answers as you can.

1 What different kinds of music are there? For example, classical, jazz, etc.
2 On what occasions and in what situations do people listen to or hear music?
3 Other than simple enjoyment, what reasons do people have for listening to music?

Listening

1 Listening

You are going to hear people talking in eight different situations which are all related in some way to music. Listen and make a note of the different kinds of music mentioned by the speakers.

2 Comprehension

A Now listen again and for questions 1–8, choose the best answer, A, B or C.

1 What situation is the speaker describing?
   A going to the doctor's   B going to the dentist's   C going to a concert

   `1  B`

2 What is this speaker annoyed about?
   A the use of personal stereos in public
   B a particular kind of music
   C all kinds of noise pollution

   `2  B  A`

3 Why does Mrs Johnson want the DJ to play *Love Hurts* on the radio?
   A Because she wants to get in touch with her son.
   B Because it's her son's birthday.
   C Because it's her son's favourite record.

   `3  A`

4 What kind of event is the speaker describing?
   A an opera   B the film version of a musical   C a rock concert

   `4  C`

5 What is the speaker's main subject?
   A a particular pop song
   B the way memories come back
   C a situation in her past

   `5  B`

I listen music while I am jogging 1. *to stop myself becoming bored* / *just for enjoyment*

6 What is this musician talking about?
   A How he learnt to play his instrument.
   B How he was taught to play his instrument.
   C How he learnt to read music.

6 *A*

7 Which question is the speaker answering?
   A What kinds of music do you enjoy?
   B What is your favourite kind of music?
   C Where do you go to listen to music?

7 *B*

8 Who is the speaker?
   A a teacher   B a musician   C a doctor

8 *C*

B Listening between the lines

1 Why do you think the second speaker's friend listens to music while he's jogging?
2 Why do you think the disc jockey on the radio says this? *You don't have to tell her where you are if you don't want to.*
3 In the fourth recording why did the audience *go mad*, so that the speaker couldn't hear the music?
4 What do you understand by this sentence from the last extract? *They have had their lives reduced to a bed and a locker.*

Grammar and practice

Have / get something done

A Look at these extracts from the interview and answer the questions which follow each sentence.

1 *I just had to get it seen to.*
   Who saw to the tooth?
2 *Actually I only had it filled – which wasn't so bad as having it taken out.*
   Why didn't the speaker fill the tooth himself?
3 *She'd like to have* Love Hurts *played for her son Michael.*
   Who played *Love Hurts*?

B Is there a difference in meaning between these two sentences?

1 *I had my tooth filled.*
2 *My tooth was filled by the dentist.*

When might a passive be used instead of *get* or *have*?

C How is the verb *have something done* used differently in these two extracts?

1 *I had my tooth filled.*
2 *They have had their lives reduced to a bed and a locker.*

D Before you continue, check your understanding of the verbs *have / get something done* in the Grammar reference on page 214.

E Rewrite these sentences using *have* or *get.* The first one has been done as an example.

1 The mechanic changed the oil in my car.
   I had the oil in my car changed.
2 The hairdresser cut my hair in a completely different style.
3 A decorator has repainted our house.
4 A friend of mine, who's an electrician, is going to repair my video next week.
5 My jacket is being cleaned at a specialist cleaner's.
6 The town hall has just been rebuilt for the council.

F Think of as many answers to these questions as you can.

1 What can you have done at the dentist's?
2 Why do people go to the hairdresser's?
3 Why do people take their cars to a garage?
4 If you didn't want people to recognize you which features of your appearance would you have changed?

G What do you have done for you, rather than doing for yourself? Make a list and compare your answers with other students.

Vocabulary

1 Health

Find ten medical words in this wordsearch. Here are their meanings.

P	A	T	R	E	A	T	O	S
U	B	A	N	D	A	G	E	U
S	L	L	I	P	A	P	E	R
H	M	I	D	W	I	F	E	G
P	L	A	S	T	E	R	A	E
B	C	O	F	O	I	N	G	O
L	U	H	C	A	T	C	H	N
U	R	T	N	E	I	T	A	P
D	E	E	S	R	U	N	F	U

1. person specially trained to help women to give birth *midwife*
2. person who looks after ill people – especially in hospital *nurse*
3. person who is ill and needs looking after *PATIENT*
4. doctor who performs operations *surgeon*
5. long strip of cloth for covering an injury *Bandage*
6. tablet *Pill*
7. patch of material which is stuck on to the skin to protect a small cut or scratch *Plaster*
8. Don't come too near me – I don't want you to __*catch*__ my cold.
9. My brother was born deaf but, using the latest techniques, the doctors have managed to __*Push*__ him.
10. In some countries doctors will not __*cure*__ people who have no medical insurance.

2 Use of English *encounter(ed)*

1. come up against (*encounter*)
2. cut down on (reduce)
3. kept up with
4. don't go along with
5. keep up with / catch up with
6. come down with
7. come up with

Use the word in capitals at the end of each line of this text to form a word which fits in the space in the same line.

While I was abroad I picked up a mystery (1)__*infection*__. My doctor **INFECT**
sent me to see a (2)__*specialist*__ because he didn't recognize my **SPECIAL**
symptoms. After a thorough (3)__*examination*__ a nurse gave me an **EXAMINE**
(4)__*injection*__ in my arm. **INJECT**
Although the arm was quite (5)__*painful*__ for several **PAIN**
days afterwards, my (6)__*recovery*__ was very quick. **RECOVER**

3 Phrasal verbs

In the listening extracts about qualifications, one of the speakers says:
I mean no-one's going to *check up on* you, are they?'
Check up on is a three-part phrasal verb.
Fill the gaps in these sentences with the correct form of three-part phrasal verbs made from the verbs and particles below. Remember that the three parts of these verbs always stay together. The first one has been done for you.

1 I've _____ a problem, which means I'll have to work all weekend.
2 The doctor said I was overweight and advised me _____ my sugar intake.
3 We couldn't buy newspapers on the island so I _____ the news by listening to the radio.
4 I agree with most of what the government does, but I _____ their plan to raise income tax.
5 My friend was running so fast that I couldn't _____ him.
6 My class was almost empty last week – nearly everyone _____ flu.
7 It's about time someone _____ a new idea for preventing colds.

Verbs	Particle 1	Particle 2
catch come cut go keep	along down up	against on with

Writing

Exam training: Stories 2 Paper 2 Part 2

1 Introduction

Stories can concentrate simply on a sequence of events or they can include descriptions of the people, places and objects involved in the events. The writing section in Unit 5 emphasized the first type of story. Re-read the summary box in Unit 5 on page 69, before continuing with this section, which focuses on the second type.

2 Model

A Read the following question and the model answer. As you read the answer for the first time, underline the sentences or phrases which say what happened.

Write a short story for your school's English newspaper. You must begin or end your story with these words:
Every time I hear that music now, it reminds me of that amazing day.

I was travelling through northern Italy, listening to a Paul McCartney cassette on my personal stereo. Although it was sunny, it was cool for April. The coach was comfortable, light and airy—occasionally, the smartly-dressed attendants brought cold drinks and delicious snacks.

Just after midday, the road started to climb and the temperature fell rapidly. When we reached the highest point of the hills, it was snowing hard. Suddenly, there was a bang, and the coach drove off the road and stopped. For a moment everything was quiet and nobody moved. In my headphones, Paul McCartney went on singing sweetly. Fortunately nobody was hurt and soon we were all chattering excitedly. The driver had lost control after a puncture. He said he couldn't change the wheel in such terrible weather conditions.

Twenty hours later the breakdown truck arrived and soon we were able to continue our journey. By the time we arrived in Milan, I was tired and hungry—I must have listened to my cassette over twenty times. Every time I hear that music now, it reminds me of that amazing day.

B Now look at the rest of the story – the parts that you did not underline. Find sentences or phrases which:
1 describe a person's appearance, character or behaviour
2 describe a place or a thing
3 describe a situation or an atmosphere
4 provide an explanation

What is the approximate proportion of narrated events to description?

3 Think, plan, write   **A** You are going to write a story in answer to the same question. Here are some questions to think about:

1 Is there a song or a piece of music that reminds you about a particular occasion or event? (If you can't think of one, choose some music you like and invent a story about the first time you heard it.)
2 Try to remember the occasion or the sequence of actions. Note these down.
3 Now try to remember something about your own feelings at the time. Add details of any other people involved, the location or situation and the atmosphere surrounding your story. Make brief notes to remind yourself.

B Make a paragraph plan. You should have at least three paragraphs. Here is a possible plan.

Paragraph 1   The beginning of the story, including a description of the situation or location and any important people.

Paragraph 2   The main event of the story, including extra descriptions of people, places or atmosphere.

Paragraph 3   The end of the story, including explanations and descriptions of people's final reactions or moods.

C Write your story in 120–180 words. Check as you write that you are including interesting or useful descriptions and explanations. Don't forget to mention your personal feelings. Include the sentence you have been given at the beginning or the end of your story.

D Read through your story. Is the proportion of narrated events to description about the same as in the model answer?

E Check your story for accuracy of grammar, spelling and punctuation.

Exam techniques

Taking the First Certificate exam

Introduction

This section gives general advice about preparing for the exam and about making the best use of your time during the exam. Everyone's different, however, so what works for one person might not be so effective for another. You should decide what is best for you.

The Exam Factfile on pages 4 – 8 will help to familiarize you with the details of the First Certificate exam. Ask your teacher for clarification, too.

Before the exam

1 Don't try to revise the whole of the English language. Spend time on the parts of the exam that you find most difficult.
2 Look back over your work and list your most frequent mistakes. Work out a revision timetable that covers these problem areas.
3 Stick to your timetable – this will help you to revise systematically.
4 Use the Exam techniques sections in each of the units and the Grammar reference and Vocabulary reference at the back of the book.

Exam day

1 Before you go into the exam, make sure you know which paper you are doing; how long it lasts; what you have to do.
2 Before you start each paper, think about or make sure you know how many exercises you have to do; how much time to spend on each exercise; how much time to allow for checking.

During the exam

1 Listen carefully to what the examiner or invigilator says.
2 Read the exam papers to make sure you know exactly what you have to do.
3 Check that you have answered every question. Don't leave any gaps or unanswered questions – make a sensible guess if necessary.
4 Keep checking your answers until time runs out.
5 Try not to be too nervous and don't panic.

Paper 1 Reading
(1 hour 15 minutes)

• Decide the order in which you are going to deal with the texts.
• Read and follow all instructions carefully.
• Read texts through quickly before doing the related tasks.
• You will not have time to read all texts in detail and it isn't necessary. Skim and scan texts for answers where possible.

Paper 2 Writing
(1 hour 30 minutes)

• Read through Part 2 of the paper and decide which of the four tasks 2–5 you are going to do.
• Decide whether to start with the letter in Part 1 or one of the Part 2 tasks.
• Spend a few minutes making a simple plan for each piece of writing. Decide on an appropriate style, layout and organization. Then think about the content of paragraphs and the language you will use, e.g. verb tenses. Keep your plan in mind while writing.
• Don't spend more than half the time on your first answer.
• Make sure you answer all the points in the question appropriately.
• Check your writing by reading it through. Try to hear your own voice and 'listen' for mistakes. Check grammar, spelling and punctuation.

Paper 3
Use of English
(1 hour 15 minutes)

- Look at the five tasks you have to do and decide which order to do them in. For example, it may be best to start with a 'mechanical' task like Part 3 and leave Part 2 until last.
- Spend about 10 minutes on each task. This will allow you at least 20 minutes to check your answers and to go back to parts you found difficult.
- If there's a question you can't answer, don't waste time worrying about it. Go on to something else.

Paper 4 Listening
(about 40 minutes)

- Listen carefully to the instructions on the cassette.
- Try to predict as much about the recordings as you can from the question paper.
- Don't panic if you don't understand everything the first time.
- Answer all the questions.

Paper 5 Speaking
(about 15 minutes for 2 candidates)

- At first the examiner will ask you a few general questions about yourself. This is to help you relax.
- When you are given the pictures, don't spend too long talking about physical details. Move on to the theme of the pictures.
- If you are working with a partner, don't dominate the conversation. Allow your partner the opportunity to talk.
- In all parts of this paper, try to show how good your English is. This means speaking correctly and fluently and with good pronunciation, using a range of vocabulary and communicating successfully.
- Above all, keep talking and stay calm.

The answer sheet

For Paper 1 Reading, Paper 3 Use of English and Paper 4 Listening, you will have to transfer your answers to a separate answer sheet. This involves one of the following: shading a small box in pencil; writing a single word or short phrase; putting a tick in a box (Paper 3 Part 4).

Remember to leave yourself enough time for this when doing Papers 1 and 3. In Paper 4, you will be given extra time after the recording has finished.

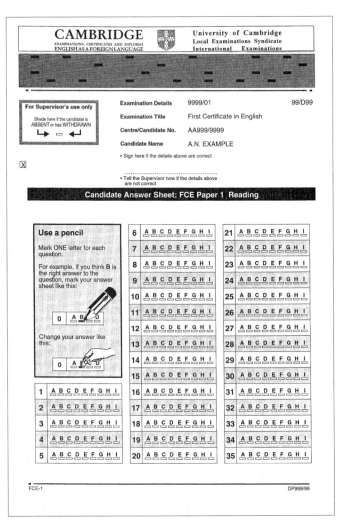

Pair work

Talking about photos, First turn (page 61)

Student A: the interviewer

I'm going to give you two pictures showing families with young children. I'd like you to talk about the pictures and say what you think it would be like growing up in these two different families.

If Student B finishes talking within one minute, ask these questions:

If you were a twin would you like to wear the same clothes as your brother or sister?

What are the advantages of having only one child from a parent's point of view?

Talking about photos, Second turn (page 61)

Student A: the candidate

Picture discussion, Activity 2 (page 149)

Student B – Photograph A

This man is taking part in a competition to see who can attract the most worms out of the ground.

General questions on the theme of competitions:

1 What kind of competitions are popular with adults and children in your country?

2 Why do people go in for competitions? Do you need special qualities to be a good competitor?

3 If you won a lot of money in a competition, what would you do with it? Would it change you?

Fluency (page 13)

Student A

Read these notes about the three applicants' good and bad points. Choose who you would most like to join the expedition. It is up to you to decide whether these people are male or female.

WM Peters

+ Has a reputation for honesty. Strong and fearless. Independent minded. Never gossips about other people behind their backs. A good photographer.
- Can be rather cold towards others. Has no interests outside trekking. Likes to be in charge.

L Palmer

+ Tends to take everything in his/her stride, and does not panic easily. Has a good sense of humour.
- Is very untidy and has no sense of direction. Snores.

F Trueman

+ Young and healthy. Has done weight-training, so would be able to carry heavy loads for long distances. An excellent cook.
- Has little experience of trekking. Is rather shy.

Arrangements (page 23)

Student A

A classmate of yours, who has just returned from a two-week holiday, phones you to ask to meet you and go through all the work he or she has missed. You are rather annoyed about this request because you don't think your classmate should have had this extra holiday. Each time your friend tries to arrange a meeting, make an excuse - apologize and say you are very busy.

Example: *I'm sorry, Monday's impossible, I'm having a driving lesson on Monday evening.*

Talking about photos, Second turn (page 61)

Student B: the interviewer

I'm going to give you two pictures of different ceremonies in which young children are given their names. I'd like you to talk about the pictures and say which ceremony is more like what happens in your country.

If Student B finishes talking within one minute, ask these questions:

Does your name have a particular meaning in your language?

Do you like your name? What would you prefer to be called?

Fluency (page 135)

Student B

You are a sumo wrestling trainer. You think Student A just needs to put on 30 kilos to be sure of winning the world championships. Both of you would then be rich and famous. Persuade Student A to eat more.

Picture discussion, Activity 4 (page 149)

Student A – Photograph B

These police officers are taking part in the Christmas Tree Patrol which operates for the two weeks before Christmas in some English forests. Their job is to deter or catch Christmas tree thieves.

General questions on the theme of the environment:

1 Should people have real Christmas trees?
2 Do you think the police force should be involved in the protection of the environment? Are there more important things they could be doing?
3 Do you think the government in your country does enough to protect the environment?

Grammar reference

Terminology

Determiner: definite article

Jimmy McGregor was the first man to swim from New Zealand to Australia. When he arrived in Australia, he was met by a TV interviewer. 'Strewth, mate,' said the Australian unbelievingly. 'How did you get to be such a good swimmer? That's an impossible distance you've just swum!'

'As you may know,' replied Jimmy, 'there are lots of lakes in Scotland and, from the age of two, my father used to take me to Loch Lomond, which is one of the biggest. He would row me into the middle, help me over the side, and leave me to swim the twenty kilometres back to the shore.'

'That must have been rather hard for a two-year-old,' said the Australian admiringly.

'Yes,' agreed Jimmy. 'However, the hardest part was fighting my way out of the sack!'

Subordinate clause

Sentence

Main clause

Modifier / intensifier: used to strengthen or weaken the meaning of adjectives and adverbs. Also: *so, very*.

Ungradable adjective: can only be used with 'extreme' modifiers like *absolutely*. Also: *huge, freezing, furious, terrified*.

Quantifier. Also: *all, both, less, some, several, a lot of*, etc.

Connective: relative pronoun

Connective: conjunction. Also: *but, so, if*, etc.

Modifier: adverb. Also: *pretty, quite*, etc

Speech marks: used to indicate the actual words that someone says.
NOTE Other punctuation marks come inside the speech marks.

Full stop: used at the end of a sentence.

Capital letter: used
1 to begin sentences
2 for all proper nouns (names, days of the week, etc.)
3 nationality adjectives
4 for the first letter of direct speech

Question mark: used at the end of a question

Determiner: indefinite article. Also: *a*.

Apostrophe: used
1 in contractions to show that one or more letters are missing
2 to indicate the possessive, e.g. *John's book*

Determiner: possessive adjective.
NOTE The demonstrative adjectives *this, that, these, those* are also determiners.

Gradable adjective: can be used with modifiers

Comma: used
1 before reporting verbs in direct speech
2 to separate items on a list
3 to divide a subordinate clause from a main clause when the subordinate clause comes first
4 after connecting adverbs
5 around non-defining relative clauses
6 in front of most conjunctions

Exclamation mark: used for emphasis instead of a full stop.

Connective: adverb. Also: *firstly, in conclusion*, etc.

Unit 1

Describing habitual actions

1 Habitual actions in the present

A The present simple
This is the usual way of expressing present habitual actions.
> *Whenever I go to town, I spend too much money.*

The present simple is also used for permanent situations.
> *My uncle lives in Bristol, but he works in London.*

B Tend to
The verb *tend to* + infinitive can be used to refer to usual or generally occurring actions.
> *She tends to get up late at weekends.*

C Other ways of expressing habitual actions in the present
1 Present continuous + *always*
This is used mainly to refer to repeated actions which the speaker finds annoying.
> *You're always complaining about my cooking.*

It can even be used when you are irritated with yourself.
> *I'm always losing my keys.*

2 *Will* + infinitive
This is sometimes used instead of the present simple to refer to behaviour which is characteristic of a particular person.
> *I'll sit for hours watching TV.*

3 *Keep* + -ing
This is often used to refer to habitual actions which are accidental or annoying.
> *I keep bumping my head on that tree.*

2 Habitual actions in the past

A The past simple
When a past simple verb refers to habitual or repeated actions it can be accompanied by a frequency expression.
> *When I worked in London, I usually got home at six o'clock.*

B Used to + infinitive
This refers to habitual past actions which no longer happen.
> *Before I had a car, I used to cycle to work .*

It can also be used to refer to actions that did not happen before, but happen now.
> *I didn't use to have foreign holidays. Now I go abroad every year.*
> *We never used to watch TV at breakfast time.*

Remember the question form of *used to*.
> *Where did you use to go for your holidays?*

Sentences with *used to* do not need frequency adverbs, although they are sometimes included for emphasis.
> *I always used to be late for school.*

C Would + infinitive
This refers to habitual past actions.
> *Every summer our parents would take us to the seaside.*

Avoid using *would* in questions and negative sentences, as its meaning can be completely different.

D The difference between *used to* and *would*
Used to can refer to permanent situations as well as habitual actions.
> *I used to be able to see Big Ben from my bedroom window.*

Would can only refer to actions, not situations. You can say *He'd catch the 7.30 train*, but not *He'd work in London*.

Used to
Used to has three forms with different meanings.

A Used to + infinitive
This refers to habitual past actions (see note **2B** above).
> *My father used to smoke 40 cigarettes a day.*

B To be used to + -ing
This means *to be accustomed to*.
> *I must go to bed early. I'm used to having ten hours sleep a night.*

C To get used to + -ing
This means *to become accustomed to*, often to something unusual or strange.
> *If you come to England, you'll have to get used to driving on the left-hand side of the road.*

NOTE Other common verbs which follow the same pattern are *look forward to* and *object to*.

Unit 2

The future
There are many ways of talking about future time in English. This is a summary of the most common forms and their uses.

1 Present continuous
The present continuous is used to refer to future actions or events which have already been arranged.
> *Are you doing anything interesting at the weekend?*
> *We're spending the summer with our friends in Greece.*

2 Will

A Will + infinitive (future simple)
The *will* future is used to talk about:
1 future facts.
> *The sun will rise at 6.30 tomorrow morning.*
2 predictions or expectations.
> *Helen and John won't be here on time. They're always late.*
3 strong intentions.
> *When Loretta retires, I'll definitely apply for her job .*
4 instant decisions about the immediate future.
> *The phone's ringing. I'll answer it.*

B Will + be + -ing (future continuous)
This form is used to talk about:
1 events or actions that will be in progress at a specific time in the future.
> *This time tomorrow, I'll be travelling through France.*
2 predicted or expected trends.
> *In the 21st century, people will be living to the age of 130.*

C Will + have + past participle (future perfect simple)
Will + have + been + -ing (future perfect continuous)
These two forms are used to talk about:
1 actions or events that will already be completed by a specific time in the future.
> *By the year 2000, I'll have left school and started work.*

2 the continuous nature of actions and events in the future.
   *On Saturday we 'll **have been living** here for three years.*

NOTES

1 *Shall* is sometimes used instead of *will* after *I* and *we*.
   *In a few days we **shall** have forgotten about the accident.*

2 *Shall* must be used to start questions which are suggestions and offers.
   ***Shall** we phone to see what time the film starts?*
   ***Shall** I carry that heavy case for you?*

3 *Going to* + infinitive

This is used to talk about:

a intentions or plans.
   *After Christmas, **I'm going to get** a job and save up.*
   *What **are you going to do** when you leave school?*

b predictions based on present evidence or knowledge.
   *My nose is tickling. I think **I'm going to sneeze**.*
   *My sister's **going to have** a baby.*

4 Present simple

This tense is used to talk about scheduled, timetabled or fixed events.
   *The match **starts** at 7.30 tomorrow evening.*

5 Other ways of referring to the future

A To be about to + infinitive

This is used to talk about actions or events which we expect to happen in the immediate future.
   *I must hurry – the train is **about to leave**.*

B To be on the point of + -ing

This expression also refers to the immediate future.
   *The train is **on the point of leaving**. Close the doors!*

Articles

1 The definite article *the*

Three of the main uses of the definite article are to refer to:

a something that has been mentioned before.
   *Bill: I've got a dog.   Ben: What's **the** dog's name?*

b something there is only one of in a particular context.
   ***The** Queen spent three days in Wales.*
   *Soon after we'd taken off, **the** pilot welcomed us on board.*

c something the speaker and listener both know about.
   ***The** film was really good – thanks for recommending it.*

It is also used in these ways:

d with superlative constructions.
   *She's **the** fastest runner in Europe.*

e with adjectives used as nouns referring to groups of people.
   *There's one law for **the** rich and another for **the** poor.*

f with the names of oceans, seas, rivers, mountain ranges.
   ***the** Atlantic, **the** Thames, **the** Alps*

g with the names of some countries and groups of islands.
   ***the** United States, **the** United Kingdom, **the** West Indies*

2 The indefinite article *a / an*

These are the main uses of the indefinite article:

a to refer to something for the first time.
   *I've got **a** dog.*

b to refer to a person or thing (but not a special person or thing).
   *Can I have **a** drink please? Tea, coffee, beer, I don't mind.*

c to refer to a person's job.
   *Alan is **a** telephone engineer.* I'm a teacher.

d with numbers.
   ***a** hundred, **a** million*

3 Zero article (Ø)

These are the main contexts in which no article is used:

a with plural countable nouns.
   Ø International footballers are paid too much money.

b with uncountable nouns.
   He used to drink Ø beer, but now he drinks only Ø water.
   They fell in Ø love while they were in Spain.

c with the names of towns, cities, states and most countries.
   Ø New York, Ø Texas, Ø Greece

d with nouns for certain places or situations.
   Suzy went into Ø hospital yesterday.
   on Ø deck, at Ø home, on Ø holiday, to Ø church, at Ø school

Unit 3

動名詞

Gerunds and infinitives

Certain verbs, adjectives and prepositions must always be followed by the gerund; others must always be followed by the infinitive. Some verbs, however, can be followed by either the infinitive or the gerund.

1 The gerund

Gerunds are verbs that behave like nouns. They are formed by adding *-ing* to the verb base and can be used in four ways.

A As the subject of a clause or sentence
   ***Eating out** can be expensive.*

B As the object of a clause or sentence
   *My brother enjoys **fishing** but he hates not **catching** anything.*

C After certain verbs

1 After verbs expressing likes and dislikes (but see **3B**2).
   *I don't enjoy **seeing** you like this.*

2 After other verbs such as:
   admit, appreciate, avoid, can't help, consider, delay, deny, finish, forgive, give up, imagine, involve, keep, mind, miss, postpone, put off, prevent, report, resist, risk, suggest.
   *Have you considered **buying** a new one?*

D After prepositions

1 After all prepositions except *to*, which is usually followed by the infinitive (see 3 below for some common exceptions).
   *On **opening** the letter, she realized it wasn't for her.*

2 After adjective + preposition combinations such as:
   nervous / worried   about
   bad / good / clever / skilled   at
   sorry / responsible   for
   interested   in
   capable / afraid / frightened / terrified   of
   bored   with
   *I'm interested in **applying** for the job.*

3 After verb + preposition combinations such as:
   apologize for, arrest someone for, be / get used to, congratulate someone on, insist on, look forward to, object to, succeed in, warn someone about.
   *My little brother insisted on **coming** with me.*

2 The infinitive

A After certain verbs

The following verbs are always followed by the infinitive:
afford, agree, arrange, ask, appear, attempt, choose, decide, expect, help, hope, intend, learn, manage, need, offer, pretend, promise, refuse, seem.

> *I can't afford **to go** on holiday this year.*

B After certain adjectives

The following adjectives are always followed by the infinitive:
amazed, certain, difficult, disappointed, easy, free, glad, happy, likely, pleased, possible, simple, sure, surprised.

> *The recipe is simple **to follow**.*

3 The gerund or the infinitive

Some verbs can be followed by the gerund or the infinitive.

A With no change of meaning

The verbs *start, begin, continue* can be followed by either the gerund or the infinitive, without changing the meaning of the sentence.

> *Jeff continued **to smoke** despite the doctor's advice.*
> *Jeff continued **smoking** despite the doctor's advice.*

B With a slight change of meaning

The meaning of the verbs *like, prefer, hate, love* changes slightly, depending on whether the gerund or infinitive follows them.

1 The gerund is more usual for general statements when the emphasis is on the enjoyment (or not) of the action.

> *Mary prefers **eating out** to **eating** at home.*

2 The infinitive is more usual for more specific statements where extra information is given.

> *Jane prefers **to eat out** because there's no washing-up to do.*

NOTE With the verb *like* + infinitive there is often the added meaning of a preferred alternative.

> *I like **to drive** there* may imply 'I prefer that means of transport to going by train or coach'.

C With a change of meaning

1 The verbs *try, stop, regret, remember, forget, mean, go on* can be followed by the gerund or the infinitive, but with a change in meaning:

Try
+ gerund to experiment in order to achieve an objective.
> *Try **going** to bed earlier and see if that helps.*

+ infinitive to attempt a difficult action.
> *Jill's been trying **to get** a job since she left school, but with no success.*

Stop
+ gerund to finish an activity.
> *Stop **talking** and get on with your work!*

+ infinitive to interrupt one activity in order to do another.
> *Roger stopped **to have** a cup of tea.*

Regret
+ gerund to be sorry about an action in the past.
> *Many people regret **marrying** young.*

+ infinitive to be sorry about what you are going to say.
> *Dr. Taylor regrets **to say** that he is unable to see patients without an appointment.*

Forget / remember
+ gerund to (not) recall an action.
> *I distinctly remember **asking** them to come after lunch.*
> *I won't forget **seeing** Christie win the gold medal as long as I live.*

+ infinitive to (not) do an action you must do.
> *Ann remembered **to lock** all the doors when she went on holiday, but she forgot **to close** the bathroom window.*

Go on
+ gerund to continue an action.
> *I'll go on **loving** you until I die.*

+ infinitive to finish one activity and start another.
> *After seven years of study, Andy went on **to become** a doctor.*

Mean
+ gerund to involve.
> *Dieting usually means **giving up** sweet things.*

+ infinitive to be one's intention.
> *I meant **to send** you a postcard but I forgot to take my address book.*

NOTE The infinitive is only possible with *mean* in perfect and past tenses.

2 The verbs of perception *see* (*watch, notice,* etc), *feel, hear, smell* have a different meaning when they are followed by the infinitive (without *to*) or a participle.

+ participle to experience part of an event
> *I noticed a man **acting** in a strange way.*

+ infinitive without *to* to experience the whole event
> *I heard my sister **come** in at 1 a.m.*

Unit 4

Comparative and superlative adjectives

1 Forms

A Regular adjectives with one syllable

Adjective	Comparative	Superlative
tall	*taller*	*the tallest*
large	*larger*	*the largest*
big	*bigger*	*the biggest*

NOTES

1 Adjectives ending in two consonants or two vowels and a consonant add *-er / -est*.
long, short, bright, smooth, cool, clean, great

2 Adjectives ending in *-e* add *-r / -st*.
nice, late, safe, strange, rude, wide

3 Many adjectives ending in a single vowel + single consonant double the consonant and add *-er / -est.*
fat, thin, flat, sad, wet

B Regular adjectives with two or more syllables

Adjective	Comparative	Superlative
heavy	*heavier*	*the heaviest*
modern	*more modern*	*the most modern*
important	*more important*	*the most important*
common	*commoner*	*the commonest*
	more common	*the most common*

NOTES

1 Adjectives ending in *-y* change *y* to *i* and add *-er / -est*.
happy, dirty, funny, tidy, busy, early, empty, dry

2 Most longer adjectives use *more* and *the most*.
comfortable, independent, insignificant, uninteresting

3 Some two-syllable adjectives can form their comparatives and superlatives in two ways: by adding *-er / -est* or with *more* and *most*.
clever, pleasant, gentle, narrow, shallow, simple, tired

C Irregular adjectives

Adjective	Comparative	Superlative
good	*better*	*the best*
bad	*worse*	*the worst*
old	*older*	*the oldest*
	elder	*the eldest*
far	*farther*	*the farthest*
	further	*the furthest*

2 Comparative and superlative adjectives in context

A More / -er + than
I'm **taller than** my brother.
My brother's **more serious than** me.
I'm **more intelligent than** he is / him.

NOTES
1 If the pronoun after *than* is not followed by a verb, use the object pronoun form – *me, him, us, them*, etc.
2 If the pronoun after *than* is followed by a verb, use the subject pronoun form – *I, he, we, they*, etc.

B The most / -est
I'm **the tallest** student in the class.
My sister's **the most intelligent** student in her school.

C Less + than / the least
That film was **less interesting than** the last one I saw.
It was **the least interesting** film I've seen all year.

3 Ways of qualifying comparative adjectives

a Use these words and phrases to refer to big differences: *far, a lot, much*.
Cars are **a lot faster** and **much more comfortable** than bicycles.
b Use these words and phrases to refer to small differences: *a bit, a little, slightly*.
The weather's **a bit hotter** than it was yesterday.

Comparative and superlative adverbs

1 Regular adverbs

The majority of adverbs are like this:

Adverb	Comparative	Superlative
slowly	*more slowly*	*the most slowly*

2 Irregular adverbs

Adverb	Comparative	Superlative
well	*better*	*the best*
badly	*worse*	*the worst*
little	*less*	*the least*
much	*more*	*the most*

3 Adverbs which are the same as adjectives

Adverb	Comparative	Superlative
fast	*faster*	*the fastest*
hard	*harder*	*the hardest*

Other adverbs of this kind are:
far, long, loud, straight.

The + comparative + the

This construction draws attention to the link between two actions or situations (when one thing happens, another thing follows). A comparative expression in the first clause is always balanced by a comparative expression in the second clause, but several grammatical patterns are possible here:
a adjective . . . adjective.
    The harder a job is, **the more rewarding** I find it.
b adverb . . . adverb.
    The sooner we start, **the quicker** we'll finish.
c adjective . . . adverb or adverb . . . adjective.
    The easier a job is, **the more quickly** I do it.
d *more* (+ noun) . . . *more* (+ noun).
    The more money Jack earned, **the more clothes** he bought.
e *less* (+ clause) . . . *less* (+ uncountable noun).
    fewer (+ plural countable noun).
    The less Bob earned, the **less food / the fewer holidays** he could afford.
f *more* (+ clause) . . . *less* (+ clause).
    The more you sleep, **the less** you do.
Other combinations of these patterns are possible. Here are some more examples.
    The harder Joe worked, **the more** he earned.
    The more he ate, **the fatter** he got.

Notice these points about *the . . . the* sentences:
1 Neither of the two clauses makes sense without the other.
2 In writing, a comma is used to separate the two clauses.
3 Both clauses need a verb.
4 In some expressions with *better*, no verbs are needed.
    Jim   When shall I come round to see you?
    Tim   **The sooner, the better**.

Other comparative constructions

1 as . . . as

This construction can be used with adjectives or adverbs to make comparisons between two things or people.
I'm **as tall as** my brother.
Trains don't travel **as fast as** planes.
In negative sentences *so* can be used instead of the first *as*.
Cats aren't **so friendly as** dogs.

2 Comparative + and + comparative

This construction can be used with adjectives or adverbs to refer to a trend.
Towards the end of film, I became **more and more frightened**.
As the exams approached, I worked **harder and harder**.
Over the last twenty years, televisions have become **less and less expensive**.

So and such

So and *such* are intensifiers which are used to add emphasis.

1 So

a *So* + adjectives (without nouns) and adverbs
    I find Spanish people **so generous**.
    Don't drive **so dangerously**. You'll have an accident.
b *So* is also used with *much, many, little, few*.
    I'm not very hungry. Don't give me **so much** food.
    I'm surprised there were **so few** people at the theatre.

2 Such

a *Such a + adjective + singular countable noun*
   Carmen is **such a kind person**.
b *Such + adjective + plural countable noun*
   Jo and Paul are **such hardworking students**.
c *Such + adjective + uncountable noun*
   When we were in Spain, we had **such warm weather**.
d *Such + a lot (of)*
   During our week in Thessaloniki we met **such a lot of** nice people and had **such a lot of** fun.

3 So / such + that clause

That clauses after *so* and *such* express results or consequences.
   Maria works **so hard that** she's always top of her class.
   John's got **such a high IQ that** he got into university when he was only 14.

Unit 5

Past Time

1 Past simple

We use the past simple tense when we want to refer to an action or event which is **finished** and:
a took place at a specific time and place in the past.
   Judy **went** to Spain in 1989.
b took place over a specific period in the past.
   She **lived** in Spain between 1989 and 1994.
c was habitual during a specific period in the past.
   When Judy lived in Spain, she **ate** dinner at about 10 p.m.

NOTE A past time reference must either be given or understood from the context.

2 Past continuous

We use the past continuous to indicate:
a a continuous event in the past (which may or may not be unfinished).
   Dick **was working** for his uncle when I knew him.
b a temporary event in the past which was in progress before another event took place.
   I'll always remember what I **was doing** when I heard about John Lennon's death.
c an event which started before another event in the past and continued.
   When Neil and Cathy eventually turned up, all the other guests **were** already **eating** their dessert.
d simultaneous, continuous actions in the past.
   While I **was trying** to phone her, she **was trying** to phone me!
e repeated actions occurring over a period of time in the past.
   Before I got my own flat, I **was** always **arguing** with my parents.

3 Past perfect

We use the past perfect to indicate a past event or situation which occurred before another past event or situation.
   I'**d been** awake for quite a while before the alarm rang.
   Although I arrived on time, Mike **had** already **left**.

NOTE A time conjunction sometimes replaces the past perfect to show which of the two past events occurred first. In this case both events can be in the simple past tense.
   Alex **phoned** me **before** he **left**.

4 Past perfect continuous

We use the continuous form when we want to emphasize the continuity and duration of this event.
   Brian **had been trying** to get a job for over a year before he was offered his present one.

5 Present perfect

We use the present perfect tense when we want to talk about:
a an event which started in the past, continues in the present and may continue into the future.
   My parents **have been** married for over twenty years.
b a recent event in the past which has relevance to the present.
   Your taxi **has arrived**.
c an event which happened in the past without saying when it happened (because we do not consider this is important).
   Have you **seen** Jill?
   I'**ve read** Hamlet but I'**ve never seen** it performed.
d an event which happened in the past but in unfinished time (with expressions like *today, this month, this year*, etc).
   I didn't see Tim last week but I'**ve been out** with him twice already this week.

6 Present perfect continuous

We use the continuous form:
a to emphasize the continuity and duration of the event.
   The Smiths **have been living** in the same house ever since they got married.
   The following verbs can be in the present perfect or the present perfect continuous tense with no real change of meaning, although the continuous form is often preferred: *live, wait, drive, smoke, work, stay, study, rain*.
   I'**ve driven** since I was eighteen.
   I'**ve been driving** since I was eighteen.
b to indicate that a continuous activity in the recent past is responsible for a present situation. This activity may or may not be unfinished.
   I'm not crying; I'**ve been peeling** onions.

Participle clauses

A participle clause contains a present participle, e.g. *seeing*, a past participle, e.g. *seen*, or a perfect participle, e.g. *having seen*. It can be used:
a to give more information about a person or thing. It can replace a relative clause.
   The woman **wearing** the funny pink hat is my aunt.
   (replaces *who is wearing*)
   The plane, last **used** in the Gulf War, is now a museum exhibit.
   (replaces *which was last used*)
b to show that the event in the subordinate clause happens at the same time as the event in the main clause. It can replace a time clause.
   Walking down the High Street on Saturday, I saw Paul.
   (replaces *As / When / While I was walking*)
c to indicate that the event in the subordinate clause comes immediately before the event in the main clause.
   Raising their glasses, they wished Darren a happy birthday.

d to show that the event in the main clause occurs because of the event in the subordinate clause. It can replace a reason clause.

> **Not understanding** *Albert's question, I was unable to give him an answer.*
> (replaces *Because /Since I didn't understand*)

e to emphasize that the event in the subordinate clause happened before the event in the main clause.

> **Having spent** *my money on a car, I couldn't afford a holiday.*

Very often the event in the main clause is the result of the event in the subordinate clause.

NOTE The subject of the participle must also be the subject of the other verb. It is not possible to say *Having a bath, the phone rang.*

Unit 6

Conditional sentences

There are four main types of conditional sentence. Each type has a distinctive pattern of verb tenses, and its own meaning.

1 Zero / present conditional (type 0)

A Form

If + present . . . present or imperative

B Meanings

This type of sentence is used to refer to conditions which are always true.

> **If Mike reads** *on the train,* **he feels** *sick.*
> (Every time Mike reads on the train, the same thing happens: he feels sick.)

This type of sentence is also used to refer to scientific facts.

> **If you put** *paper on a fire,* **it burns** *quickly.*

It is also used to give instructions.

> **If** *the phone* **rings**, **answer** *it.*

In zero or present conditional sentences *when* or *whenever* can be used instead of *if.*

2 First conditional (type 1)

A Form

If + present simple . . . *will* future

B Meaning

This type of sentence is used to predict likely or probable results in the future, if a condition is met.

> **If we don't leave** *now,* **we'll miss** *the train.*
> **If we leave** *now,* **we won't need** *to hurry.*

First conditional sentences are often used to express promises, warnings and threats.

> **If you pass** *your exams,* **I'll give** *you a job.*
> **If you don't turn** *that music down,* **you'll go** *deaf.*

C Some modal verbs can be used instead of *will.*

> *If we leave now, we* **may** *catch the train.*
> *If you come to London again, you* **must** *call and see us.*

3 Second conditional (type 2)

A Form

If + past simple . . . *would / could / might*

B Meaning

This type of sentence is used to speculate about imaginary or improbable situations (the implication is that the conditions will *not* be met).

> **You'd feel** *healthier* **if you did** *more exercise.*
> **If you went** *to Africa,* **you'd have** *to have several injections.*
> (It's not likely you'll go to Africa, but it is possible.)

Second conditional sentences can refer to unreal situations.

> **If people didn't drive** *so fast,* **there wouldn't be** *so many fatal accidents.*
> (Actually people do drive fast and there are a lot of fatal accidents.)
> **If I were taller**, **I'd play** *basketball.* (Being taller is impossible for me.)

Second conditional sentences are often used to express advice.

> **If I were** *you,* **I wouldn't drive** *so fast.*

C Might / could

Might and *could* can be used instead of *would* in the main clause of second conditional sentences to show uncertainty.

> *If you did more exercise,* **you might feel** *healthier.*

4 Third conditional (type 3)

A Form

If + past perfect . . . *would / might / could have* + past participle

B Meaning

This type of sentence looks back at the past and speculates about possibilities which didn't happen.

> **If I'd had** *your address,* **I'd have sent** *you a postcard.*
> (I didn't have your address, so I didn't send you a postcard.)
> **You might not have crashed** *into the bus* **if you'd been driving** *more slowly.*

NOTE When the *if* clause comes before the main clause, it is followed by a comma. When the *if* clause comes after the main clause, there is no comma between the clauses.

5 Mixed conditional sentences

A Form

If + past perfect . . . *would / could / might*

B Meaning

This type of sentence, which is a mixture of a third conditional sentence and a second conditional sentence, links a completed past action with a present result.

> **If I hadn't broken** *my leg,* **I would go** *on holiday with you.*
> **I'd have** *a better job now,* **if I'd worked** *harder when I was at school.*

6 Other ways of introducing conditions

A Unless

Unless can sometimes be used instead of *if not.*

> **Unless** *we leave now, we'll miss the train.*
> (If we don't leave now, we'll miss the train.)

B As long as

As long as is used to emphasize a condition.

> *I'll lend you the money you need* **as long as** *you promise not to waste it.*

C Provided (that)

Provided (that)… and *Providing (that)…* mean 'on condition that' and are slightly more formal than *if*.

> *You can come on holiday with us **provided that** you do some of the cooking.*

Unit 7

Relative clauses

1 Form and use

a A relative clause gives extra information.

b It is introduced by a relative pronoun: *who (whom), which, that, whose* or they may be no relative pronoun, Ø.

c The choice of relative pronoun depends on whether:
   - it is the *subject* or *object* or *possessive* of a relative clause.
   - it refers to a *person* or *thing*.
   - the relative clause is *defining* or *non-defining*

d Relative clauses are common in spoken and written English. However, *non-defining* relative clauses are more common in written English than in spoken English.

2 Defining and non-defining clauses

a The information given in a defining relative clause is *essential* to the meaning of the sentence.
   > *The man **who lives at number 36** has been arrested.*
   > *The fingerprints **that were found on the gun** were his.*
   A defining relative clause makes clear *which* person or thing we are talking about.

b The information given in a non-defining relative clause is *not* essential to the meaning of the sentence.
   > *Mr. White, **who lives at number 36,** has been arrested.*

c Punctuation is important in *non-defining* relative clauses. A comma is put before the relative pronoun and at the end of the clause, unless this is also the end of the sentence. In *defining* relative clauses there are no commas.

3 Relative pronouns

A In defining relative clauses

		Person	Thing
1	Subject	*who (that)*	*that (which)*
2	Object	*Ø (that, who, whom)*	*Ø (that, which)*
3	Possessive	*whose*	*whose (of which)*

NOTE The pronouns in brackets are less commonly used.

1 As subject
   > *People **who (that)** go to university are not necessarily more intelligent than people who don't.*
   > *The universities **that (which)** opened in the sixties were all campus universities.*
   Who and *which* are more usual in writing. *That* is more usual in speech when referring to things.

2 As object
   > *That's the woman **(Ø, that, who, whom)** I saw.*
   > *It was her car **(Ø, that, which)** Philip crashed into.*
   The relative pronoun is frequently omitted, particularly in speech. *Whom* is formal and is used mainly in writing.

3 As possessive
   > *That's the man **whose** house was burgled last week.*
   > *We arranged to meet at a place **whose** location (the location **of which**) was to be kept secret.*

NOTE We usually use *that* (not *which*) after the following words: *all, any(thing), every(thing), few, little, many, much, no(thing), none, some(thing)*, and after superlatives. When the pronoun refers to the object, *that* can be omitted.
   > *It was something **that** could have happened to anyone.*
   > *It was the most difficult exam **(that)** I'd ever taken.*

B In non-defining relative clauses

		Person	Thing
1	Subject	*who*	*which*
2	Object	*who(m)*	*which*
3	Possessive	*whose*	*whose (of which)*

1 As subject
   > *Jim Kerr, **who** is lead singer with the rock band 'Simple Minds', comes from Edinburgh.*
   > *St. Andrews University, **which** is the oldest university in Scotland, is the Scottish equivalent of Oxford.*

2 As object
   > *Alice asked Richard Gere, **who (whom)** she had immediately recognized, for his autograph.*
   > *Mr James had been driving a brand-new car, **which** his father had given him for his birthday.*

NOTE *That* can never be used in non-defining clauses.

3 As possessive
   > *The author, **whose** latest novel is a bestseller, spent the afternoon signing copies of his book.*
   > *The restaurant, **whose** name he could not remember, was one of the best he had ever eaten at.*

NOTES

1 In non-defining relative clauses, *which* can refer to a whole clause.
   > *He climbed the mountain wearing only a T-shirt and trainers, **which** was a stupid thing to do.*

2 In non-defining relative clauses, after numbers and words like *many, most, neither, some*, we use *of* before *whom* and *which*.
   > *Dozens of people had been invited, most **of whom** I knew.*

4 *Where, why* and *when*

Where, why and *when* can be used instead of a relative pronoun after a noun which refers to a place, a time or a reason.

a In defining relative clauses *why* and *when* can be omitted.
   > *I'd like to live in a country **where** it's summer all year round.*
   > *Do you know the reason **(why)** Kate's changed her mind?*
   > *June is the month **(when)** many couples get married.*

b In non-defining relative clauses *when, where* and *why* cannot be omitted.
   > *Aileen was brought up in Scotland, **where** she was born, but she emigrated after her marriage.*
   > *The town is quieter after lunch, **when** everyone is having a siesta.*

5 Relative clauses and prepositions

A preposition can either come before the relative pronoun (more usual in formal English) or at the end of the relative clause (more usual in informal English).

The Hilton Hotel, at which we stayed while we were in New York, is expensive.

The Hilton Hotel, which we stayed at while we were in New York, is expensive.

A Defining relative clauses

	Formal	Informal
Person	*whom*	Ø
Thing	*which*	Ø

The man to whom I spoke gave me different information.
The man I spoke to gave me different information.
The car in which the robbers got away had been stolen.
The car the robbers got away in had been stolen.

B Non-defining relative clauses

	Formal	Informal
Person	*whom*	*who*
Thing	*which*	*which*

The hotel manager, to whom I spoke about my dissatisfaction, suggested I write to you.
The hotel manager, who I spoke to about my dissatisfaction, suggested I call you.

Modifying adjectives and adverbs

A Some adjectives and adverbs can be used to intensify or reduce the strength of gradable adjectives and adverbs like *big* and *fast*. The most common modifying adverbs, in order of strength, are *very*, *rather*, *quite* and *fairly*.

Norman did it fairly quickly.
That book was quite interesting.

The following words can be used instead of *very* : *extremely*, *really*, *incredibly*, *terribly*. Of these, only *extremely* is used in formal English. *Pretty* can be used as an alternative to *rather*.

B The meaning of these words depends on the intonation.
1 *My dad's fairly active for a man of 60.* (Weak stress on *fairly*, strong stress on *active*) = more active than you would expect a man that age to be.
2 *My dad's fairly active for a man of 60.* (Equal stress on both words) = reasonably active.
3 *My dad's fairly active for a man of 60.* (Strong stress on *fairly*) = active but not especially so.

C *Rather* and *quite*
1 *Rather* has a similar meaning to *quite* and *fairly* but is often used with adjectives and adverbs which have the idea of something bad, or which the user disapproves of.
   Michael's rather old for her.
With approving adjectives and adverbs and rising intonation it means *better than expected*.
   I don't usually like Spielberg films, but his latest is rather good.
2 *Quite* can be used with ungradable adjectives like *enormous* and *incredible*, and strong gradable adjectives like *essential* to mean *absolutely* or *totally*.
   Edmund's journey was quite unnecessary.
3 *Rather* and *quite* can also be used with nouns.
   We had quite a good meal.

Unit 8

Speech

1 Direct speech

We can report what someone has said in two ways.
a We can report their actual words.
b We can report the idea they expressed.
When we report a person's actual words in writing, we put speech marks on either side of the words and use an appropriate verb, e.g. *say, tell, ask*.
   'I'll be late home tomorrow,' Bob said.
See the Terminology section on page 199 for notes on the use of punctuation in direct speech.

2 Reported speech

When we report the idea and not the actual words that a person says we often have to make certain changes. These changes are usually to verb tenses, pronouns, word order, and time and place references.

3 Reported statements

A Changes in verb tenses
When the reporting verb is in the past tense, e.g. *said*, we usually move the tenses in the sentence we are reporting one step back in time.

Direct speech	Reported speech
Present simple ——————⟶	Past simple
'I'm a nurse,' she said.	*She said she was a nurse.*
Present continuous ————⟶	Past continuous
'I'm not going,' he said.	*He said he wasn't going.*
Past simple ——————————⟶	Past perfect
'Tony did it,' she said.	*She said Tony had done it.*
Present perfect ——————⟶	Past perfect
'I haven't read it,' she said.	*She said she hadn't read it.*
Past continuous ————————⟶	Past perfect continuous
'I was lying,' he said	*He said he'd been lying.*
'Will' future ————————⟶	Would
'I'll get it,' she said.	*She said she would get it.*
Can ——————————————⟶	Could
'I can speak French,' he said.	*He said he could speak French.*
May ——————————————⟶	Might
'I may be late,' she said.	*She said she might be late.*
Must ——————————————⟶	Had to
'I must go,' he said.	*He said he had to go.*

NOTE The past perfect and the modals *might, ought to, could, should* and *would* do not change in reported speech.

B No changes in verb tenses
1 When the reporting verb is in the present tense, e.g. *says*, we do not change the tense of the original verb. For example when we are reading what someone says in a newspaper or letter, e.g. *Darren says he's been too busy to write before*, or when we are passing on a message, e.g. *Lucy says she'll be late.*
2 When the reporting verb is in the past tense and we want to emphasize that the statement is still true we can keep the same tense if we wish.
   'Bill is my cousin' She said Bill is her cousin.

C Changes in time and place words

Some typical changes that may have to be made are:

Direct speech	Reported speech
today	*that day*
tomorrow	*the next day, the following day*
yesterday	*the previous day, the day before*
two days ago	*two days before, two days earlier*
now	*then*
here	*there*
come	*go*

Unless time and place words are reported at the same time and in the same place as they were originally said, they change.

'Marie phoned yesterday.' (said on Monday) *He said (that)*
Marie had phoned two days ago / on Sunday. (said on Tuesday)

D Other changes

1 Pronouns may change when we are reporting speech. This depends on who is reporting.
'I'll give *you* a lift.' (Jack to Barbara)
Jack said **he** *would give* **me** *a lift.* (Barbara to Peter)

2 The determiners *this, that, these, those* may change to *the*.
'**These** jeans are too tight,' Cyril said.
Cyril said **the** *jeans were too tight.*

3 The pronouns *this* and *that* may change to *it*.
'Give me **that**!' Jayne said.
Jayne told me to give **it** *to her.*

E Reporting verbs

We can use the verbs *say* and *tell* to report statements. The structure after these verbs is *say (that)* + clause:
Richard **said (that) he would be late**.
and *tell someone (that)* + clause:
Richard **told me (that) he would be late**.
That is frequently omitted in spoken English.

4 Reported questions

A Changes

We make the same changes to verb tenses, time and place words and pronouns as we do when we report statements. We also change the form of the original question into a statement and omit auxiliary verbs (*do, does, did*) and question marks.
'When are you arriving?'
He asked me when I was arriving.
If there is no question word in the original we must use *if* or *whether* (*if . . . or not*).
'Do you understand?'
He asked her if / whether she understood.

B Reporting verbs

To report questions we can use the verb *ask* or the structure *want to know*.
'Are you enjoying yourself?' Mr Jones asked.
Mr Jones **wanted to know** *if I was enjoying myself.*

5 Reported functions

A Reporting advice, commands, requests and warnings

We can report these kinds of speech using the verbs *advise, tell, ask* and *warn* + personal object pronoun + infinitive.
'You really should stop!' (advice)
She **advised me to** *stop.*
'Don't interrupt me!' (command)
He **told me not to** *interrupt him.*

'Could you close the door please?' (request)
She **asked me to** *close the door.*
'If you tell anyone, I'll . . . !' (warning)
She **warned me not to** *tell anyone.*

NOTES

1 The structure after *ask* is different when we are reporting a request or a question.
'Can you remind me please?' (request)
He **asked me to** *remind him.*
'Can you come tomorrow?' (question)
She **asked me if I could** *come the next day.*

2 The structure after *tell* is different when we are reporting a command or a statement.
'Come on! Hurry up!' (command)
She **told us to** *hurry up.*
'It doesn't start till 8.' (statement)
He **told us (that)** *it didn't start until 8.*

B Reporting suggestions

We can report suggestions with the verb *suggest* + clause.
So, for example, to report 'Let's stay in.' :
She suggested that we (should) stay in.
She suggested that we stayed in.
She suggested staying in.

NOTE You cannot use the infinitive in this structure.

Unit 9

1 Making suggestions

Some common expressions used for making suggestions are:
Why don't you [1] **/ we** [2] *go to the USA for your / our holiday?*
You [1] **/ we** [2] *could visit New York while you're / we're there.*
Let's [2] *go to the travel agent's this afternoon to book our ticket.*
What / How [3] *about phoning first to see how much it is?*
I suggest you [1] **/ we** [2] *think about it a bit more first.*

NOTES

1 These expressions do not include the speaker.
2 These expressions include the speaker.
3 These expressions could (but may not) include the speaker.

2 Giving advice

Here are some ways of expressing advice.
I don't think you should *eat so much.*
You ought to *eat less fast food.*
You ought not to *eat so much fast food.*
You shouldn't *drink so much – it's not good for you.*
If I were you, I'd *go on a diet.*
If I were in your position / shoes, I'd *do more exercise.*
You'd better *be careful what you eat.*
You'd better not *eat any more sweets. You'll be sick!*
Whatever you do, don't *eat any more cake – it's very fattening.*

3 Giving warnings

a Here are some expressions used for giving warnings.
Don't *play around with fireworks,* **or you might / could** *be badly injured.*
Look out! Be careful!

b *Otherwise* can be used instead of *or* to warn what will happen if advice is not followed.
Work hard **otherwise** *you'll fail your exam.*

4 Regrets and criticisms

Should have + past participle is often used to express regrets or criticisms about past actions.

> *I **shouldn't have spent** so much money at the weekend. (regret)*
> *You **should have remembered** you brother's birthday.*
> *(criticism)*

NOTE *ought (not) to have* can be used instead of *should have*.

5 Use of *should, ought to, could*

A Should
1 Advice
> *You **should** go and see Casablanca – it's a brilliant old film.*
2 Obligations
> *I **should** get my father a card – it's his birthday tomorrow.*
3 Probability
> *If the train's on time, **we should** arrive at 3.30.*
> (It is likely / probable that we will arrive at 3.30.)

B Ought to
1 Advice
> *You **ought** [1] **to** stop smoking – it's very bad for you.*
2 Obligations
> *I really **ought** [2] **to** pay the telephone bill tomorrow.*
3 Theory
> *John **ought to** be here by now [3] – I hope he hasn't had an accident.*

NOTES
1 *Ought to* expresses less personal advice than *should*.
2 *Ought to* here indicates that the speaker probably won't pay the bill tomorrow.
3 *Ought to* here means *was due to* or that it was expected.

C Could
1 Suggestions
> *You **could** call a taxi.*
2 Past ability
> *When I was five **I could** swim 500 metres.*
3 Possibility
> *My car **could** break down at any time – it's very old.*
4 Request for permission
> ***Could I** come in please?*

Contrasting ideas

Here are the most common ways of contrasting ideas.

1 But

But is a conjunction which contrasts ideas in one sentence.
> *I want to leave school **but** my parents won't let me.*

2 However

However contrasts ideas in different sentences.
> *My parents want me to go to college. **However**, I have other ideas.*

However is most commonly used at the beginning of a sentence, but it can also come in the middle or at the end.
> ***However**, I have other ideas.*
> *I, **however**, have other ideas.*
> *I have other ideas, **however**.*

3 Despite / in spite of

Despite can be used to contrast ideas in one sentence.
a *Despite* + noun or gerund
> ***Despite** my headache, I took the exam.**

> ***Despite** feeling ill, I took the exam.*
b *Despite* the fact (that) + clause
> ***Despite** the fact that I felt ill, I took the exam.*

In all the above sentences, *despite* can be replaced by *in spite of*.

* **NOTE** It is only correct to use *despite* + *-ing* when the subject of the *-ing* form is the same as the subject of the verb in the main clause. You cannot say *Despite speaking more slowly, I still couldn't understand him.*

4 Although

Although is a conjunction which is used to contrast ideas in one sentence. It can be used before or after the main clause.
> ***Although** it was raining hard, we took the dog for a walk.*
> *We took the dog for a walk, **although** it was raining hard.*

Even though is often used in conversation instead of *although*. It puts greater emphasis on the contrast between the ideas.

Unit 10

Modal verbs

1 Obligation and necessity

A Must

Must + infinitive is used for strong obligations which express the authority of the speaker or writer. So, it is used:
1 for formal rules or laws.
> *Passengers **must** fasten their seat belts for take-off.*
2 for suggestions, advice or recommendations that the speaker or writer feels strongly about.
> *You **must** come to my party. Everyone's going to be there.*

B Have to

Have to + infinitive is used for strong obligations which express the authority of a third person, rather than the speaker or writer. So, it is used:
1 when the speaker wants to show they are not responsible for imposing the obligation, or do not agree with it.
> *I'll be late home tonight. I **have to** work late. My boss said so.*
2 when the speaker or writer is reminding someone about a rule or law.
> *I'm sorry, but you **have to** wear a seat belt in the back of cars now.*

C Have got to

Have got to is a more informal than *have to*. So, it is often used:
1 for direct commands.
> *You **'ve got to** stop wasting your money.*
2 for emphasis.
> *I don't care how hard I have to work, I**'ve** just **got to** pass this time.*

D Need to

Need to is used to express needs or necessities, rather than strict obligations.
> *If we're going to work together I **need to** know about your background and experience.*

E Negatives
1 *Mustn't* expresses prohibition (negative rules and laws or strong advice).
> *Drivers **must not** exceed the speed limit.*
> *You **mustn't** blame yourself. It's not your fault.*

2 *Do not have to / have not got to* express lack of obligation or necessity.

> You **don't have to** wear a uniform, but you can if you like.

3 *Do not need to / needn't* + infinitive are used to express lack of obligation or necessity and are similar in meaning to *do not have to*.

> There are no lessons tomorrow, so I **don't need to** get up early.
> You **needn't** tell me your phone number if you don't want to.

4 *Did not need to* + infinitive means 'It was not necessary, so we didn't do it'.

> The train was delayed so we **didn't need to** hurry.

5 *Needn't have* + past participle means 'It was not necessary, but we did it in spite of this'.

> We had to wait for half an hour on the platform because the train was delayed. We **needn't have** hurried after all.

2 Permission and prohibition

A *Can / can't*

This is one of the commonest ways of expressing permission and prohibition.

> **Can I** use the phone, please?
> In Spain **you can't** leave school until the age of 16.

NOTE

May I . . . ? means the same as *Can I . . . ?*, but is more formal and more polite.

B Other expressions of permission

> **You're allowed to buy** cigarettes when you're 18.
> We **were only permitted to take** photographs in certain places.
> My parents **let me stay out** late at weekends.

C Other expressions of prohibition

> You **aren't allowed to** go abroad without a passport.
> Smoking **is not permitted** in most cinemas.
> You **are not permitted to** smoke in this theatre.
> People **are forbidden to** smoke on the Underground.
> The workers **have been prohibited from** striking.
> Nigel **has been banned from** driving for six months.

Adverbs

1 Types of adverb

There are six main types of adverb or adverb phrase:

A Adverbs that describe **how** something is done (**manner**)
quickly / badly / quietly / well / forwards / in a hurry

B Adverbs that describe **where** something is done (**place**)
abroad / upstairs / somewhere / on the table

C Adverbs that describe **when** something happens (**time**)
tomorrow / on Friday / now / for six months / a year later

D Adverbs that describe **how often** something happens (**frequency**)
sometimes / often / never / hardly ever

E Adverbs that describe to what extent something is true (**degree**)
quite / almost / very / rather / fairly

F Adverbs that express an **opinion** (**viewpoint**)
obviously / surprisingly / actually / amazingly

2 Position of adverbs in sentences

Here are some useful guidelines.

A Adverbs of manner, place and time

1 These are usually placed towards the end of sentences.

> I knew I'd left my shoes **upstairs**.
> I got home **late**, so I opened the door **quietly**.

2 If two or three adverbs of manner, place or time are used in the same sentence, they are usually put in this order: **manner-place-time**.

> I waited **patiently downstairs all afternoon**.

3 Some adverbs and adverb phrases of manner, place and time can start a sentence for emphasis.

> **Quietly** I opened the door.
> **Tomorrow** I'm going to the dentist's.

4 Adverbs of manner, place and time cannot be placed between a verb and its object. So, you cannot say: *I opened* **quietly** *the door.*

B Adverbs of frequency

1 When used with simple verb tenses, frequency adverbs are placed before the verb.

> I **always** walk to work.

2 When used with auxiliary verbs, frequency adverbs are placed after the first auxiliary verb.

> I've **never** seen a live football match.

3 Frequency adverbs always come after the verb **to be**.

> Wherever I go, I'm **always** late.

4 Some frequency adverbs can start a sentence for emphasis. The most common are: *frequently / occasionally / sometimes / usually / (very/quite) often.*

> **Sometimes** I stay up all night.

C Adverbs of degree

These are usually placed before the words they modify.

> It's **almost** six o'clock.
> The film was **quite** interesting.

D Adverbs expressing a viewpoint

These are often placed at the beginning of sentences.

> **Amazingly** it didn't rain all weekend.

3 Too, enough, very

A *Too*

Too means *more than is needed or wanted* and is used in these ways:

1 *Too* + adjective or adverb

> It's **too hot** in here. Can I open a window?
> You're driving **too fast**. Slow down.

2 *Too* + adjective or adverb + *for*

> This food is **too hot for** me. I can't eat it, I'm afraid.
> You're walking **too slowly for** me. Hurry up!

3 *Too* + adjective or adverb (+ *for* + object) + *to* + verb

> My father was **too ill to look after** himself.
> That film was **too frightening for us to watch**. That's why we left before the end.

4 *Too* + quantifier (+ noun)

> I ate **too much (food)** at lunchtime, so I don't feel hungry now.
> I'll never finish the exam. There's **too little time** left.

B Enough

Enough means *sufficient / as much as is needed* and is used in these ways:

1 Adjective or adverb + *enough*
  Holidays are never **long enough**.
  I didn't go to bed **early enough** *last night.*
2 Adjective or adverb + *enough* + *for* + noun or pronoun
  My car isn't **big enough for the whole family**.
3 Adjective or adverb + *enough* + *to* + verb
  My parents didn't think we were **old enough to get** *married.*

C Very

Very simply gives emphasis and is used in these ways:
1 *Very* + adjective
  Concorde is a **very fast** *plane.*
2 *Very* + adverb
  I can walk **very quickly**.
3 *Very* + quantifier
  I'm on a diet, so I'm eating **very little**.

D Too, enough or very

Compare these three sentences:
  The holidays are **very long**. (We don't know how the speaker feels about this.)
  The holidays are **too long**. (The speaker doesn't like this.)
  The holidays are **long enough**. (This is just right.)

Adjective order

Adjectives placed in front of the noun they describe are usually in the following order.
1 **your opinion** (enjoyable / horrible / boring)
  an **enjoyable** *film*
2 **dimension (size)** (*large / tiny / heavy*)
  a disgusting **little** *insect*
3 **age** (*old / young / modern*)
  a beautiful tall **young** *woman*
4 **shape** (*round / square / rectangular*)
  a large old **oval** *painting*
5 **colour** (*green / black / red*)
  a small square **black and white** *photograph*
6 **where from** (*French / Russian / Danish*)
  an ugly modern **American** *car*
7 **material made of** (*silver / paper / plastic*)
  a pink Japanese **silk** *blouse*

It is unusual to use more than three adjectives in front of a noun.

Unit 11

Certainties and possibilities

1 Indicating attitudes to facts

If we are absolutely sure of our facts, we generally use a full verb to express this certainty.
  Craig **wasn't** *at home yesterday afternoon.*
If we are not absolutely sure of our facts, we can use the modal verbs *must, can't, may, might, could* to indicate how sure we are.

2 Expressing near certainty

If we are almost sure of our facts, and this certainty is based on evidence, we can make statements using *must* or *can't*.

A If we are talking about a present situation we use *must* or *can't* + infinitive without *to*.
  My doctor **must be** *married. She wears a wedding ring.* (I am almost certain she is married.)
  Angus **can't be** *English. He's got a Scottish accent.* (I am almost certain he isn't English.)
We can also use the continuous form of the verb.
  Virginia **must be going** *to play tennis. She's carrying a racket.* (I am almost certain she is going to play tennis.)

B If we are talking about a past situation we use *must* or *can't* + *have* + past participle.
  Sandra **must have passed** *her driving test because I saw her driving a car on her own.* (I am almost certain she has passed her test.)
  Fiona and Neil **can't have enjoyed** *their holiday because they haven't said anything about it.* (I am almost certain they didn't enjoy their holiday.)
We can also use the continuous form of the verb.
  I'm sorry I'm late. You **must have been waiting** *for ages!*

NOTE The negative of *must* in this case is *can't*, not *mustn't*.

3 Expressing possibility

If we are not sure of our facts but we think that they are possibilities, we can make statements using *could, may* or *might*.
a If we are talking about a present situation we use *could, may, might* + infinitive without *to*.
  Paula **could be** *on holiday.* (Maybe she's on holiday.)
  Claude **may have** *flu.* (Perhaps he's got flu.)
b If we are talking about a past situation we use *could, may, might* + *have* + past participle.
  Freda **might have overslept**. (It's possible that she's over slept.)
c It is also possible to use continuous forms.
  Julie **might be visiting** *her mother .*
  The missing girl **may have been wearing** *a blue skirt.*

NOTES
1 There is no real difference in meaning between *may, might* and *could*.
2 The negative forms of *may* and *might* are *may not* and *might not*. It is not usual to use a contracted form.
  The defendant **may not be telling** *the truth.* (It's possible that he isn't telling the truth.)
3 The negative form of *could* is *couldn't*. It's meaning is similar to *can't*.
  He **couldn't be lying**. (I am almost certain he isn't lying.)

Wishes

1 Use

We use *wish* to talk about situations we would like to change but can't either because they are outside our control or because they are in the past.

2 Tenses

The tense of the verb after *wish* does not correspond to the time we are wishing about; it changes. The verb tense is one step back in time (as in reported speech. See page 207).

A A wish about a present or future situation is expressed with a past tense.

Situation	Wish
I'm an only child	I wish I **wasn't** an only child.
I can't drive	I wish I **could** drive.
Rod isn't coming to the party	I wish Rod **was coming**.

NOTE In formal English we say I / he / she / it were / weren't.

B A wish about a past situation is expressed with a past perfect tense.

Situation	Wish
I've lost my best pen	I wish I **hadn't lost** it.
I didn't remember	I wish I'**d remembered**.

3 Wish . . . would.

We use wish . . . would:

a when we want to complain about a present situation.

Situation	Wish
A dog is barking	I **wish** that dog **would** stop barking!
The road is icy	I **wish** you **wouldn't** drive so fast

NOTE We can't say I wish I would . . .

b when we are impatient for an event outside our control to happen.

Situation	Wish
You're waiting for the bus	I wish the bus **would come**.

NOTES

1 It is not possible to use wish . . . would with the verb be unless we are complaining. We say I wish it were Friday and not I wish it would be Friday.

2 If we want a future event to happen or not happen, and this event is possible and not just a desire, we use the verb hope + present simple.

> I hope I pass my exams.

3 If only can often be used in place of wish with no real change of meaning.

> If only Sue was here. She'd know what to do.

Unit 12

The passive

1 Verbs that can be used in the passive

Most transitive verbs can be used in the passive. A transitive verb is a verb which has an object, e.g. catch.

> The police **caught the thief.**

Intransitive verbs cannot be used in the passive. An intransitive verb is a verb which does not have an object, e.g. fall.

> Rodney **fell** and hurt his leg.

2 Form of the passive

The passive is formed with the verb be in the appropriate tense + the past participle of the main verb. In the case of modals, e.g. could, must, it is formed with the modal + be + past participle.

Tense	Subject	Verb 'be'	Past Participle
present simple	Letters	are	delivered twice a day.
present continuous	Redmond	is being	watched.
past simple	The Loch Ness Monster	was (first)	seen in 565 A.D.
past continuous	Our hotel room	was being	cleaned when we arrived.
present perfect	Antiques worth over £10,000	have been	stolen.
past perfect	They	had been	warned about the danger.
future	You	will be	paid on Friday.
modals	Food	should be	eaten before the sell-by date.

NOTE In informal English get can sometimes be used instead of be to form the passive. The agent is not generally mentioned.

> Nigel **got stopped** for speeding.

3 Choosing active or passive form

In an active sentence, the subject is the person or thing that does the action.

> **Liverpool** beat Manchester United.

In a passive sentence, the subject of the verb is the person or thing affected by the action.

> **Manchester United** were beaten by Liverpool.

When we want to focus on the person or thing **affected** by the action instead of the **doer** of the action (the agent) we use the passive.

4 Including the agent (doer)

When we use the passive we can choose to include the agent or not. The agent is the person or thing responsible for the action.

> The record is held **by Carl Lewis**.

We do not include the agent:

a when the agent is not important.
   We do not say: Trespassers will be prosecuted **by the landowner**.

b when we do not know who the agent is and would have to use the words 'somebody' or 'a person'.
   We do not say: My car has been stolen **by somebody**.

c when the agent is obvious.
   We do not say: The thief was sentenced to five years imprisonment **by the judge**.

d when the agent has already been mentioned.
   We do not say: Some of Stephen King's books have been written **by him** under the pseudonym Richard Bachman.

5 Verbs with two objects

Some verbs can have two objects – a direct object (DO) and an indirect object (IO).

> Lady Markham's late husband had given **the painting** (DO) **to the gallery** (IO).
> Lady Markham's late husband had given **the gallery** (IO) **the painting** (DO).

Both objects can be the subject of the passive verb.

> **The painting** had been given to the gallery by her late husband.
> **The gallery** had been given the painting by her late husband.

When one of the objects is a person, it is more usual for this to be the subject.

>**Bobby** *was given a new bike for his birthday.*
>
>and not   *A new bike was given to Bobby for his birthday.*

6 Passive constructions with the infinitive

a When we want to pass on information but we do not know whether the information is true or not, or we do not want to say where the information came from, we can use the passive form of these verbs *think, believe, report, consider, know, say, expect* followed by the infinitive.

b When the information is about a present situation, we use the passive + infinitive.

>*The Queen* **is believed to be** *one of the richest people in the world.*
>
>*Mr Smith* **is thought to be staying** *with friends.*

c When the information is about something in the past, we use the passive + the past infinitive (*to have* + past participle).

>*Cher* **is said to have had** *a face-lift.*

Unit 13

Talking about ability

1 *Can, be able to*

Can and *be able to* are the verbs most commonly used to express ability. Sometimes it is possible to use either verb without changing the meaning of the sentence. Sometimes, however, we have to use *be able to* as there is no appropriate form of *can*.

Infinitive	——	*to be able to*
Present	*can*	*am / is / are able to*
Future	——	*will be able to*
Past	*could*	*was / were able to*
Present perfect	——	*have / has been able to*

See **4** below for uses of *could*.

2 Present ability

A To talk about a general ability in the present both forms are possible but *can* is more usual.

>*Adrian* **can** *cook really well.*
>
>*(He* **is able to** *cook really well)*

B To talk about a learned ability in the present *can* is more usual. *Know how to* can be used as an alternative to *can*.

>**Can** *you play chess?*
>
>*Do you* **know how to** *play chess?*

3 Future ability

To talk about an ability in the future we use the future form of *be able to*.

>**Will I be able to** *play better after I've had some lessons?*

4 Past ability

A To talk about a general ability in the past both forms are possible.

>*Before his accident, Ben* **could** *run as fast as the best of them.*
>
>*Before his accident, Ben* **was able to** *run as fast as the best of them.*

B To talk about an ability to do something in the past on one particular occasion, it is not possible to use *could*. We must use the past tense of *be able* or *manage* + infinitive or *succeed in* + *-ing*.

>*Although she had lost a lot of blood, the doctors* **were able to save** *the girl's life.*
>
>*Despite the difficult conditions, the doctors* **managed to perform** *the operation successfully and* **succeeded in saving** *the man's leg.*

NOTE If the event was unsuccessful, it is possible to use *couldn't* as well as the past tense forms of *be able to, manage to, succeed in*.

>*Although he did his best, he* **couldn't** *finish it in time.*

5 'Conditional' ability

A To talk about a hypothetical ability in the present or future we can use *could* or *would be able to*.

>*I* **could** *probably jump higher if I had longer legs.*
>
>*I* **would** *probably* **be able to** *play better if I concentrated more.*

B To talk about a hypothetical ability in the past we usually use *could* + *have* + past participle although we can also use *would have been able to*.

>*Even if he'd got into the final, he* **couldn't have beaten** *Christie.*
>
>*Even if he'd run faster than he'd ever run, he* **wouldn't have been able to beat** *Christie.*

6 Other structures used to talk about ability

A To talk about aptitude and capacity for doing something we can use *be capable of* + *-ing*.

>*Eddie* **is** *certainly* **capable of breaking** *the world record.*

B To talk about how well we do something we can use the structure *be good (brilliant* etc)/ *bad (terrible* etc) *at* + noun or gerund.

>*I* **have** *never* **been good at sports**.
>
>*I* **was** *particularly* **bad at running**.

Question tags

1 Form

A A question tag consists of the verb *be* or an auxiliary (*do, have*) or modal auxiliary (e.g. *can, should*) + subject pronoun. It is added to an affirmative or negative statement.

B As a general rule, if the statement is in the affirmative then the question tag goes in the negative and vice-versa.

>*It's 5 o'clock,* **isn't it?**
>
>*There* **aren't** *enough glasses,* **are there?**

C If there is an auxiliary verb or a modal auxiliary verb or *be* in the statement, it is repeated in the question tag.

>*You* **haven't** *seen Stuart,* **have you?**
>
>*You* **can** *come,* **can't you?**
>
>*I'm a bit early,* **aren't I?**

D If there is a full verb in the statement, the auxiliary verb *do* is used in the question tag.

>*His plane* **arrives** *at 10 p.m.,* **doesn't it?**
>
>*It* **snowed** *this time last year,* **didn't it?**

NOTE When *have* is a full verb and not an auxiliary verb we use the auxiliary *do* in the question tag and not *have*.

>*They* **had** *a good time,* **didn't they?**

E After imperatives we can use the following forms: *will you? would you? can you? could you?*

>*Take that to Mary,* **will you?** (**would you?** is more formal)

*Speak up, **can you?*** (***could you?*** is more formal)
The effect of the question tag here is similar to 'please'.

NOTE After a negative imperative only *will you?* is possible.
*Don't make a mess, **will you?***

F After statements containing negative words like *nothing,
nobody, none,* we use an affirmative question tag.
*Nothing was stolen, **was it?***
*Nobody was hurt, **were they?***

NOTE With words like *nobody, somebody* we use the plural
pronoun *they.*

2 Use and intonation

We usually use question tags:

a to ask for confirmation of something. This is like a real
question, and the question tag is said with rising
intonation.
David's married, isn't he? (I think he is married but I want
you to answer 'Yes he is' or 'No he isn't'.)
He isn't arriving tomorrow, is he? (I didn't think he was
arriving tomorrow but I'm not sure and I want
confirmation of when he is arriving.)

b to ask other people if they agree with us. In this case the
question tag is said with falling intonation.
Alf's a good pianist, isn't he? (I expect you to say 'Yes'.)
You don't know Tom, do you? (I expect you to say 'No'.)

Unit 14

Cause and effect

1 *Make*

The verb *make*, which means *to cause to (be)*, is used in two
different ways.

a *Make* + object + adjective
*Going to bed late will **make you overtired**.*
*Exercise **makes you fit**.*

b *Make* + object + infinitive (without *to*)
*Aerobic exercise **makes your heart beat** faster.*
*Horror films **make me laugh**.*

NOTE If the subject of the verb is a person, *make* often means
to force or compel.
*My father **made me finish** my homework.*
*The customs officer **made me empty** my suitcase.*

2 Other expressions of cause and effect

a *Bring about* + object
*Going to India **has brought about a complete change** in the
way he looks at the world.*

b *Cause* + object / *cause* + object + *to* + verb
*Too much exercise **can cause** insomnia.*
*Seeing that terrible accident **has caused him to pay more
attention** to his own driving.*

c *Result in* + noun
*Getting plenty of rest before an exam **can result in an
improved performance**.*

d *Lead to* + noun
*Her inability to express herself clearly **has led to all kinds of
problems**.*

Expressing purpose

Here are some common ways of talking about purpose.

1 *To* + infinitive
*People work **to earn** money.*

2 *In order to* + infinitive
*Nick went to Germany **in order to learn** the language.*
***In order not to be** recognized, Martin wore a disguise.*

3 *So as to* + infinitive
*William went into town by bus **so as to avoid** the usual
parking problems.*
***So as not to wake** her parents, Juliet took her shoes off
when she went upstairs.*

NOTE *In order to* and *so as to* are more formal than *to.*

4 *So that* + clause
*I turned the light on **so that I could see** what I was doing.*

Causative verbs

Have something done and *get something done* are both used to
refer to actions which are done for the subject rather than by
the subject. Causative verbs are used instead of passive verbs
to show that the subject causes the action to be done.

1 *Have something done*
*I don't know how to repair cars, so I'm **having mine
repaired** at the garage round the corner.*

2 *Get something done*
*I really must **get my eyes tested**. I'm sure I need glasses.*
***Get** your hair **cut**!*

NOTE The differences between *have* and *get something done*
are that *have* is slightly more formal than *get*, and that *get* is
more frequent than *have* in the imperative form.

3 *Non-causative uses of have and get*
Have and *get* are also used to refer to events which
happened to someone, but were outside their control.
*After being late for work every day for two weeks, Billy **had
his pay reduced**.*
*I stood so close to the fire that **I got my legs burnt**.*

Vocabulary reference

This section comprises vocabulary related to the main topics in each unit. Most of the words listed are used in this book or in the Workbook; others have been added where they might be useful. The following abbreviations are used:
n – noun vb – verb adj – adjective

Unit 1

Places

1 Buildings for living in
apartment
bedsit
block
  apartment block
  block of flats
bungalow
cottage
flat
floor
  on the ground /
  first / top floor
house
  detached house
  semi-detached
  house
  terraced house
storey
  a ten / multi-
  storey building

2 Other buildings and facilities
car park
castle
cathedral
church
office
  office block
park
post office
pub
seafront
shop
  baker's
  butcher's
  chemist's
  department store
  dry cleaner's
  fishmonger's
  fish-shop
  greengrocer's
  grocer's
  ironmonger's
stationer's
sweet shop
tobacconist's
travel agent's
skyscraper
station
  bus station
  fire station
  police station
  railway station
town hall

3 Communities
city
  capital city
port
resort
  holiday resort
  seaside resort
  ski resort
town
village

4 Parts of communities
area
  country area
  residential area
  rural area
  urban area
centre
  city centre
  town centre
district
outskirts
  on the outskirts
region
residential area
suburb
  in the suburbs
  suburban (adj)

5 Geographical features
bay
beach
cliff
coast
  on the coast
countryside
flat (adj)
forest
hill
  hilly (adj)
lake
mountain
  mountainous
  (adj)
plain (n)
river
sea
  by the sea
seaside
  at the seaside
shore
stream (n)
valley
wood
  woody / wooded
  (adjs.)

Unit 2

Weather

1 Temperature
chilly
cold
cool
freezing
hot
mild
scorching
warm

2 Describing weather
breeze
  breezy
bright
clear
cloud
  cloudy
damp
drizzle
  drizzly
dry
dull
fog
  foggy
hailstone
lightning
rain
  raindrop
  rainfall
  rainy
shower
  showery
snow
  snowfall
  snowflake
  snowy
storm
  stormy
sun
  sunny
  sunshine
thunder
wet
wind
  windy

3 Verbs
blow
freeze
hail
pour (with rain)
rain
shine
snow

Unit 3

Entertainment and the Arts

1 Venues
art gallery
cinema
concert hall
exhibition centre
museum
opera house
stadium
theatre

2 People
actor
artist
audience
backing group
ballerina
choreographer
cast
composer
conductor
dancer
director
drummer
guitarist (lead /
  bass)
magician
musician
orchestra
painter
pianist
playwright
producer
saxophonist
sculptor
singer
vocalist
violinist

3 Events
ballet
concert
exhibition
film
play
opera

4 Interiors and equipment
aisle
box
circle
curtain
footlight
gallery
lighting
microphone
orchestra pit
row
screen
scenery
set
speaker
stage
stalls
wings
workshop

5 Arts and crafts
carving
drawing
knitting
painting
pottery
sculpture
sewing

6 Materials
canvas
charcoal
clay
cloth
paint
papier-mâché
plaster
plastic
steel
stone
wood
wool

7 Other related words
dubbed dialogue
encore
interval
lines
part
performance
plot
photography
review
scene
script
subtitles

8 Verbs
applaud
boo
conduct
exhibit
perform
play (a part)

Unit 4

Families and other relationships

1 Families
aunt
brother
  elder / older
  brother
cousin
daughter
father
grandchild
  granddaughter /
  son
  grandfather /
  mother
  grandparent(s)
great-grandchild
husband
  ex-husband
in-laws
  son-in law, etc.
mother
niece
nephew
parents
sister
son
step-father
  step-daughter,
  etc.
twin
  twin-sister /
  brother
uncle
widow (woman)
widower (man)
wife
  ex-wife

2 Marital status
divorced
engaged
married /
  unmarried
separated
single
widowed

3 Other relationships
acquaintance
boss
colleague
employee
employer
fiancé / fiancée
friend
  best friend
  girlfriend /
  boyfriend
neighbour
partner

4 Verbs

get divorced (from) / engaged (to) / married (to)
get on (well) with someone
go out with someone
marry someone
start / end a relationship with someone

Jobs

accountant
actor
air steward
architect
assistant
  personal assistant
  shop assistant
author
baker
barman / barmaid (bar person)
builder
businessman / woman / executive
butcher
caretaker
chef
civil servant
clerk
computer operator/ programmer
cook
decorator
dentist
designer
director
  company director
  film director
doctor
driver
  bus / taxi / train driver
dustman (refuse collector)
economist
editor
electrician
engineer
farmer
fisherman
fishmonger
flight attendant
hairdresser
head teacher
jeweller
journalist
judge
lawyer
lecturer
manager
miner
musician

news reader / news presenter
nurse
optician
painter
photographer
pilot
plumber
police officer
politician
porter
printer
prison officer / warder
receptionist
sailor
salesman / saleswoman
scientist
secretary
soldier
solicitor
surgeon
tailor
teacher
telephonist
telephone operator
travel agent
TV cameraman
TV presenter
vet
waiter
writer

Unit 5

Sport

1 Sports

athletics (do)
badminton (play)
basketball (play)
boxing
cycling
diving
football (play)
golf (play)
gymnastics (do)
hockey (play)
horse-racing
ice-skating
motor-racing
riding
rugby (play)
skiing
snooker (play)
squash (play)
surfing
swimming
tennis (play)
volleyball (play)
weightlifting
windsurfing

2 People

athlete
badminton player
basketball player
boxer
cyclist
diver
footballer / football player
golfer
gymnast
hockey player
jockey
ice-skater
racing driver
rider
rugby player
skater
skier
snooker player
squash player
surfer
swimmer
tennis player
volleyball player
weight-lifter

3 Equipment

ball
  football
  hockey ball
  golf ball
bat
cue
golf club
hockey stick
ice-skates
racing car
racket
saddle
sailboard
skis
shuttle cock
surfboard

4 Places

circuit
court
course
gym
pitch
ring
rink
stadium

5 Verbs

beat
box
catch
cycle
dive
draw
hit
kick
lose
miss
pass
pot

practise
race
ride
save
score (a point / a goal)
serve
shoot
skate
ski
swim
surf
tackle
train
throw
volley
win

6 Related words

amateur (adj / n)
ace
basket
captain
cup
game
goal
kit
match
medal
net
professional (adj / n)
race (n / vb)
record
referee
skill
spectators
team
whistle

Unit 6

The body

1 Head and shoulders

chin
cheek
ear
eye
  eyebrow
  eyelash(es)
forehead
hair
head
lip(s)
mouth
neck
nose
nostril
jaw
shoulder
tooth (teeth)
tongue
throat

2 Arms and hands

elbow
finger
  index finger
  middle finger
  little finger
(finger)nail
fist
forearm
hand
  left / right hand
palm
thumb
wrist

3 Legs and feet

ankle
calf
foot (feet)
heel
hips
knee
leg
shin
thigh
toe
  big toe
  little toe
toenail

4 Trunk

bottom
chest
back
stomach (tummy)
waist

5 General words

blood
bone
hair
muscle
skin

6 Verbs with parts of the body

eyes
  blink
  glance
  stare
  wink
finger
  point
  scratch
foot
  kick
hands
  clap
  punch
  shake
  slap
  smack
head
  nod
  shake

lips
  kiss
mouth
  eat
  mutter
  talk
  taste
  whisper
nose
  breathe
  smell
  sniff
shoulders
  shrug
teeth
  bite
  chew
toe
  stub
tongue
  lick
throat
  swallow

Colours

1 Colours

beige
black
blue
  navy blue
  royal blue
  sky blue
brown
cream
golden
green
  bottle green
  lime green
grey
orange
pink
purple
  mauve
  violet
red
  crimson
  scarlet
silver
white
yellow

2 Words describing colours

bright
dark
light
pale

Animals

Types of animal (with examples)

birds
  eagle
  pigeon
  sparrow

domestic animals
  cow
  horse
  pig
fish
  cod
  sardine
  shark
household pets
  cat
  dog
  rabbit
insects
  ant
  mosquito
  wasp

mammals
  mouse
  rhinoceros
  whale
reptiles
  alligator
  snake
  turtle
wild animals
  fox
  kangaroo
  lion
zoo animals
  chimpanzee
  elephant
  giraffe

Unit 7

Describing people

1 Age
Age categories
baby
toddler
child
teenager
young man / woman
youth *men only; often has negative associations; often used in connection with crime*
middle-aged (man / woman)
elderly (man / woman) *more polite word than 'old'*

Precise ages
She is twenty-one (years old).

Imprecise ages
He's in his teens.
She's in her early / mid- / late twenties.
He's about thirty. She's forty something.
He's fiftyish.   She's sixty odd.

2 Height
He's average height. *average is a relative measurement*
She's above average height. *more common in formal or written language*
She's petite. *used for girls and women, it means short but dainty and feminine*
He's short.
She's tall(ish) / short(ish). *the suffix -ish means quite*
She's taller / shorter than average. *more common in spoken or informal language*

3 Build
Women and men
He's fat / overweight.
She's slim. *pleasingly thin*
He's thin. *often used in a negative way*
She's skinny. *too thin*
Women
She's got a good figure.
She's plump. *pleasantly fat; more polite than 'fat'*

Men
He's got a paunch. *a large, protruding stomach*
He's stocky. *short and strong*
He's well built. *strong, largish but not fat*

4 Hair
Length
long / short
medium-length / shoulder-length
mainly used to describe women's hair
Colour
(jet) black
fair / dark
ginger / red
grey / going grey
light-brown / medium-brown / dark-brown
mousy
natural blond / dyed blond *written blonde for women*
white
Type
curly / spiky / straight / wavy
He's bald / going bald. / He's got a bald patch.
He's got a receding hairline. *more formal*
His hair's receding. *less formal*
Style
She's wearing her hair down / loose / up / in plaits / in a pony-tail.
She's got a fringe / side parting / centre parting.
Order of adjectives
The usual order is: length+colour+type
She's got short, blonde curly hair.
or *(length)+type +colour*
She's got wavy, blonde hair. *however, 'straight' usually comes before the colour*

5 Complexion
She's got a fair / dark / olive / pale / tanned complexion.
He's got a clear / good / spotty complexion.
She's got freckles / spots.

6 Distinguishing features
He's got a beard / moustache. He's clean-shaven.
He's got bushy eyebrows / a scar / a tattoo.
She wears glasses.

Unit 8

Crime

1 Crimes
arson
assault
blackmail
burglary
fraud
hijacking
hooliganism
kidnapping
mugging
murder
(armed) robbery
shoplifting
smuggling
terrorism
theft
vandalism

2 Criminals
arsonist
blackmailer
burglar
hijacker
hooligan
kidnapper
mugger
murderer
robber
shoplifter
smuggler
terrorist
thief
vandal

3 Justice and punishment
appeal
barrister
caution
cell
community service
court
court case
death penalty
defence
fine (n / vb)
gaol (Br) jail (US)
guilty
(life) imprisonment
innocent
judge
jury
justice
lawyer
(first) offence
(life) sentence
prison
probation
prosecution
punishment
  capital punishment
  corporal punishment
remand home
solicitor
trial
verdict
witness

4 Verbs
arrest
ban
break in
break out
break the law
burgle
charge
commit a crime
escape
get away
get away with
hold up
investigate
rob
steal

5 Other words
alibi
armed
burglar / car alarm
legal (illegal)

store detective
weapon

Unit 9

Travel

1 Air
airport
check-in (n) / check in (vb)
fly (vb)
land (vb)
landing (n)
plane
take-off (n) / take off (vb)

2 Land
bicycle (bike)
bus
  bus station
car
coach
  coach station
lane
motorbike
motorway
rail
  go by rail
railway
  railway station
road
  main road
  minor road
taxi
traffic
train
tube
underground

3 Sea
boat
crossing
ferry
port
sail
sea
set sail
ship
voyage

4 Verbs
board (boat / plane)
go by (boat, train, etc.)
go on board
hitch-hike (vb)
  go hitch-hiking
set off

5 General
destination
journey
passenger
route

travel
travel agent
trip

Holidays

camp (vb)
  go camping
charter flight
cruise
excursion
(youth) hostel
hotel
luggage
motel
package holiday
self-catering
  holiday
sightseeing
  go sightseeing
(suit)case
tour
  tourism
  tourist

Unit 10

Clothes

W = women's
clothes / M =
men's clothes

1 General

anorak
belt
blouse (W)
cardigan
dress (W)
gloves
jacket
jeans
jumper
mac(k) /
  mackintosh
overall(s)
overcoat
pullover
raincoat
scarf
shirt
  sweat-shirt
  T-shirt
tie
skirt (W)
  mini-skirt (W)
shorts
socks
suit
sweater
trousers

2 Headgear

beret
cap
hat
helmet

3 Footwear

boots
plimsolls
sandals
slippers
shoes
trainers

4 Underwear

bra (W)
knickers (W)
pants
tights (W)
vest

5 Night-wear

dressing-gown
night-dress /
  nightie (W)
pyjamas

6 Sportswear and swimwear

jogging suit
tracksuit
bikini (W)
swimming costume
/ swim-suit (W)
swimming trunks
  (M)

7 Other things that are worn

contact lenses
earrings
glasses
hairband
jewellery
ring

8 Fashion

designer (n/adj)
fashion
  fashionable
  fashion-conscious
trend
  trendy (adj)
unfashionable

Materials

1 Artificial

plastic
nylon
polyester

2 Natural

cotton
denim
leather
linen
rubber
silk
suede
wool (n)
  woollen (adj)

Patterns

check (n / adj)
  checked (adj)
flowery (adj)
patterned (adj)
plain (adj)
spot (n)
  spotted (adj)
stripe (n)
  striped (adj)
tartan (n / adj)

Space

astronaut
cosmonaut
earth
gravity
launch (v)
moon
orbit
planet
space
  space craft
  space shuttle
  space station
  space suit
weightless (ness)

Unit 11

Science and technology

1 Machinery (general terms)

appliance
engine
gadget
machine

2 People

inventor
researcher
scientist
technician

3 Adjectives

battery- / mains-
  operated
high-tech
mobile
portable
remote controlled
scientific
technical

4 Inventions

computer
communications
  satellite
microchip
microscope
microwave
robot
speedometer
thermometer

5 Verbs

discover
experiment
invent
research

6 Other words

fax (facsimile copy)
  (n / vb)
lab (laboratory)
patent (n / vb)

The environment

1 Natural disasters

drought
earthquake
flood
tidal wave
typhoon
volcanic eruption

2 Environmental issues

acid rain
aerosol
animal welfare
battery hen
bottle-bank
carbon monoxide
climate
conservation
endangered species
energy
  nuclear
  solar
exhaust fumes
fertilizers
forest fires
global warming
greenhouse effect
(non)-renewable
  resources
nuclear
  fallout
  reactor
oil-slick
ozone layer
pesticide
pollution
protected animal
rain forest
unleaded petrol
waste
  nuclear
  radio-active
wildlife

3 Politics

environmental
  group
green issues
pressure group

4 Verbs

cut down
destroy
dispose (of)
dump
protect
pollute
recycle
save
throw away
use up

Unit 12

Celebrations and festivals

1 Types of gathering

barbecue
christening
family gathering
fete
funeral
get-together
anniversary party
party
  birthday party
  cocktail party
  dinner party
  fancy dress party
wedding

2 Other words

band
banner
bonfire
commemorate
costume
firework display
flag
float
parade
procession
site

Food and drink

1 Types of meal

barbecue
buffet
four-course meal
picnic
snack
TV dinner

2 Condition of food

fresh
off
past its sell-by date
raw
ripe
rotten
stale
tender

tough
undercooked
unripe
overcooked

3 Taste and texture

bitter
bland
creamy
crisp
crunchy
hot
mild
salty
savoury
sickly
sour
spicy
stodgy
sweet
tasteless

4 Containers

bottle
box
can
carton
jar
packet
pot
tin

5 Quantities

bar
litre
loaf
lump
piece
pint
portion
slice
spoonful

6 Verbs

Cooking food
bake
boil
cook
fry
grill
heat
microwave
poach
roast
steam
stew

Preparing food
add
beat
blend
chop
dice
grate
melt
peel
shred
slice

spread
stir
whisk
Preparing drinks
add
fill
mix
pour
shake
stir
**Eating and
drinking**
bite
chew
swallow
sip

7 Other words
crumbs
fast food
(non-)fattening
helping
pastry
slimming
sticky

Sleep

doze
dream
fast asleep
nap
nightmare
snore
stretch
toss and turn
wide awake
yawn

Unit 13

The mind

1 Adjectives
articulate
brainy
bright
gifted
imaginative
intelligent

2 Verbs
analyse
calculate
forget
infer
memorize
realize
recognize
remember
work out

3 Other words
brain
emotion
genius
idea

intellect
knowledge
logic
memory
mind
skill
talent
thought
virtuoso

The senses

1 Senses
hearing
sight
smell
taste
touch

2 Verbs
catch a glimpse
glance
glimpse
hear
listen
look at
notice
observe
scan
see
stare
watch

3 Other words
(colour) blind
deaf
eyesight
hard of hearing
short- / long-
 sighted

Money

**1 Banking and
investing**
account
bank statement
bankrupt
borrow
budget (n / vb)
cash
cashier
cheque
 traveller's cheque
credit (card)
currency
debt
deposit (n / vb)
exchange rate
interest (rate)
invest
investment
lend
loan
mortgage (n / vb)
owe
pay
save

savings
shares
withdraw

2 Earning
bonus
earn
earnings
income
 gross
 net
rise
salary
wage

**3 Buying and
spending**
bargain
bill
cost (n / vb)
expense
instalments
price
purchase (n / vb)
purse
receipt
reduction
refund (n / vb)
spend
wallet

**4 Giving,
receiving and
paying**
collection
donate
 donation
fee
fine (n / vb)
grant
income tax
inherit
inheritance
pension
pocket money
rent (n/vb)
scholarship
tip (n / vb)
winnings

**5 Related
adjectives**
affluent
broke
generous
hard-up
mean
poor
prosperous
rich
stingy
wealthy
well off

**6 Verbs and
expressions**
add up
go up / down

make ends meet
pay back
pay into
put down
put towards
run out
save up
take out

**7 Other words
and expressions**
profit
property
valuable
value
waste of money
wealth
worth
worthless

Unit 14

Education

1 General
educate
education
educator
qualification
qualify (vb)
revise
revision

2 Subjects
archaeology
art
business studies
dance
drama
economics
games (sport)
geography
geology
history
home economics
foreign (modern)
 languages
maths
music
physical education
psychology
religious education
science
 biology
 chemistry
 physics
sociology
technology

3 People
graduate
head-teacher
infant
lecturer
pupil
schoolboy
schoolgirl

student
teacher
undergraduate

**4 Types of
school**
boarding school
 boarder
day school
mixed school
nursery school
primary school
 infant school
 junior school
secondary school
university

5 Exams
cheat
examine (v)
examiner
examination
fail
get through
pass
take / sit an exam
 retake / re-sit
revise for
test (n / vb)

6 Qualifications
certificate
degree
 BA / MA / BSc /
 MSc / PhD
diploma

Health

1 People
dentist
doctor
general practitioner
midwife
nurse
patient
specialist
surgeon

2 Places
hospital
operating theatre
surgery (doctor's /
 dental)
waiting room
ward

3 Treatment
bandage
check-up
dose (of medicine)
drugs
injection
 give someone an
 injection
medicine
 take medicine
operation
pain-killer

pill
plaster
tablet
tranquillizer

4 Illnesses
ache
 ear ache
 headache
 stomach ache
 toothache
cancer
cold
cough
flu
heart attack
heart disease
infection
 infectious
 (disease)
pain
virus

5 Minor injuries
bruise (n / vb)
cut (n / vb)
graze (n / vb)
wound (n / vb)

6 Verbs
catch
 catch flu
cure
heal
hurt
injure
operate on
prescribe
 prescription (n)
treat
 treatment (n)

7 Adjectives
fit
ill
sick
 feel sick
 be sick (vomit)
healthy
 unhealthy
painful
unwell
well

8 Other words
ambulance
emergency
first aid
health insurance
recover (vb)
 recovery
temperature

Lexical phrases

All these phrases are in the Student's Book and the unit number for each is given as a reference. Phrases such as these are commonly tested in Paper 3.

1 With key verbs

break
break a journey 9
break someone's heart 9

bring
bring something to a standstill 6
bring yourself to do something 6

change
change a wheel 14
change your mind 10

come
come true 5

cost
cost the lives (of people) 5

do
do a course (in a subject) 6
do an experiment on 6
do damage to 9
do harm to someone 6
do research into 9
do the trick 9
do well 14

fall
fall in love with 4

find
find work 10

get
get hold of 8
get into an argument 9
get married 1
get someone into trouble 6
get something under way 5
get time off 1

give
give birth 11
give someone a ring (phone) 7
give someone the sack 1

go
go ahead 5
go cycling etc. 10
go downhill 11
go mad 14
go to the trouble to do sthing 2
go to waste 5
go wrong 4

have
have something for breakfast 1
have a break 10
have a/little choice 11
have a day off (work) 8
have a degree 14
have a flair for 9
have a good time 2
have a good view of 1
have a baby 2
have fun 9
have no idea about something 6
have objections to 10
have something in common 10
have something to eat 4
have stitches 7

keep
keep a straight face 6
keep fit 3
keep going 2
keep hold of 8

lay
lay a finger on someone 7

lose
lose control 14
lose touch with 14
lose your temper 9

make
make a difference 9
make a profit 13
make a recovery (from illness) 2
make ends meet 13
make enquiries into something 6
make it (to the top) 14
make (a) noise 9
make sure 10
make your mind up 14

pass
pass an exam 14

play
play a part in 6
play a trick on 6
play for a team 6
play music 9
play squash 10
play the guitar 6
play the part 12

put
put right 12

reach
reach a conclusion 9

run
run a business 6
run the risk of (+vb +-ing) 2

see
see the funny side of something 5

set
set a bad example 8
set fire to 12
set free 8
set light to 1

speak
speak a language 10

spend
spend energy 5
spend time (+vb +-ing) 5

take
take a chance 5
take a look at 9
take a photograph 2
take a test 10
take action 6
take care to do sthg 2
take measures 12
take part in 5
take place 3
take someone to one side 7
take something seriously 6
take steps to do something 6
take time 5
take time off 8

2 Prepositional phrases

at
at 9.30 2
at a fast rate 6
at all times 9
at any rate 13
at the same time 13
at a speed of 29,000 kph 10
at lunchtime 5
at my desk 3
at one point 13
at public expense 6
at risk from 2
at the age of 2
at the beach 5
at the beginning 9
at the cost of 6
at the end 7
at the end of the day 14
at the foot (bottom) of the page 12
at the front 14
at the same time 13
at the moment 10
at their feet 3
shout at someone 9
throw something at someone 9

by
by rail / train 9
by the time 7

for
for ages 6
for a moment / a couple of
   minutes 5
for example 6
for goodness sake 12
for some reason 6
for the better 11
a bed for the night 9
ask for trouble 9
perfect for (+vb +-ing) 10
responsible for 6
jump for joy 14
value for money 12

from
from my point of view 6
from the word go 14
from time to time 6

in
in 1944 9
in addition (to this) 10
in an emergency 10
in business 14
in charge (of) 2
in contrast 8
in control 4
in general 6
in his late seventies 7
in March 10
in my (early) thirties 4
in my experience 4
in my heart 14
in my opinion 10
in my own time 7
in my situation 10
in my view 3
in opposite directions 10
in public places 14
in short 3
in space 10
in the 1960s 3
in the 21st century 2
in the end 14
in the first place 4
in the front row 3
in the light of 9
in the limelight 4
in the middle of 2
in the morning 3
in the street 3

in the summer of 1989 10
in their teens 3
in these circumstances 2
in this way 2
in three days' time 2
in (serious) trouble 7
an improvement in 9
bear in mind 9
interest(ed) in 6
man in the street 12
one in ten 8

into
trick someone into doing
   something 6

of
of course 10
terrified of 14

on
on average 9
on balance 14
on fire 11
on Friday (morning) 2
on my own 2
on that date 12
on the line 5
on the market 2
on the pavement 3
on the phone 2
on the right track 11
on the safe side 2
on the screen 9
on the tip of my tongue 13
on the whole 4
on tiptoe 6
on the Equator 5
on the one hand 14
on the other hand 4
on the top 7
on the train 14
on the way (to work) 14
on top of that 10
on your side 12
an attack on someone 6
based on 6
to dawn on someone 5
keen on 6

out
out of place 10
out of sight 8
out of this world 1

over
over a period of time 6
over the age of 21 8
over the centuries 8
(all) over the world 7

to
to my surprise 10
allergic to 6
harmful to 9
thanks to 9

under
under (the same) conditions 10
under threat 6

until
until March 3

with
compete with 4
co-operate with 10
deal with 9
familiar with 9
nothing to do with someone 8
replace something with
   something else 10

3 Other expressions

a close shave 5
a high price to pay for something 1
a near thing 5
above all 9
as far as (person) is concerned 1
I can't be bothered 7
I can't do a thing about it 5
I can't wait 2
I suppose so 2
I'll get it (phone) 2
It's a shame 5
It's hard to say 7
It's (not) my fault 2
It's me (phone) 1
It's not like him 7
It's not surprising 3
It's up to me 8
It's worth (+vb +-*ing*) 8
might as well 5
none the worse 5
safe and well 5
short of breath 8
sick to death 8
someone my own age 1
the other day 6
the wider world 14
there's no doubt about it 11
there's no point (+vb +-*ing*) 8
there's nothing you can do 7
these days 4
this time next week 2
with minutes to spare 5

4 Sentence starters

All being well 2
Another advantage is 8
Anyway 6
As a general rule 9
As far as I can see 6
As far as I can remember 4
As it was 7
At any rate 13
At the same time 13
Believe it or not 14
Everyone knows that 2
Given the circumstances 5
If you ask me 2
It doesn't matter where (what / when / who) 2
It seems likely that 14
Let's face it 10
Not knowing what else to do 5
One important thing is 3
That's not the end of the story 2
The funny thing is 2
The problem is / was 9
The thing is 2
The trouble is 6
What gets me is 12
When it comes to it 4

Irregular verbs

Infinitive	Past simple	Past participle
be	was / were	been
beat	beat	beaten
become	became	become
begin	began	begun
bend	bent	bent
bite	bit	bitten
bleed	bled	bled
blow	blew	blown
break	broke	broken
bring	brought	brought
build	built	built
burn	burnt, burned	burnt, burned
burst	burst	burst
buy	bought	bought
catch	caught	caught
choose	chose	chosen
come	came	come
cost	cost	cost
cut	cut	cut
deal	dealt	dealt
do	did	done
draw	drew	drawn
dream	dreamt, dreamed	dreamt, dreamed
drink	drank	drunk
drive	drove	driven
eat	ate	eaten
fall	fell	fallen
feed	fed	fed
feel	felt	felt
fight	fought	fought
find	found	found
fly	flew	flown
forbid	forbade	forbidden
forget	forgot	forgotten
forgive	forgave	forgiven
freeze	froze	frozen
get	got	got; (*US*) gotten
give	gave	given
go	went	gone
grow	grew	grown
hang	hung, hanged	hung, hanged
have	had	had
hear	heard	heard
hide	hid	hidden
hit	hit	hit
hold	held	held
hurt	hurt	hurt
keep	kept	kept
know	knew	known
lay	laid	laid
lead	led	led
lean	leant, leaned	leant, leaned
learn	learnt, learned	learnt, learned
leave	left	left
lend	lent	lent
let	let	let
lie	lay	lain
light	lit	lit

Infinitive	Past simple	Past participle
lose	lost	lost
make	made	made
mean	meant	meant
meet	met	met
pay	paid	paid
put	put	put
read	read	read
ride	rode	ridden
ring	rang	rung
rise	rose	risen
run	ran	run
say	said	said
see	saw	seen
sell	sold	sold
send	sent	sent
set	set	set
shake	shook	shaken
shine	shone	shone
shoot	shot	shot
show	showed	shown, showed
shrink	shrank, shrunk	shrunk
shut	shut	shut
sing	sang	sung
sink	sank	sunk
sit	sat	sat
sleep	slept	slept
smell	smelt, smelled	smelt, smelled
speak	spoke	spoken
spell	spelt, spelled	spelt, spelled
spend	spent	spent
spill	spilt, spilled	spilt, spilled
spin	spun	spun
spoil	spoilt, spoiled	spoilt, spoiled
spread	spread	spread
stand	stood	stood
steal	stole	stolen
stick	stuck	stuck
sting	stung	stung
strike	struck	struck
sweep	swept	swept
swell	swelled	swollen, swelled
swim	swam	swum
swing	swung	swung
take	took	taken
teach	taught	taught
tear	tore	torn
tell	told	told
think	thought	thought
throw	threw	thrown
wake	woke	woken
wear	wore	worn
win	won	won
wind	wound	wound
write	wrote	written

Phrasal verbs

This list includes all the useful phrasal verbs which appear in the reading texts and listening passages of this book and which may be tested in First Certificate. Phrasal verbs which are part of a specific vocabulary exercise in the units are printed in **bold**. The number refers to the unit in which the phrasal verb first appears. Words in italics show the meaning of the verb in this particular context. Examples of contexts are given in brackets.

account for 3
add up *make sense* 4
blow up *enlarge* 2
break down (car) 6
break out *escape* 6
break out (war) intrans. 7
break up (from school) 2
break up (into small pieces) 2
break up (meeting) intrans. 2
break up (relationship) 2
bring (problems) **on** (oneself) 9
bring about 8
bring back (memories) 9
bring in (law) 9
bring out *produce* 9
bring someone **round** (after accident) 9
bring up 9
bring up on (be brought up on) 2
build up (pressure) 11
bump into 6
burn off (calories) 3
burst into (flames) 12
carry out (a survey) 6
carry out (work) 2
carry out (an experiment) 10
carry round 7
catch up with 14
check up on 14
clean up 12
clear up 12
cloud over 2
come across *find* 11
come back 3
come from 3
come in 4
come out 5
come out in (freckles) 7
come round *regain consciousness* 11
come round *visit* 11
come up *happen unexpectedly* 11
come up against 14
come up with 11
cut down on 14
cut off (be cut off) 2
cut (something) down 9
cut up 3
divide up 13
drink up 12
drop off 12
dry up 5

eat up 12
end up 7
file away 12
fill up (a car) 12
find out 5
fit in 7
fit in with 13
fly by *pass quickly* 1
gang up (on) 8
get away *escape* 12
get away from 1
get back 12
get by *manage* 12
get down *depress* 12
get into 11
get through 1
get on *continue* 5
get on *progress* 12
get on with *have good relations with* 12
get out *escape* 12
get out *leave* 3
get over *recover* 12
get through 8
get together *collect* 5
get up *rise* 2
get up (wind) 2
give away (a secret) 6
give back 8
give in (to) intrans. 10
give up (a job) 1
give up (+vb +-*ing*) *stop doing something* 2
go along with 14
go back 8
go down *fall in temperature* 1
go down with 14
go into *enter* 3
go off *explode* 8
go off *go bad* 8
go on (to do something) 2
go on (to university) 4
go on *happen* 1
go out *stop burning / being alight* 8
grow on *like more* 3
go over *review* 8
go through *search* 8
go up 8
go with *look good with* 8
go without 12
grow up 1
hand in (homework) 2
hang around 8
hang on *wait* 2
hang on to 1
hang out 10

head back 5
head off 3
hold up *rob* 6
hurry up 1
keep at 3
keep up with 14
knock over 8
laugh at (someone) 10
leave over 3
let (someone) **down** *disappoint* 6
let off 5
lie down 2
light up (a cigarette) 8
listen to 10
live (it) up 3
live on 10
lock up 5
look after (yourself) 2
look at *examine* 4
look for 2
look forward to (+vb +-*ing*) 5
make into 13
make up (the numbers) 6
move into 12
move on to (something else) 9
pass on 13
pass out *faint* 6
pay back 13
pay for 13
pay into 13
pick (something) up (skill) 14
pick up (cold) 1
pick up *collect* 5
pick up (an atmosphere) *sense* 4
pile up 2
point (something) out (to someone) 9
pop out (eyes) 6
pull on 7
push back 5
push towards 8
put (something) down 9
put off *delay* 3
put off *discourage* 3
put off *distract* 3
put (something) **up** (on the wall) 2
put on (weight) *gain* 3
put on *switch on* 3
put on (clothes) 10
put out 12
put towards 13
put up (hand) *raise* 2
put up (price) *raise* 2
put up (tent) 2
put up *accommodate* 2
put up with 10
rip (someone) off 9
run out (of milk) 8
save up 13
see to 12
sell up 11
send off for 10
set off *leave* 5

set out *leave* 5
set out (to do something) *start* 10
set up 12
settle down 1
settle into 5
show off (abilities) 4
shut out 1
sit down 3
sleep through 5
slip out 5
slow down 8
smarten up 7
sort out 12
speed up 2
split up 6
sum up 6
take after *resemble* 4
take away 8
take back *retract* 4
take down *write* 4
take in 5
take off (clothes) 10
take off (plane) 5
take on (a meaning) *assume* 4
take out (tooth) 14
take over (company) 4
take round 5
take through 5
take to *like* 4
take up (a career) 10
take up (a story) 6
take up *start doing* 4
tear up 12
think of 7
throw away 5
throw on (clothes) 1
throw out 7
tidy up 12
touch down (plane) 7
track down 2
try on (clothes) 10
try (something) out 14
turn against 8
turn down *reduce* 7
turn down *refuse* 7
turn off 14
turn into 1
turn out *attend* 6
turn out *happen* 2
turn out (to be) 7
turn (someone) away (from) 9
turn up 7
use up 12
wait for 7
wake up 5
watch out for 9
wear out (clothes) intrans. 10
wipe out 11
work out (a scheme) trans. 6
work out (a problem) 5
work out *succeed* 4
wrap up 12
write down 10
write up 12

Index

Page numbers in roman refer to the units; numbers in **bold** refer to the Grammar reference.

Acknowledgements

The Publisher and authors would like to thank the following for their kind permission to reproduce articles, extracts and adaptations of copyright material:

p.9 adapted from Fiona Malcolm: 'For my next trick', photograph by David Secombe, in *Sunday Times Magazine*, © Times Newspapers Ltd, 1991, by permission. p.15 extract from Molly Parkin: 'Bad Habits' reproduced from *Marie Claire*/European Magazines 1989/Robert Harding Syndication. p.26 extract from Tim Radford: 'The struggle to beat the cold', © The Guardian. p.36 adapted from Brendan Martin: 'Talking to . . . Elton John', in *Woman's Realm*, by permission of the author. p.39 adapted from: 'My kind of day - Roger Black', © Radio Times. p.50 adapted from Mandy Bruce: 'Whose finger is on the button in your house?', illustration by Graham Thompson, reproduced from *Woman*, © Woman/Solo Syndication, by permission. p.64 adaptation of 'It happened to me . . .' reproduced from *Woman*, © Woman/Solo Syndication, by permission. p.73 extract from Ruth Fisher: 'Torture - but it's worth it', © The Observer. p.76 extract from Alun Rees: 'Soccer team's pigeons put to flight by cut-out moggies', © The Daily Express. p.78 extract from: 'The Shape of things to come', © Essex County Standard. p.88 adapted from: 'Nature's artful dodgers', © Focus Magazine. p.111 adapted from: 'The evil weed', © The Independent. p.119 extract from Sandy Sulaiman: 'Toys for the grown-up boys', © The Guardian, by permission. p.120 (on cassette) adapted from Alison Leigh Jones: 'Are your kids playing with danger?' in *Woman* , © Woman/Solo Syndication, by permission. pp. 124-5 abridged from Katie Wood: 'Eurorailing', first published in National Student Extra, January 1992, by permission of the author. pp.128-9 adapted from: 'Is the Chunnel back on course?' © Yellow Advertiser. p.139 extract from: 'Britain's space ambassador', © Focus Magazine. pp.152–3 extract from Nigel Hawkes: 'Scientists obsessed - playing with fire', in *World* Magazine (BBC), by permission of the author. p.161 extracts from 'Lowdown of Friday the 13th', in the *Observer Magazine*, © The Observer. pp.171-2 extracts from: 'Memories are made of this', © Focus Magazine. p.184 adapted from James Kanter: 'Stars who did their own thing', © The Guardian.

Every effort has been made to trace the owners of copyright material in this book, but we should be pleased to hear from any copyright owner whom we have been unable to contact, in order to rectify any errors or omissions. p.28 adapted from Jan Vijg: 'Long life' in Plus Magazine. p.56 from an article by Catherine Charnaud in The Indy. p.76 article by Genevieve Muinzer: 'A year of living dangerously', in *Woman*. p.112-3 adapted from: 'Capital punishment', in *The Indy*. p.119 letter from *She*, writer unknown. p.158 article by Paul Haddlesey: 'ZZzzz', in *Scoop*.

The Publisher and authors are grateful to the University of Cambridge Local Examinations Syndicate for permission to reproduce the sample answer sheet on page 196.

Illustrations by:
Richard Deverell
Nicki Elson
Sophie Grillet
Sue Hillwood-Harris
John Holder
Shaun Letham
David Loftus
Fiona MacVicar
Colin Mier
Margaret Morgan
Oxford Illustrators
Colin Salmon
Susan Scott
Technical Graphics, Oxford University Press
Graham Thomas

Location photographs by:
Emily Andersen
Philip Dunn
David Mansell

Studio photographs by:
Norman McBeath
Stephen Oliver

The Publisher and authors would like to thank the following for their permission to reproduce photographs:
Action Plus; Allsport (U.K.) Ltd; Altered Image; Arcaid; Art Directors Photo Library; Liam Bailey Studio; BBC; Brainwaves; Collections; Colorific!; Lupe Cunha; James Davis Travel Photography; Hulton Deutsch; East Anglian Daily Times; Mary Evans Picture Library Ltd; Robert Estall; Genesis Space Photo Library; The Ronald Grant Archive; Jeremy Green; Sally and Richard Greenhill; The Guardian; Guglielmo Gulvin; Robert Harding Picture Library Ltd; Hitachi (U.K.) Ltd; Impact Photos Ltd; Kenwood Ltd; Tony Lees; Lawson Clarke; Life File; Magnum Photos Ltd; Mirror Syndication international Ltd; National Geographic; Network Photographers Ltd; Gavin Newman; Photofusion Ltd; Popperfoto; J C Poulmarsh; Punch Cartoon Library; Retna Pictures Ltd; Rex Features Ltd; Royal Shakespeare Company Tour Publicity; Science Photo Library Ltd; Sony U.K. Ltd; Frank Spooner Pictures Ltd; Tony Stone Images; The Sunday Times; Telegraph Colour Library; The Times Newspaper; Torbay News Agency Service; TRIP; Universal Pictorial Press and Agency Ltd; Vandystadt; John Walmsley; Wenn; Zanussi Ltd.

The authors are grateful to the following people for their help:
Tony Kidd, Beverley Jackson, Pete and Chris Proctor, Madame Larivière (le Gai Logis), Maison Urwin.

The Publisher and authors would like to thank all the teachers and students who contributed to the research and development of the first edition. The following people and institutions who piloted and reported on the material deserve special thanks:
Kerry Allen; Ann Ayton, ILA; Simone Aronsohn; Deborah and Sarah Boodt; Elizabeth Curry, Frontisterio Papoutsi-Mitta; Raquel Reyes Delgado; Mrs Detsika; Carolyn Frenzel, Nick Love and Helen Gialias, Anglo-Continental; Tony Gill and Lorraine Kelly, Language Studies Ltd; Jesus Gimeniz and Joaquim Silos, Today School; Jill Grimshaw; Clare Hindley, Central School; Tim Hoggard; David Jones, ETC (UK); Mrs Katsianou; Mr Kontogeorgis; Mrs Koumatou; Clare McGinn, King Street College; Rita Misaelidou; Maria Moumtzi and Mrs Angelaki; Rhian Owen, Esade; Mr and Mrs Papageorgiou; Mr Papalexiou; Athina Papasotiriou, Frontisterio Haralambidis; Lilly Sell and Susan Barber, Lake School; Mrs Sigizi; Costas Sotiriou; Pete Staboglis and George Trigas; Gisela Szypytko, Anglo World; George Tavridis, Nikos Avramides, Melinda Tsagarouli, Kelly Webb, Fany Antoniou, Helen Konstantinidi, Kathy Kontogianni and Iraklis Papadopoulos, Strategakis Central School; Lesley Thompson; Tony Triggs; Deborah Watson; Louise Webb and Margie Johnson, Eurocentres; Clare West; Saraita Whan and Imogen Arnold, Godmer House; Peter Wilson, Dickens School; Stephen Yeats; Mrs Zazani.

The Publisher and authors would like to thank those teachers and students who participated in the post-publication trialling of the first edition. The following deserve special thanks for their helpful feedback:
Kiki Eglezi, Stratigakis School of English, Thessaloniki; David Heathfield, Isca School of English, Exeter; Doris Haralamtidis, The Scholar, Athens; Sarah Keith, International Language Academy and House of English, London; Peter Lambourne, Anglo World, London; Anne Matthews, Eurocentre, Cambridge; Rita Misailidou, Ipsiladio School of English, Thessaloniki; Nina Rosa da Silva, Eurocentre Victoria, London; Steve Vassilakopoulos, Thessaloniki; Clare West, English Language Centre, Hove.

The Publisher and authors would also like to thank the following for their valuable advice and detailed comments on the manuscript of this new edition:

Mark Harrison; Sarah Keith; Nina Rosa da Silva; Clare West.

Oxford University Press, Great Clarendon Street, Oxford OX2 6DP

Oxford   New York
Athens   Auckland   Bangkok   Bogota   Bombay
Buenos Aires   Calcutta   Cape Town   Dar es Salaam   Delhi
Florence   Hong Kong   Istanbul   Karachi   Kuala Lumpur
Madras   Madrid   Melbourne   Mexico City   Nairobi
Paris   Singapore   Taipei   Tokyo   Toronto   Warsaw

and associated companies in
Berlin   Ibadan

OXFORD and OXFORD ENGLISH are trade marks of Oxford University Press

First edition: *First Certificate Masterclass* © Oxford University Press 1994
New edition: *New First Certificate Masterclass*   © Oxford University Press 1996

ISBN 0 19 432829 5

First published 1996
Seventh impression 1998

No unauthorised photocopying

Printed in Spain by Mateu Cromo, S.A. Pinto (Madrid)